HILLMAN MINX
HILLMAN HUSKY

Owner's Workshop Manual

by S.F. Page

Models Covered

D0301027

1390 c.c. Minx Series I	–	May 1956 – September 1957
1390 c.c. Minx Series II	–	September 1957 – September 1958
1390 c.c. Husky Series I	–	January 1958 - March 1962
1494 c.c. Minx Series III	–	September 1958 – October 1959
1494 c.c. Minx Series IIIA	–	October 1959 - October 1960
1494 c.c. Minx Series IIIB	–	October 1960 - August 1961
1592 c.c. Minx Series IIIC	–	August 1961 - August 1963
1390 c.c. Husky Series II	–	March 1962 - August 1963
1390 c.c. Husky Series III	–	August 1963 - July 1966
1592 c.c. Minx Series V	–	August 1963 - September 1965

© J.H. HAYNES & CO. LTD. 1971

SBN 900550 09 0

J.H.Haynes and Company Limited

Sparkford. Yeovil. Somerset

distributed in the USA by
HAYNES PUBLICATIONS INC.
9421 WINNETKA AVENUE
CHATSWORTH LOS ANGELES
CALIFORNIA 91311 USA

ACKNOWLEDGEMENTS

My thanks are due to the Rootes Group for the assistance given in the supply of technical material and illustrations, to Castrol Ltd., for supplying the lubrication chart, and also to those private owners who have enthusiastically provided information and given practical advice.

Although every care has been taken to ensure the accuracy and completeness of the information given in this manual no liability can be accepted for damage, loss or injury caused by any errors or omissions.

PHOTOGRAPHIC CAPTIONS
& CROSS REFERENCES

For ease of reference this book is divided into numbered chapters, sections and paragraphs. The title of each chapter is self explanatory. The sections comprise the main headings within the chapter. The paragraphs appear within each section.

The captions to the majority of photographs are given within the paragraphs of the relevant section to avoid repetition. These photographs bear the same number as the sections and paragraphs to which they refer. The photograph always appears in the same Chapter as its paragraph. For example if looking through Chapter Ten it is wished to find the caption for photograph 9:4 refer to section 9 and then read paragraph 4.

To avoid repetition once a procedure has been described it is not normally repeated. If it is necessary to refer to a procedure already given this is done by quoting the original Chapter, section and sometimes paragraph number.

The reference is given thus: Chapter No. /Section No. Paragraph No. For example Chapter 2, section 6 would be given as: Chapter 2/6. Chapter 2, Section 6, paragraph 5 would be given as Chapter 2/6:5. If more than one section is involved the reference would be written: Chapter 2/6 to 7 or where the section is not consecutive 2/6 and 9. To refer to several paragraphs within a section the reference is given thus: Chapter 2/6. 2 and 4.

To refer to a section within the same Chapter the Chapter number is usually dropped. Thus if a reference in a Chapter 4 merely reads 'see section 8', this refers to section 8 in that same Chapter.

All references to components on the right or left-hand side are made as if looking forward to the bonnet from the rear of the car.

HILLMAN MINX SERIES IIIB ESTATE CAR

HILLMAN MINX SERIES V DE-LUXE SALOON

INTRODUCTION

In 1931 the first Hillman Minx family saloon was introduced to the motoring public. Subsequently this model has been completely revised and redesigned five times up to the introduction of the 1.6 litre engined model.

The 30 odd years of the Hillman Minx evolution is represented by six basic body styles on which numerous modifications have been employed.

Since however, there are now very few of the earlier cars still running, the models dealt with in this manual are those from the introduction of the Series I with 1,390 c.c. overhead valve engine, which replaced the Mk. VIII in October 1954, to the last of the 1,592 c.c. models (September 1965).

In May 1956 the Minx Series I Saloon DeLuxe, Convertible, and special saloon were introduced and provided an entirely new concept in body design. A new sloping bonnet was fitted together with a narrower and larger grille with the sidelights located at the end of the horizontal bar. The headlamps were hooded and a wrap around rear window used. In this instance the chassis numbers started at A1600001.

In September 1957 the Series II models were introduced and remained basically the same as the previous model except for the radiator grille, which was slightly redesigned, the horizontal bar disappearing and the words 'Hillman' appearing in script. A different camshaft was also fitted which resulted in the engine developing maximum power (51 b.h.p.) at 4,400 r.p.m. instead of 4,600 r.p.m. Manumatic transmission was an optional extra on this model.

In January 1958 the Husky Estate car was introduced and used the same 1,390 c.c. engine as the Minx Series II. The wheelbase of the Husky was 7'2" as opposed to the 8' of the Minx.

September 1958 saw the introduction of the Series III, the main difference being the replacement of the 1,390 c.c. engine with a bored out 1,494 c.c. unit. Production started with chassis number A1900001. A restyled one piece grille was fitted with 'HILLMAN' in capitals above it. The fascia panel was also restyled.

In October 1959 the Series IIIA made its appearance with chassis number for the DeLuxe version starting at B1000001 and for the special saloon B0000001. The main mechanical change was the introduction of a remote control floor gear change, with the column change optional, except on special models. The power of the engine was increased to 56.5 b.h.p. at 4,600 r.p.m. and a new close ratio gearbox fitted. The mesh radiator grille was divided by five central horizontal bars and the sidelights were made rectangular instead of circular as previously. The rear lights were also altered to oval shaped units and combined the stop, tail and indicator lights. Small curved tail fins were adopted and larger brakes fitted. A Smith's 'Easidrive' Automatic transmission was available as an optional extra.

In October 1960 the most important change was the fitting of a hypoid rear axle, and with modifications to the gearbox was known as the Series IIIB. Production commenced at chassis number B1100001. At the same time the special saloon was replaced by the Minx Saloon, which had a new aluminium grille similar to the DeLuxe model. A better air filter and a larger oil pump were also fitted.

Finally in August 1961 the last of the III Series models - the IIIC made its appearance from chassis number B0200001. This made use of a larger 1,592 c.c. engine. Alterations to the suspension comprised the fitting of greaseless nylon inserts on the outer track rod ball joints. The popular centre floor gearchange was standardised on all models. The previous Hillman Minx Series was discontinued and the models were known as the DeLuxe Saloon with a '1600' motif on the front doors.

Meanwhile the Husky had continued in production virtually unaltered. In March 1962 the Series II model had been introduced. This had a lower roof line and a new radiator grille.

In August 1963 the Series V was introduced and was completely restyled with a redesigned grille and a lower bonnet line. Various improvements were made to the gearbox and suspension and all greasing points were dispensed with. The fascia panel was redesigned. Separate front seats and disc brakes on the front wheels were fitted as standard. At the same time a restyled Husky, the Series III, appeared with a lower bonnet line and an improved gearbox and greaseless suspension.

The model designations were not changed for the Motor Show in October 1964, but a new all synchromesh gearbox and $7\frac{1}{2}$ in. diaphragm clutch were introduced together with a dished steering wheel and redesigned front seats. The Series V continued in production until September 1965.

This manual describes in detail the method employed in servicing and overhauling the mechanical and electrical components of Hillman models and shows how they can be maintained in good condition to ensure long life and reliability for which these cars have become famous.

The strip and rebuild sequences show how the major assemblies are dealt with and can be studied in conjunction with the text and exploded illustrations.

Because there are no special skills needed in the stripping down, and rebuilding or replacing, of the mechanical parts it follows that there is no particular reason why the average owner should not be able to carry out such work, provided always that the job is tackled properly, and that a reasonable kit of tools is readily available.

Here then is a manual which will show the enthusiastic, mechanically inclined Hillman owner how he can best maintain and repair his car, without constant recourse to expensive tools and equipment.

DIMENSIONS AND CAPACITIES

Wheelbase-Minx	8 ft. 0in. (243.8 cm.)
-Husky	7 ft. 2in. (218.5 cm.)
Track (Tread)-Front	4 ft. 1in. (124.4 cm.)
-Front (Minx Series V)...	4 ft. 3¾ in. (131.4 cm.)
-Rear	4 ft. 0½ in. (123.2 cm.)
Overall Length-Minx Series I	13 ft. 4½ in. (407.7 cm.)
-Minx Series II to IIIC	13 ft. 6.7 in. (413.2 cm.)
-Minx Series V	13 ft. 5½ in. (410.2 cm.)
-Husky	12 ft. 5½ in. (379.8 cm.)
Overall Height-Saloon (Minx 1 to IIIC)	4 ft. 11½ in. (151 cm.)
-Saloon (Minx V)	4 ft. 10 in. (147.3 cm.)
-Estate Car	5 ft. 1 in. (155 cm.)
-Convertible	4 ft. 10 in. (147.3 cm.)
-Husky - Series I	5 ft. 2 in. (157.5 cm.)
- Series II, III	4 ft. 11½ in. (151.1 cm.)
Overall Width-Minx Series I to IIIB	5 ft. 0¾ in. (154.3 cm.)
-Minx Series IIIC, V..	5 ft. 1 in. (155 cm.)
-Husky	5 ft. 0½ in. (153.7 cm.)
Ground Clearance (unladen)-Saloon	7 in. (17.8 cm.)
-Estate Car	7 in. (17.8 cm.)
-Convertible	5½ in. (13.9 cm.)
-Husky	6½ in. (16.5 cm.)
Turning Circle-Minx I, early II	34 ft. 3 in. (10.43 m.)
-Minx later II onwards...	36 ft. (10.97 m.)
-Husky with Burman 'P' type steering..	31 ft. 6 in. (9.59 m.)
-Husky with Burman 'F' type steering..	33 ft. 6 in. (10.2 m.)
Weight (approx.) with fuel and water-Minx I (Saloon)	2200 lbs. (998 kgs.)
-Minx I, II (Estate Car) ...	2335 lbs. (1059 kgs.)
-Minx II (Saloon)..	2142 lbs. (971 kgs.)
-Minx III, IIIA, IIIB(Saloon)..	2230 lbs. (1011 kgs.)
-Minx III, IIIA, IIIB(Estate car)	2353 lbs. (1067 kgs.)
-Minx IIIC (Saloon)	2225 lbs. (1009 kgs.)
-Minx V	2200 lbs. (998 kgs.)
-Minx IIIC (Estate car) ...	2329 lbs. (1056 kgs.)
-Husky I, II	2080 lbs. (943 kgs.)
-Husky III	2061 lbs. (935 kgs.)
Towing Capacity (Max.)-Minx I to IIIB, Husky	15 cwt. (762 kgs.)
-Minx IIIC to V	17 cwt. (863 kgs.)
Engine (including filter)..	8 pints (9.6 U.S. pints; 4.5 litres)
Engine (excluding filter)..	7 pints (8.4 U.S. pints; 3.9 litres)
Gearbox	2¾ pints (3.3 U.S. pints; 1.56 litres)
Rear Axle	1¾ pints (2.1 U.S. pints; 1 litre)
Cooling System-Minx I to IIIC; Husky I, II	13¼ pints (15.9 U.S. pints; 7.5 litres) with heater
-Minx V; Husky III..	12½ pints (15.1 U.S. pints; 7.1 litres) with heater
Fuel tank-Minx-Series I to IIIC	7¼ gallons (8.7 U.S. gallons; 33 litres)
-Series V.	10 gallons (12 U.S. gallons; 45.4 litres)
-Husky	6¼ gallons (7.5 U.S. gallons; 28.4 litres)

ROUTINE MAINTENANCE

DAILY

Radiator - Check water level (use soft or rain water).

WEEKLY

Battery - Check electrolyte level (to top of separators only).

Tyres - Check pressures (including spare).

250 miles (400 KM.).

Engine - Check oil level in sump.

1,000 miles (1,600 KM.).

Radiator - Check water level (use soft or rain water).

Battery - Check electrolyte level.

Tyres - Check pressure (including spare wheel).

Engine Sump - Check oil level.

Brakes and Clutch - Check master cylinder fluid level and top up if necessary.

Steering Linkage and Front Suspension:-

Lubricate stub axle ball joint and swivel pin.

Lubricate track rod joints.

Lubricate suspension link bushes.

Lubricate idler lever bushes.

Propeller Shaft - Lubricate universal joints.

2,000 miles (3,200 KM.).

Radiator - Check water level (use soft or rain water).

Battery - Check electrolyte level.

Tyres - Check pressure (including spare wheel).

Engine Sump - Drain when hot. Refill with new oil of recommended grade.

Brakes and Clutch - Check master cylinder fluid level and top up if necessary.

Steering Linkage and Front Suspension:-

Lubricate stub axle ball joint and swivel pin.

Lubricate track rod joints.

Lubricate suspension link bushes.

Lubricate idler lever bushes.

Propeller Shaft - Lubricate universal joints.

3,000 miles (4,800 KM.) or three months if 3,000 miles not covered.

Radiator - Check water level (use soft or rain water).

Battery - Check electrolyte level.

Wheels - Change all wheels diagonally.

Tyres - Check pressures (including spare wheel).

Engine Sump - Check oil level.

Distributor:-

Oil automatic timing mechanism.

Grease cam profile.

Oil contact breaker moving contact pivot.

Oil shaft and cam bearing.

Check contact breaker gap, clean and adjust if necessary and reset ignition timing.

Accelerator - Oil control linkage and pedal fulcrum.

Gearbox - Check oil level.

Gearshift Mechanism - Lubricate. Column change only.

Clutch - Check master cylinder fluid level and top up if necessary. Oil withdrawal lever jaw pin (slave cylinder to withdrawal lever). Check free movement at end of withdrawal lever (adjustable clutch only) and adjust if necessary. Inspect hydraulic pipe connections for leaks.

Brake and Clutch Pedals - Oil pivot bushes and linkage joints.

Brakes - Check master cylinder fluid level and top up if necessary. Inspect hydraulic pipe connections, pipe lines and unions for leaks. Test and adjust if necessary. Lubricate handbrake cable and linkage.

Steering Unit - Top up.

Steering Linkage and Front Suspension:-

Lubricate stub axle ball joint and swivel pin.

Lubricate track rod joints.

Lubricate suspension link bushes.

Lubricate idler lever bushes.

Propeller Shaft - Lubricate universal joints.

Rear Axle - Check level and top up.

Body - Oil door strikers, locks, hinges, bonnet and boot hinges and locks (including tailgate hinges and locks on Estate car). Check drain holes in lower edge of each door.

6,000 miles (9,600 KM.) or six months if 6,000 miles not covered.

Radiator - Check water level (use soft or rain water).

Battery - Check electrolyte level.

Wheels - Change all wheels diagonally.

Tyres - Check pressures (including spare wheel).

Oil Filter - Drain when hot. Renew element.

Engine Sump - Drain when hot. Refill with new oil of recommended grade.

Sparking Plugs - Clean and check gaps.

Distributor:-

Oil automatic timing mechanism.

Grease cam profile.

Oil contact breaker moving contact pivot.

Oil shaft and cam bearing.

Check contact breaker gap, clean and adjust if necessary, and reset ignition timing.

Generator - Lubricate rear bearing.

Carburetter - Clean float chamber.

Fuel Pump - Clean filter and sediment chamber.

Fan Belt - Check tension and adjust if necessary.

Accelerator - Oil control linkage and pedal fulcrum.

Gearshift mechanism - Lubricate. Column change only.

Gearbox - Drain (when hot) and refill with fresh oil.

Clutch - Check master cylinder fluid level and top up if necessary. Oil withdrawal lever jaw pin (slave cylinder to withdrawal lever). Check free movement at end of withdrawal lever (adjustable clutch only) and adjust if necessary. Inspect hydraulic pipe connections for leaks.

Brake and Clutch Pedals - Oil pivot bushes and linkage joints.

Brakes - Check master cylinder fluid level and top up if necessary. Inspect hydraulic pipe connections, pipe lines and unions for leaks. Test and adjust if necessary. Lubricate handbrake cable and linkage.

Steering Unit - Top up.

Steering Linkage and Front Suspension:-
Lubricate stub axle ball joints and swivel pin.

Lubricate track rod joints.

Lubricate suspension link bushes.

Lubricate idler lever bushes.

Propeller Shaft - Lubricate universal joints.

Rear Axle - Drain (when hot) and refill with fresh oil. Clean breather hole.

Body - Oil door strikers, locks, hinges, bonnet and boot hinges and locks (including tailgate hinges and locks on Estate car). Check drain holes in lower edge of each door.

Electrical Equipment - Check all lights for correct operation, including stop/tail lights and instrument illumination.

12,000 miles (19,200 KM.) or twelve months if 12,000 miles not covered.

Radiator - Check water level (use soft or rain water).

Battery - Check electrolyte level. Clean terminals and smear with petroleum jelly.

Wheels - Change all wheels diagonally.

Tyres - Check pressures (including spare wheel).

Oil Filter - Drain when hot. Renew element.

Engine Sump - Drain when hot. Refill with new oil of recommended grade.

Air Cleaner - Clean and renew filter element. (See handbook).

Sparking Plugs - Renew.

Distributor:-
Oil automatic timing mechanism.
Grease cam profile.
Oil contact breaker moving contact pivot.
Oil shaft and cam bearing.
Check contact breaker gap, clean and adjust if necessary, and reset ignition timing.

Generator - Lubricate rear bearing.

Starter Motor - Check fixing bolts for tightness.

Carburetter - Clean float chamber.

Fuel Pump - Clean filter and sediment chamber.

Fan Belt - Check tension and adjust if necessary.

Valve Rockers - Check and adjust clearances.

Cylinders - Check compression pressures. (See Page xx).

Accelerator - Oil control linkage and pedal fulcrum.

Gearshift Mechanism - Lubricate. Column change only.

Gearbox - Drain (when hot) and refill with fresh oil.

Clutch - Check master cylinder fluid level and top up if necessary. Oil withdrawal lever jaw pin (slave cylinder to withdrawal lever). Check free movement at end of withdrawal lever (adjustable clutch only) and adjust if necessary. Inspect hydraulic pipe connections for leaks.

Brake and Clutch Pedals - Oil pivot bushes and linkage joints.

Brakes - Check master cylinder fluid level and top up if necessary. Inspect hydraulic pipe connections, pipe lines and unions for leaks. Test and adjust if necessary. Lubricate handbrake cable and linkage.

Steering Unit - Top up.

Steering Linkage and Front Suspension:-
Lubricate stub axle ball joint and swivel pin.

Lubricate track rod joints.

Lubricate suspension link bushes.

Propeller Shaft - Lubricate universal joints.

Rear Axle - Drain (when hot) and refill with fresh oil. Clean breather hole.

Hub Bearings - Check lubrication and end float.

Body - Oil door strikers, locks, hinges, bonnet and boot hinges and locks (including tail gate hinges and locks on Estate car). Check drain holes in lower edge of each door.

General - Check all bolts for tightness with particular attention to propeller shaft couplings, shock absorbers, rear springs 'U' bolts, bottom link fulcrum pin securing bolts, bolts securing front crossmember to frame, exhaust system.

24,000 miles (38,400 KM.)
In addition to the 12,000 miles (19,200 km.) service, the following should be carried out:-

Clean the commutators of both the generator and starter motor, and inspect the brush gear.

LUBRICATION CHART

EVERY 250 MILES

ENGINE.
Check oil level and replenish.
if necessary, with **Castrol GTX**
in summer and winter.
After the first 500 miles and there-
after every 6,000 miles, (2,000 miles,
Series I, II, III, IIIa & IIIb models), drain
off old oil while warm and refill with fresh
Castrol GTX in summer and winter.
Note: Owners are advised that more
frequent sump draining periods are
desirable if the operation of the car
involves:—
   (1) Frequent stop/start driving.
   (2) Operation during cold weather,
       especially when appreciable
       engine idling is involved.
   (3) Where much driving is done under
       dusty conditions.
OVERSEAS
Air temperature above 21°C. **Castrol XL**
Air temperature 27°C. to -7°C.
Castrolite
Air temperature -0°C. to -18°C.
Castrol Z
Air temperature below -15°C.
Castrol ZZ
Capacities: Series 1—8pts., others—7pts.
+ 1pt. for filter.

EVERY 3,000 MILES
Including 250 &
1,000 mile services.

STEERING UNIT.
Apply **Castrol Hi-press Gear Oil** with
the oil gun at the nipples indicated.
Series III, IIIa, IIIb, IIIc, V, VI & Husky
Series II & Husky III Box type is fitted,
check level and top up if necessary
with **Castrol Hypoy** every 6,000 miles.
Note: LHD models lubricate on full right
lock. RHD models lubricate on full
left lock.
OVERSEAS
Air temperature above -12°C.
Castrol Hi-press Gear Oil
Note—Box type use **Castrol Hypoy**
Air temperature below -12°C.
Castrol Hypoy Gear Oil

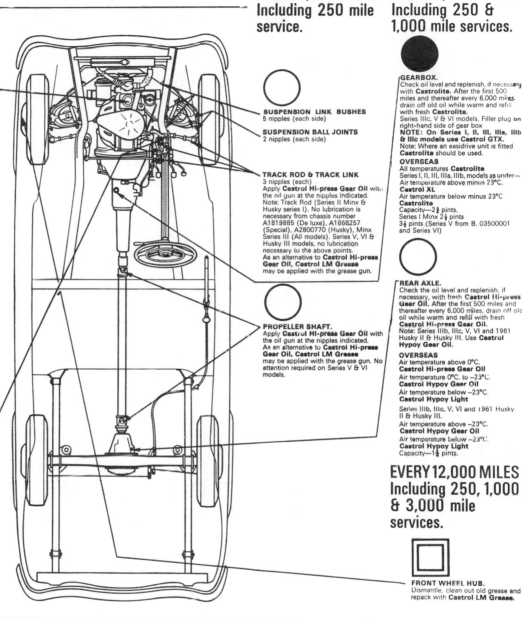

EVERY 1,000 MILES
Including 250 mile
service.

SUSPENSION LINK BUSHES
5 nipples (each side)

SUSPENSION BALL JOINTS
2 nipples (each side)

TRACK ROD & TRACK LINK
3 nipples (each)
Apply **Castrol Hi-press Gear Oil** with
the oil gun at the nipples indicated.
Note: Track Rod (Series II Minx &
Husky series I). No lubrication is
necessary from chassis number
A1819885 (De luxe), A1868257
(Special), A2800770 (Husky), Minx
Series III (All models). Series V, VI &
Husky III models, no lubrication
necessary to the above points.
As an alternative to **Castrol Hi-press
Gear Oil, Castrol LM Grease**
may be applied with the grease gun.

PROPELLER SHAFT.
Apply **Castrol Hi-press Gear Oil** with
the oil gun at the nipples indicated.
As an alternative to **Castrol Hi-press
Gear Oil, Castrol LM Grease**
may be applied with the grease gun. No
attention required on Series V & VI
models.

EVERY 3,000 MILES
Including 250 &
1,000 mile services.

GEARBOX.
Check oil level and replenish, if necessary
with **Castrolite**. After the first 500
miles and thereafter every 6,000 miles,
drain off old oil while warm and refill
with fresh **Castrolite**.
Series IIIc, V & VI models. Filler plug on
right-hand side of gear box.
NOTE: On Series I, II, III, IIIa, IIIb
& IIIc models use Castrol GTX.
Note: Where an easidrive unit is fitted
Castrolite should be used.
OVERSEAS
All temperatures **Castrolite**
Series I, II, III, IIIa, IIIb, models as under—
Air temperature above minus 23°C.
Castrol XL
Air temperature below minus 23°C
Castrolite
Capacity—2½ pints.
Series I Minx 2½ pints
3½ pints. (Series V from B. 03500001
and Series VI)

REAR AXLE.
Check the oil level and replenish, if
necessary with fresh **Castrol Hi-press
Gear Oil**. After the first 500 miles and
thereafter every 6,000 miles, drain off old
oil while warm and refill with fresh
Castrol Hi-press Gear Oil.
Note: Series IIIb, IIIc, V, VI and 1961
Husky II & Husky III. Use **Castrol
Hypoy Gear Oil**.
OVERSEAS
Air temperature above 0°C.
Castrol Hi-press Gear Oil
Air temperature 0°C. to -23°C.
Castrol Hypoy Gear Oil
Air temperature below -23°C.
Castrol Hypoy Light
Series IIIb, IIIc, V, VI and 1961 Husky
II & Husky III.
Air temperature above -23°C.
Castrol Hypoy Gear Oil
Air temperature below -23°C.
Castrol Hypoy Light
Capacity—1½ pints.

EVERY 12,000 MILES
Including 250, 1,000
& 3,000 mile
services.

FRONT WHEEL HUB.
Dismantle, clean out old grease and
repack with **Castrol LM Grease**.

EXPLANATION OF SYMBOLS

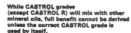

While **CASTROL** grades
(except **CASTROL R**) will mix with other
mineral oils, full benefit cannot be derived
unless the correct **CASTROL** grade is
used by itself.

CASTROL GTX.
An ultra high performance
motor oil approved for
use in the engine in
summer and winter.
CASTROLITE should be
used in the gearbox on
certain models.

**CASTROL HI-PRESS
GEAR OIL.**
An extreme pressure
lubricant of medium viscosity
for the rear axle, steering gear
box and chassis lubrication
Mk IIIb, IIIc, V, VI and 1961
Husky II & Husky III, use
CASTROL HYPOY.
CASTROL LM GREASE
may be used as an alternative
for all chassis grease nipples.

**CASTROL LM
GREASE.**
Recommended for
the wheel bearings.
May also be used
for chassis lubrication

RECOMMENDED LUBRICANTS

	Engine	Air Cleaner	Gearbox	Propeller Shaft	Rear Axle (Spiral bevel)	Rear Axle (Hypoid)	Front Suspension	Front Wheel Hubs	Steering Unit Type P	Steering Unit Type F	Gearshaft, accelerator, handbrake linkages. Brake, clutch pedal pivots. Door, bonnet, boot hinges, locks & catches
SHELL	x 100 Multigrade 10W/30	x 100 Multigrade 10W/30	x 100 Multigrade 10W/30	Spirax 140 EP or Retinax A	Spirax 140 EP	Spirax 90 EP	Spirax 140 EP or Retinax A	Retinax A	Spirax 140 E.P.	Spirax 90 EP	x 100 Multigrade 10W/30
B.P.	Viscostatic 10W/40	Viscostatic 10W/40	Viscostatic 10W/40	Energrease L. 2.	Gear Oil G.P. 90/140	Gear Oil G.P. 90/140	Energrease L. 2.	Energrease L. 2.	Gear Oil G.P. 90/140	Gear Oil G.P. 90/140	Viscostatic 10W/40
FILTRATE	10W/30 Multigrade	10W/30 Multigrade	10W/30 Multigrade	Super Lithium Grease	E.P. Gear 90	E.P. Gear 90	Super Lithium Grease	Super Lithium Grease	E.P. Gear 90	E.P. Gear 90	10W/30 Multigrade
STERNOL	WW Multigrade 10W/40	WW Multigrade 10W/40	WW Multigrade 10W/40	Ambroline L.H.T.	Ambroleum E.P. 90	Ambroleum E.P. 90	Ambroline L.H.T.	Ambroline L.H.T.	Ambroleum E.P. 90	Ambroleum E.P. 90	WW Multigrade 10W/40
DUCKHAM'S	Q.5500	Q.5500	Q.5500	L.B.10 Grease	Hypoid 90	Hypoid 90	L.B.10. Grease	L.B.10. Grease	Hypoid 90	Hypoid 90	Q.5500
CASTROL	Castrolite	Castrolite	Castrolite	Castrolease L.M.	Hypoy 90	Hypoy 90	Castrolease L.M.	Castrolease L.M.	Hypoy 90	Hypoy 90	Castrolite
ESSO	Extra Motor Oil 10W/30	Extra Motor Oil 10W/30	Extra Motor Oil 10W/30	Multipurpose Grease H	Gear Oil G.P. 90/140	Gear Oil G.P. 90	Multipurpose Grease H	Multipurpose Grease H	Gear Oil G.P. 90	Gear Oil G.P. 90	Extra Motor Oil 10W/30
MOBIL	Mobiloil Special 10W/30	Mobiloil Special 10W/30	Mobiloil Special 10W/30	Mobilgrease M.P.	Mobilube GX. 90	Mobilube GX. 90	Mobilgrease M.P.	Mobilgrease M.P.	Mobilube GX. 90	Mobilube GX. 90	Mobiloil Special 10W/30

When operating at sustained air temperatures above 80°F (27°C) or below 32°F (0°C) a local Rootes Dealer should be consulted. If a monograde oil is preferred, or if the engine numbers are earlier than B.03500001 (Minx), B.21100001 (Husky), the local Rootes Dealer should be consulted.

12

SAFETY PRECAUTIONS

Whenever you start work on your car PLAY SAFE. It is worth a little extra effort to make sure the likelihood of an accident is minimised.

When you are going to do any work involving the engine, or the electrical system, disconnect the battery and preferably remove it from the car. The reason for this is mainly to prevent short circuiting of the electrical system, since this can result in setting fire to the wiring looms in some instances. Or again, the dropping of a spanner on a battery terminal will result in a shower of sparks and if the short circuit is continued the battery will be permanently damaged. Better to spend a few moments removing the terminals to cut the electrical supply than to have to buy a new battery, or worse, to have a burnt out car.

When you have to work underneath the car, which will invariably involve pushing, pulling and lifting on the underside, first jack up the car and then support it very firmly indeed. DO NOT RELY ON PILES OF BRICKS AT EACH CORNER, OR OLD OIL DRUMS PUSHED UNDERNEATH THE CORNERS OF THE BODY. These may give way and you will be trapped. If at all possible, use good timber, preferably under the four wheels, in order to get the height. Alternatively, if you are working on the front end, use a pair of timber ramps to lift the front wheels well off the ground. The drawing below shows the construction of two suitable ramps made of timber used by the author to lift his car about 9 inches from the ground. The unit is screwed together, mainly with 2 inch wood screws. The back panels are 9 inches deep and I used 2 pieces, 5 inches wide, leaving a gap of 2 inches in the centre, rather than having the extra cost of a 12 inch wide board. Do not forget to put blocks against the rear wheels to prevent there being any chance of the car running back down the ramps when you put pressure on any part of the vehicle from underneath.

DO NOT RUN THE ENGINE OF THE CAR IN A CLOSED GARAGE. This advice seems to be given more times than it is taken, and neglect of this simple precaution has resulted in many people having become seriously ill.

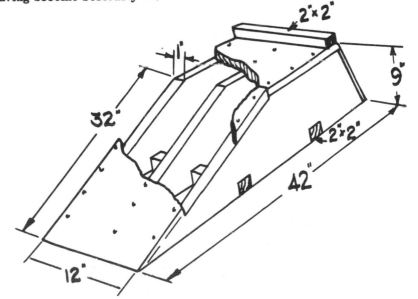

TOOLS AND EQUIPMENT

One of the greatest problems which any enthusiast faces when carrying out mechanical repairs or overhauls is the lack of the right tool for use at the right moment. This does not mean that special equipment as used by main service depots must be bought and used, since this would make repair work uneconomic, but it does mean that good quality tools must be readily available in order to carry out the work reasonably, easily and accurately. For those readers who would like to know all the tools required for the jobs listed in this manual, the author has looked around his own workshop and the following list has catered for most of the major work done over the years.

A set of socket wrenches. These are a must, and it is essential they are of good quality. Unfortunately there are quantities of imported socket wrenches available which, when applied to tight or rusted nuts or bolts, are too weak to handle them so, instead of turning the bolt or nut, the inside of the socket is torn away. Alternatively the handle may be too weak to take more than a limited torque and either twists or the edges tear away. So forget cheap tools, and wait a while longer until a good set can be afforded. This will pay off in the long run. One must not despise the good quality open ended spanner, since this can often be used where a socket cannot be fitted. The crankshaft pulley nut requires a spanner of $1\frac{1}{4}$ in. across flats, but the rest of the engine can be dismantled and reassembled with socket spanners of the following sizes:-

Whitworth.	$\frac{3}{16}$"	$\frac{1}{4}$"	$\frac{5}{16}$"	$\frac{3}{8}$"	
A. F.	$\frac{7}{16}$"	$\frac{1}{2}$"	$\frac{9}{16}$"	$\frac{5}{8}$"	$\frac{11}{16}$"	$\frac{3}{4}$"

My own set of socket and open spanners has been in constant use now for over 20 years, the set is still intact and every part is still usable. The cylinder head bolts of your car will put some of the biggest stresses into spanners, especially when the bolts are loosened.

A set of feeler gauges is essential, covering the full range either as individual feelers or as a combination. Take care of the very thin blades, as these can soon become twisted and broken if treatment is harsh.

Other tools such as screwdrivers, hammers, mallets, files and so on are to be found in every enthusiasts garage/workshop and are in general a matter of choice. As a rule it is not a good practice to rely on adjustable spanners for most jobs, since these frequently slip, and barking one's knuckles tends to make the work on the car a chore rather than something to be enjoyed. A car jack is another essential tool. Nothing particularly expensive such as a trolley jack is necessary, but a good sturdy screw or hydraulic jack will pay for itself over and over again. When you are carrying out repairs underneath your car DO NOT rely on the flimsy jack provided with the car. This is intended only to lift the appropriate side of the car when you have a puncture and need to change a wheel.

One thing which is needed when carrying out major repairs is an ample supply of rag, and for this avoid two types. Avoid that fluffy woollen material which, when you wipe the oil dirt from a part, leaves behind a series of fibres. Also avoid that stiff, non-absorbant type of rag which never seems to dry away the paraffin or remove the dirt.

For electrical work it will be found that long shanked socket type spanners having wooden handles are just the tools for getting at the distributor point securing nuts, or the small nuts securing terminals to instruments. These are especially handy when the small nut is difficult to return, since the nut is placed in the spanner and then offered to the thread of the screw or bolt in places where fingers are too big.

In these days when the majority of keen do-it-yourself motorists have their own electric drill, the uses for this equipment on major car repair and overhaul work are endless. From the drilling of holes to accept self tapping screws when fitting up accessories, to the cleaning of engine valves and removal of carbon from the cylinder heads, the list of uses is too great to detail here.

A pair of wire strippers is a useful and inexpensive piece of equipment for those who like to carry out their own electrical repairs and installation of electrical equipment, since the wire can be easily stripped along just the length required. In general soldering of modern wire connectors is not necessary, and I must admit that it is some years since I have used a soldering iron on any car electrical equipment.

To drift out worn bushes a good brass or bronze drift is essential, and where such bushes have to be cut out with a chisel, a sharp edge is a must. The type of chisel depends upon the location, but in general about four types cover most requirements.

Always check a replacement part with the old one before attempting to fit it. There are so many components in the modern spare parts store that it is easy for a mistake to occur, or for the part of one model to be very slightly different from year to year. Kits of parts are available for overhauling units such as fuel pumps and universal joints and these include all the parts and gaskets which should be renewed when the component is overhauled. They are well worth buying and usually cost much less than an exchange replacement unit.

PRACTICAL HINTS WHEN DISMANTLING

If rag is scarce, save it for the final cleaning and use newspapers for initial cleaning away especially such large parts as cylinder blocks, gearbox cases and rear axle casings.

Paraffin in a deep tin is preferable to petrol for cleaning all the METAL PARTS, but under no circumstances allow paraffin or petrol near the rubber parts and pipes of either the clutch or brake hydraulic system.

Before cleaning down any dismantled parts take care to plug up exposed holes, otherwise dirt will get into them and may be a cause of subsequent troubles. For example blocked up water holes in a cylinder head will cause localised heating and pre-ignition.

If a bolt refuses to come out, and a hammer has to be applied, do not hammer the end of the bolt, but fit the nut back into place until the end of the nut and the end of the bolt are flush, and then hammer. It will usually be found that four or five good, smart blows of the hammer will do far more good with a lot less damage than a number of taps.

Where parts such as the steering drop arm joint are naturally very tight, get hold of a puller tool. Any attempt to hammer such parts will only result in the parts being bent, which means that they will have to be replaced.

Where underfloor parts are bent they should be either replaced or repaired by someone having correct checking equipment. Any attempt to heat them up and straighten them in a vice may well have the effect of cracking the part which will lead to failure of that part.

If the car is likely to be dismantled for a period of time do not trust to your memory. Label all electrical terminals and similar parts as soon as they have been dismantled.

CHAPTER ONE

ENGINE

CONTENTS

SPECIFICATIONS

ENGINE SPECIFICATION & DATA - 1,390 c.c.

Engine - General

Type	4 cylinder in line o.h.v. pushrod operated
Bore	3.00 in. (76.2 mm.)
Stroke...	3.00 in. (76.2 mm.)
Cubic capacity	1,390 c.c. (84.82 in.)
Compression ratio - High C	9.0 to 1
- Low C	7.0 to 1
Compression pressure - High C ...	150/155 p.s.i.
- Low C ...	125/130 p.s.i.
Torque - High C	69.75 lb/ft. at 2,400 r.p.m.
- Low C	66.30 lb/ft. at 2,200 r.p.m.
Firing order..	1 - 3 - 4 - 2
Engine mountings	One rubber mounting on each side of the front of the engine. One rubber mounting under gearbox.

Camshaft & Camshaft Bearings

Camshaft drive	From crankshaft by Duplex chain
Camshaft bearings	3 steel shell white metal lined, replaceable
Camshaft journal diameters	1.7470 in. to 1.7477 in.
End float	.002 in. to .003 in. (.05 to .07 mm.)
End thrust	Taken by location plate at front
Chain tensioner...	Spring blade
Chain lubrication..	Oil jet

Connecting Rods & Big & Little End Bearings

Material & type...	Steel forged H section
Length between centres	5.749 in. to 5.751 in.

Big end bearings..	Steel shell white metal lined
Small end bearings	Bushed
Big end, end float	.0012/.0075 in. (.030 to .190 mm.)
Big end bearing running clearance ...	.005 in. to .002 in. (on dia.)

Camshaft & Main Bearings

Main journal diameter	2.2495 to 2.2490 in. (57.137 to 57.125 mm.)
Crankshaft end thrust..	Taken by thrust washer on centre bearing
End float	.002 in. to .004 in. (.05 mm. to .102 mm.)
Number of bearings	3
Bearing material..	Steel shell white metal lined
Max. undersize of re-grinding... ...	– 0.06 in. (1.52 mm.)

Cylinder Block

Material	Cast iron
Water jackets	Full length of bore
Max. oversize with or without liners ..	.040 in. (1.016 mm.)

Cylinder Head

Material	Cast iron
Torque loading of cylinder nuts.. ...	41 to 43 lbs/ft.
Size to cylinder head studs..	$\frac{3}{8}$ in. U.N.F.
Gasket - Type	Varnished steel pressing
- Thickness	.022 in. in position (.56 mm.)

Gudgeon Pin

Type	Tubular fully floating
Location	Circlip
Diameter graded..	High grade .8752 to .8751 in. (painted white)
	Medium grade .8751 to .8750 in. (painted green)
	Low grade .8750 to .8549 in. (painted yellow)
Oversize available	.8782 to .8780 in.
Class of fit...	Push fit at 68°F.

Lubrication System

Type	Pressure and splash - Wet sump
Pump type	Eccentric lobe type
Intake type...	Gauze filter on pump
Pump drive	Skew gear on camshaft
Normal pressure (hot)	30 to 50 p.s.i. at 50 m.p.h.
Filter type & make	Full - flow - fram or Tecalemit
Filter model	Fram F.F.42378 : Tecalemit PSK.1663
Makers filter element number	Fram F.C.41721 : Tecalemit F.P.3305/101
Sump capacity (including filter).. ...	8 pints (4.5 litres)

Pistons & Piston Rings

Piston type & material	'T' Slot. LO-EX alloy tin plated
Number of rings - Compression ...	2 (2nd ring tapered)
- Scraper..	1/2 (A lower scraper ring was fitted in engines after following chassis numbers. De-Luxe HC. A1828633 De-Luxe LC. A1830548. Special HC.A1869876.Special A1870919. Manumatic HC.A1829472. LC.A1832543
Ring clearance between ring and groove	.0015 to .0035 in.
Ring gap fitted	.014 in. to .009 in.
Lubrication	Splash and oil jet in connecting rod

ENGINE

Valves, Guides & Valve Springs

Position	Overhead
Operation	Pushrod and rocker
Head diameter - Inlet..	1.374 in. to 1.370 in. (34.90 to 34.80 mm.)
- Exhaust	1.114 to 1.110 in. (28.30 to 28.22 mm.)
Angle of seat in block..	45°
Angle of valve face	45°
Stem diameter - Inlet..	.3110 to .3105 in. (7.9 to 7.89 mm.)
- Exhaust	.3100 to .3095 in. (7.874 to 7.861 mm.)
Valve stem clearance in guide - Inlet	.0015 to .003 in. (.04 to .075 mm.)
- Exhaust	.0025 to .004 in. (.06 to .10 mm.)
Length of valves (Inlet & Exhaust) ...	4.66 in. (118.35 mm.)
Type of spring	Dual
Spring retention...	Cup and split cotters
Valve spring - Fitted length	Inner 1.46 in. (37.1 mm.) Outer 1.58 in. (40.1 mm.)
- Load fitted	Inner 26.6 lbs.
	Outer 53.7 lbs.
Guides	Detachable : .5640 in. to .5636 in.
	Overall diameter
	Inlet 2.15 in. long
	Exhaust 2.42 in. long

When fitted the top of the valve guides to be 0.58 in. (14.7 mm.) above bottom of spring pocket

Working clearance (engine hot or cold)

- Inlet	.012 in. (.30 mm.)
- Exhaust	.014 in. (.35 mm.)

Timing	Minx I	Minx II
- Inlet opens	11° B.T.D.C.	14° B.T.D.C.
- Inlet closes	55° A.B.D.C.	41° A.B.D.C.
- Exhaust opens	53° B.B.D.C.	50° B.B.D.C.
- Exhaust closes	13° A.T.D.C.	5° A.T.D.C.

ENGINE SPECIFICATION & DATA - 1,494 c.c.

The engine specification is identical to the 1,390 c.c. engine except for the differences listed below.

Engine - General

Bore	3.1102 in. (78.999 mm.)
Cubic capacity	1,494 c.c. (91.17 cu. in.)
Compression ratio - High C	8.5 to 1
- Medium C.. ...	7.8 to 1
- Low C	7.0 to 1
Compression pressure - High C.. ...	170/180 p.s.i.
- Medium C...	155/165 p.s.i.
- Low C.. ...	140/150 p.s.i.
B.H.P. (net)(25 mm.choke) - High C..	49.2 at 4,400 r.p.m.
(22 mm.choke) - High C..	46.5 at 4,400 r.p.m.
(25 mm.choke) - Low C..	46.0 at 4,200 r.p.m.
(22 mm.choke) - Low C..	42.0 at 4,100 r.p.m.
Torque (25 mm.choke) - High C..	78.3 lb/ft. at 2,100 r.p.m.
(22 mm.choke) - High C..	73.5 lb/ft. at 1,800 r.p.m.
(25 mm.choke) - Low C..	73.7 lb/ft. at 2,000 r.p.m.
(22 mm.choke) - Low C..	71.0 lb/ft. at 2,000 r.p.m.

Valves, Guides & Valve Springs

Timing..	14° B.T.D.C.
	41° A.B.D.C.
	50° B.B.D.C.
	5° A.T.D.C.

CHAPTER ONE

Connecting Rods & Big & Little End Bearings
Big end bearings .. ..   Steel shell copper/lead indium lined
Big end bearing running clearance ...   .002 in. to .0015 in. (.05 to .03 mm.)

ENGINE SPECIFICATION & DATA – 1,592 c.c.

The engine specification is identical to the 1,390 c.c. engine except for the differences listed below.
Engine – General

Bore	3.2102 in. (81.539 mm.)
Cubic capacity	1,592 c.c. (97.1 cu. in.)
Compression ratio	8.3 to 1
Compression pressure	165 to 175 p.s.i.
B.H.P. (net)	52.8 at 4,100 r.p.m.
Torque..	86.8 lbs/ft. at 2,100 r.p.m.

Connecting Rods & Big & Little End Bearings
Big end, end float ... ...   .0037 to .002 (.093 to .050 mm.)

Gudgeon Pin
Diameter graded.. ... ...   High grade .9377 to .9376 in. (painted white)
                                            Medium grade .9376 to .9375 in. (painted green)
                                            Low grade .9375 to .9374 in. (painted yellow)

Pistons & Piston Rings

Piston type & material	Slotted aluminium alloy tin plated
Number of rings – Compression ...	2
– Scraper..	1
Ring gap fitted – Top ring	.032 to .024 in. (.81 to .61 mm.)
– 2nd, 3rd ring.. ...	.014 to .009 in. (.35 to .22 mm.)

Valves, Guides & Valve Springs

Head diameter – Inlet	1.436 to 1.432 in. (36.77 to 36.37 mm.)
– Exhaust..	1.176 to 1.172 in. (29.87 to 29.76 mm.)

TORQUE WRENCH SETTINGS

Cylinder head nuts	48 lb/ft.
Main bearings	55 lb/ft.
Big end bearings:	
Minx I to IIIB, Husky	17 lb/ft.
Minx IIIC onwards	24 lb/ft.
Flywheel securing bolts	40 lb/ft.

1. GENERAL DESCRIPTION

The 1,592 c.c. engine was developed from the 1,494 c.c. unit which in turn was developed from the 1,390 c.c. Rootes Group engine introduced in 1954. The 1,592 c.c. engine remained substantially unchanged despite model restyling.

A rigid, three-bearing crankshaft runs in white metal shells. Valve operation is by side mounted duplex chain driven camshaft. The cylinder head, having combustion chambers of essentially bath-tub shape is of cast iron, the valves operating vertically in the head.

Compression ratio is normally 8.3 : 1 with optional ratios of 6.9 or 7.8 used for specific conditions or markets. The oil filter has a replaceable unit of either Fram or Tecalemit make and should be changed every 6,000 miles of running.

Wear rate is generally good, and it can be normally expected that a major overhaul is not required until the engine has covered at least 50,000 miles.

Above average accessibility of the power unit makes it easy for the owner to work on, and cylinder head overhaul, usually only necessary after extended mileages, is simple to carry out.

The oil filter is mounted upside down to enable it to be easily unscrewed from the top, thus needing care when the filter is changed to make sure that surplus oil does not leak away

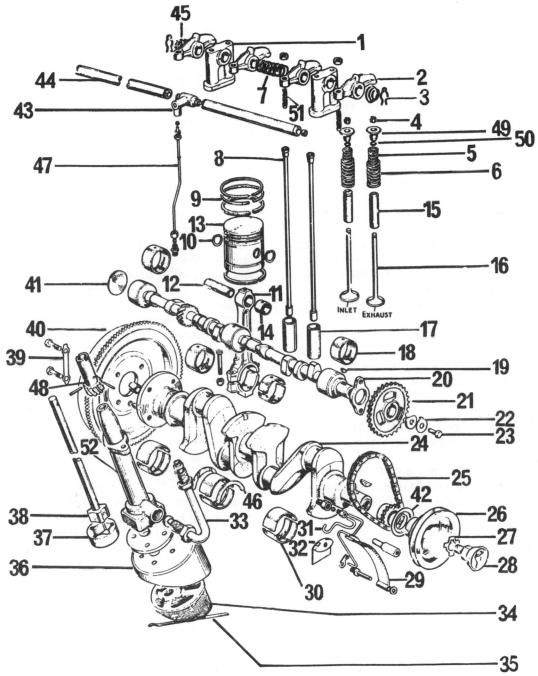

Fig. 1.1. EXPLODED VIEW OF WORKING PARTS.

1 Rocker pedestal. 2 Rocker arm. 3 Rocker arm retaining clip. 4 Valve collets. 5 Inner valve spring. 6 Outer valve spring. 7 Rocker arm spacer spring. 8 Pushrod. 9 Piston rings (4). 10 Gudgeon pin retaining circlip. 11 Connecting rod and end. 12 Gudgeon pin. 13 Piston. 14 Small end bush. 15 Valve guide. 16 Valve. 17 Camshaft followers. 18 Camshaft bearing. 19 Woodruff key. 20 Camshaft retaining plate. 21 Camshaft sprocket. 22 Tab washer. 23 Sprocket retaining bolt. 24 Crankshaft. 25 Duplex timing chain. 26 Bottom fan pulley. 27 Tab washer. 28 Starting handle dog. 29 Timing chain tensioner. 30 Crankshaft main bearing shells. 31 Oil pipes. 32 Pivot plate. 33 Oil pipe. 34 Oil pump 'pick-up' filter. 35 Filter retaining lever. 36 Filter body. 37 & 38 Oil pump rotors. 39 Tab washer. 40 Flywheel/starter ring. 41 Camshaft end plate. 42 Oil seal protector plate. 43 Rocker gear oil feed. 44 Rocker shaft. 45 Rocker arm spacing spring. 46 Thrust washer. 47 Rocker gear oil feed pipe. 48 Distributor and oil pump drive skew gear. 49 Valve spring retainer. 50 Valve stem oil seal. 51 Rocker arm adjusting screw. 52 Oil pump drive shaft casing and pump body.

all over the working area.

It is important to stress that, because this manual covers a number of models, there are small differences of procedure in dismantling and reassembly, but since the engines are so basically similar, such differences are very small, and are noted in the text where important.

2. MAJOR OPERATIONS WITH ENGINE IN PLACE

The following major operations can be carried out to the engine with it in place in the body frame:-

1. Removal and replacement of the cylinder head assembly.
2. Removal and replacement of the sump.
3. Removal and replacement of the big end bearings.
4. Removal and replacement of the pistons and connecting rods.
5. Removal and replacement of the timing chain and gears.
6. Removal and replacement of the camshaft.

3. MAJOR OPERATIONS WITH ENGINE REMOVED

The following major operations can be carried out with the engine out of the body frame and on the bench or floor:-

1. Removal and replacement of the main bearings.
2. Removal and replacement of the crankshaft.
3. Removal and replacement of the oil pump.
4. Removal and replacement of the flywheel.

4. METHODS OF ENGINE REMOVAL

The engine of all models covered by this manual can be readily removed from the car in the general sequence detailed. There are minor differences according to the model and year, and also if a car has been provided with one of the speed conversions available, but in general the following sequences apply.

The engine can be removed with or without the gearbox, but in view of the weight of the engine it will be found easier to leave the gearbox in the chassis, or alternatively to remove the gearbox from the car first. On cars fitted with the Easidrive automatic transmission the engine and the transmission must be lifted out as a unit and this will require suitable block and tackle or a portable lifting crane.

5. ENGINE REMOVAL

1. Turn on the water drain taps found at the bottom of the radiator and on the side of the cylinder block. Do not drain the water in your garage or the place where you will remove the engine if receptacles are not available to catch the water.

2. Disconnect the battery by removing the earth lead. For safety from electrical shocks it is best to remove the battery from the car.

3. With a suitable container in position unscrew the drain plug at the bottom of the sump and drain off the engine oil. When the oil is drained screw the plug back in lightly to ensure it is not mislaid.

4. Unscrew the nuts securing the exhaust pipe to the manifold, loosen the support clip and lower the pipe or remove it.

5. Unbolt the clutch slave cylinder and move to one side.

6. Remove any brackets connecting the clutch bellhousing to the sump frame bolts and disconnect the fuel pipe securing clip. Remove the cover plate from the bellhousing.

7. If the car is fitted with a steering column gear change, disconnect the operating rod from the lever and remove the bell crank lever and its mounting bracket.

8. Unbolt the bonnet hinges and lift off the bonnet.

9. Unscrew the clips securing the top and bottom water hoses from the engine ends. Also disconnect the heater inlet and outlet hoses (if fitted).

10. Unscrew the four bolts securing the radiator unit to the mounting plate and lift the radiator from the car. Close the drain tap.

11. Disconnect the throttle and choke cables at the carburetter end.

12. Disconnect the generator leads, pull away the plug leads and also remove the lead to the centre of the coil. Unclip the distributor cover and lift away. Make sure that the plug leads are clearly marked indicating which lead terminates at which plug. Place a piece of clean rag over the distributor to prevent dirt entering. Disconnect starter motor wiring.

13. Remove the water temperature gauge lead. Disconnect the oil pressure gauge pipe, where fitted, and disconnect the fuel supply pipe at the fuel pump.

14. Remove the air cleaner.

15. Unbolt the ignition coil, after first removing the two leads on the coil terminals. On earlier models these are secured with nuts, on later models they clip in position.

16. If lifting tackle is not available, at least two other people will be needed to lift the engine clear. First take the weight off the front of the engine to allow the two front mounting rubbers to be removed. This can be assisted by the use of a jack under the engine sump

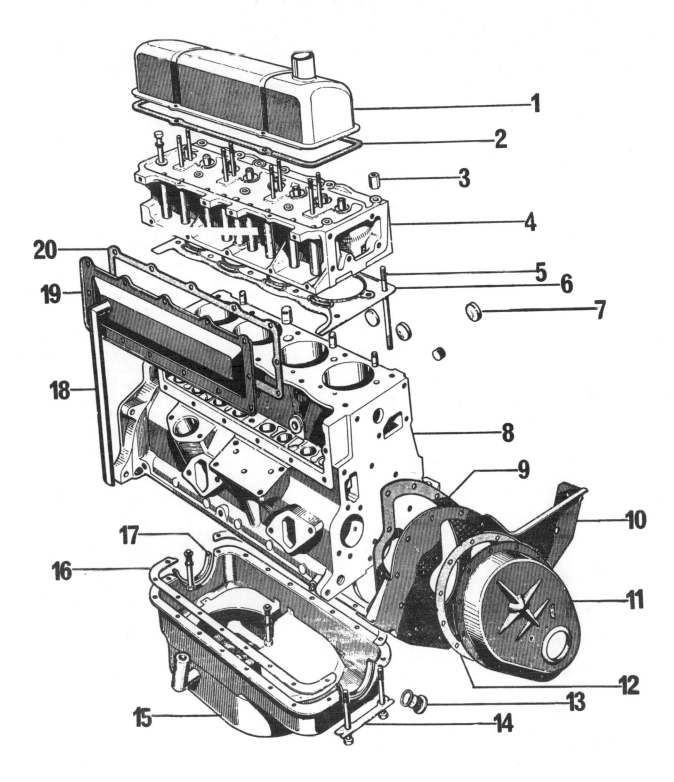

Fig. 1.2. CYLINDER BLOCK AND ASSOCIATED PARTS.

1 Rocker cover. 2 Rocker cover gasket. 3 Cylinder head nut. 4 Cylinder head. 5 Cylinder head stud. 6 Cylinder head gasket. 7 Core plug. 8 Engine block. 9 Engine front plate gasket. 10 Engine front plate. 11 Timing chain cover. 12 Timing chain cover gasket. 13 Sump plug and seating ring. 14 Sump retaining bolts and tab plate. 15 Sump.

provided a board of timber is placed between the jack and the sump to spread the load.

17. At the rear of the engine, remove all the bolts securing the bellhousing to the crankcase, draw the engine forward to free the drive shaft splines and then lift directly upwards out of the car.

18. Where no lifting tackle is available, the actual lifting can be done with a strong rope passed around the front end and rear end of the engine, passed up to a piece of sound 4 x 2 timber or similar, one person taking each end of the timber across the car, with a third person guiding the engine out of the car.

6. DISMANTLING THE ENGINE - GENERAL

It is best to mount the engine on a dismantling stand, but as this is frequently not available, then it is best to stand the engine on a strong bench so as to be at a comfortable working height. Failing this, it can be stripped down on the floor. During the dismantling process the greatest care should be taken to keep the exposed parts free from dirt. As an aid to achieving this aim, it is a very sound scheme to thoroughly clean down the outside of the engine, removing all traces of oil and congealed dirt. A good grease solvent such as 'Gunk' will make the job much easier, as, after the solvent has been applied and allowed to stand for a time, a vigorous jet of water will wash off the solvent and all the grease and dirt. If the dirt is thick and deeply embedded, work the solvent into it with a wire brush.

Finally wipe down the exterior of the engine with a clean rag and only then, when it is finally quite free from dirt, should the dismantling process begin. As the engine is stripped, clean each part in a bath of paraffin or petrol. Never immerse parts with oilways in paraffin, i.e. the crankshaft, but to clean wipe down carefully with a petrol damped rag. Oilways can be cleaned out with pipe cleaners. If an air line is present all parts can be blown dry and the oilways blown through as an added precaution.

Re-use of old engine gaskets is a false economy and can give rise to oil and water leaks, if nothing worse. To avoid the possibility of trouble after the engine has been re-assembled always use new gaskets throughout. Do not throw the old gaskets away as it sometimes happens that an immediate replacement cannot be found and the old gasket is then very useful as a template. Hang up the old gaskets as they are removed on a suitable hook or nail.

To strip the engine it is best to work from the top down. The sump provides a firm base

on which the engine can be supported in an upright position. When the stage where the sump must be removed is reached the engine can be turned on its side and all other work carried out with it in this position.

Wherever possible, replace nuts and bolts and washers finger-tight from wherever they were removed. This helps avoid later loss and muddle. If they cannot be replaced then lay them out in such a fashion that it is clear from where they were removed.

7. DISMANTLING THE ENGINE

1. Removal of the inlet and exhaust manifold is simple except for the two inboard nuts. A normal open ended spanner will not turn these nuts because there is not sufficient room to give the initial loosening turn. Therefore a hammer and chisel or small drift is needed, several sharp raps with the hammer being sufficient to make the first turns of each nut. The next few turns can be made by levering the nut around with a screwdriver until it is possible to apply a $\frac{1}{4}$ in. open ended spanner to the end of each nut, (see photo), and complete the unscrewing. If these two nuts appear to be well rusted, apply a few drops of penetrating oil, and leave for a few minutes for the oil to work, then proceed as above.

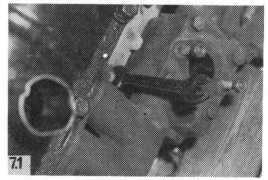

2. The four slot headed screws are undone with a long screwdriver (see photo), and the rocker cover removed.

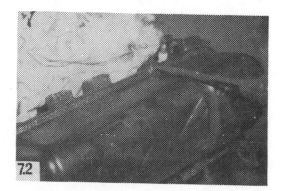

Fig. 1.3. Layout of the 1,592 c.c. power unit.

3. Unscrew the oil supply pipe union in the centre of the rockers, and then unscrew the eight bolts securing the rocker pedestals evenly (see photo), and lift the two banks of rockers.

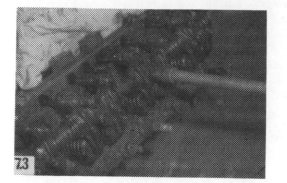

4. The eight valve push rods are lifted out, each being placed in its correct position in a piece of cardboard having a large F for the front. This helps to ensure that these push-rods can be returned to their correct position on reassembly. (See photo).

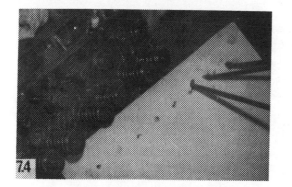

5. Unscrew the two bolts securing the ignition distributor and lift this away, followed by the oil filter and the base of this filter, which is secured by four bolts.

6. It is necessary to remove this base in order to obtain access to one of the valve side plate cover bolts, which, although it can be unscrewed, cannot be extracted with the filter base in position

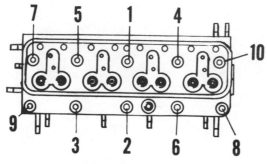

Fig. 1.4. The order in which to tighten or loosen the cylinder head nuts.

7. The small bolts around the cover plate are then removed and the plate lifted away.

8. Next, if there is a small-bore rubber hose between the water pump and the thermostat chamber on the filter side of the engine, unscrew the top clip of this hose.

9. Unscrew all the cylinder head bolts, working from the centre outwards in the sequence given in Fig. 1.4 in order that the cylinder head is released evenly (see photo), and lift the cylinder head away together with the gasket.

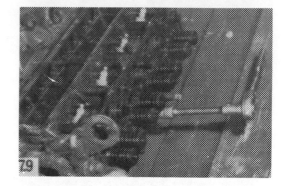

10. Turning now to the front of the engine, the bolts securing the water pump in position are removed with an open ended spanner, noting that the top bolt is in fact a cheese headed bolt, requiring a screwdriver to hold the bolt while the nut is released.

11. The crankshaft jaw nut is removed with a large open-ended spanner, or with the use of a tommy bar through holes in the jaw on some models. Note that where this jaw nut is secured with a locking washer, the tab of this washer must be tapped up with a chisel or drift.

12. With the nut off, two of the valve rocker pedestal bolts can be screwed into the two tapped holes in the crankshaft pulley to form a puller tool. (See photo).

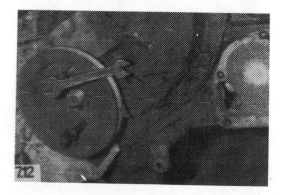

13. Pieces of flat steel will be needed behind the bolts which are then screwed in alternately a half turn at a time. This will gradually withdraw the pulley, leaving a woodruff key in the crankshaft.

14. The bolts around the outside of the timing case can now be unscrewed, together with a small hexagon headed bolt in the lower centre of some engines, and the cover is lifted away exposing the timing wheels and chain. (See photo).

15. Withdraw the timing wheels complete with the timing chain with the aid of two levers applied together to withdraw the sprocket evenly from its spigot. Two strong screwdrivers would be perfectly adequate for this job. (See photo).

16. With the timing wheels removed, unscrew the two setscrews securing the camshaft flange thrust plate, and gently pull the camshaft forward, taking care not to allow the cams to scrape along the bearing surfaces.

17. If the bearings are found to be damaged, they must be drawn out of their bores in the cylinder block. For this a Churchill tool number R.G. 32 will be needed, this puller tool being passed through the bearing in order to draw it out towards the front, as seen in Fig.1.5.

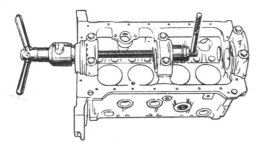

1.5. Churchill tool No. R.G. 32 being used to withdraw the camshaft bearings.

18. The clutch unit is marked with a punch to assist reassembly, and then the six bolts securing the unit to the flywheel are unscrewed, one turn at a time until the pressure is released, the clutch then being removed as a unit.

19. To remove the oil sump unscrew and remove the eighteen bolts around the flange to allow the sump to come away with its gasket. (See photo).

20. If the sump is being dropped with the engine in the car, leave one bolt in position on each side to take the weight while the remaining bolts are being removed. NOTE that on some models the dipstick tube is secured by a clip bolted to the oil pump cover on the outside of the cylinder block, and this bolt must be unscrewed and the clip removed before the sump can be taken away.

21. With the sump away, the oil pump is removed by first unscrewing the large nut of the union of the supply pipe. (See photo).

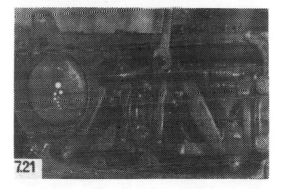

22. Then unscrew the two bolts securing the oil pump flange to the cylinder block. (See photo).

23. The oil pump body is a snug fit in the cylinder block bore and will require the use of two levers or sturdy screwdrivers to ease it away.

7.22

7.28

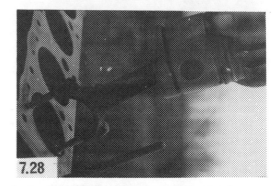

7.28

24. The pump casing is a light alloy casting and therefore should not be hammered to release it.

25. Initial release is achieved by applying a brass drift to the top of the pump shaft to drive it downwards, and if this does not free it so that it can be drawn downwards by hand, a pair of levers should be inserted between the flanges to complete the removal.

26. No doubt the surface of the spigot will be covered with a gummy substance and this should be removed by well washing in petrol in order to restore the surface for reassembly. Any attempt to scrub the surface with sandpaper will be detrimental to the fit between the two parts. If the oil pump has been working satisfactorily, then it can be well cleaned down and placed to one side.

27. Before attempting to remove the pistons and con rods, mark each half of the big end bearings with a centre punch, marking one punch mark on the camshaft side of each half of the big end bearing nearest the front of the engine, two punch marks on the second, three on the third and four on the back big end. (See photo). This will ensure that the con rods are refitted to their correct cylinders and also that they are assembled the right way round.

7.27

28. It will be seen that self locking nuts are used to secure the big end bearing caps, and with these removed, the connecting rod and piston is withdrawn through the top of the cy-

linder. (See photo).

29. If the big end bearings have not been marked, it will be found that a forging flash is left on the squirt hole side of the connecting rod, and this lines up with a similar flash on the cap. This squirt hole, which is drilled through a small projection on one side of the connecting rod must be assembled to the right hand (thrust) side of the cylinder walls when the engine is viewed from the rear.

30. The piston rings comprise a chromium plated top compression ring, evident by its much brighter appearance than the other two rings. The second compression ring has a narrower face toward the top of the piston, and this ring is marked 'Top' to indicate the narrower edge. The scraper ring is the lower of the three, and is a slotted ring.

31. On some of the earlier engines a fourth scraper ring is fitted in the lower groove of the piston. If examination of the piston rings show them to be in good condition, and the vertical clearance in the grooves is about 0.0015 to 0.0035 in. then the rings can be left in position.

32. If a cylinder block has to be replaced, for example following a crack due to freezing, while it is normal practice to supply the blocks separately, it is useful to obtain a set of suitably graded pistons to suit the particular block. The cylinder grade indication will be found

stamped on two machined bosses at each end of the cylinder block below the level of the cylinder head on the manifold side. The piston grade and weight figures are stamped on the top face of each piston. If the cylinder block is to be rebored then a set of pistons to suit the new diameters will have to be supplied.

33. Having removed the clutch mechanism (paragraph 18 above), it is now possible to remove the flywheel should this be necessary.

34. Bend back the locking tabs from the four set bolts which hold the flywheel to the flywheel flange on the rear of the crankshaft.

35. Now remove the bolts and lift the flywheel away from the crankshaft flange taking extreme care not to damage the teeth on the starter ring. NOTE: Should the crankshaft tend to rotate when pressure is put on the flywheel set bolts with a spanner the crankshaft can be locked by inserting a wooden wedge between the crankshaft and the side of the block inside the crankcase.

8. ENGINE REASSEMBLY - GENERAL

To ensure maximum life with minimum trouble from a rebuilt engine, not only must everything be correctly assembled, but everything must be spotlessly clean, all the oilways must be clear, locking washers and spring washers must always be fitted where indicated and all bearing and other working surfaces must be thoroughly lubricated during assembly. Before assembly begins renew any bolts or studs the threads of which are in any way damaged, and whenever possible use new spring washers. Apart from your normal tools, a supply of clean rag, an oil can filled with engine oil (an empty plastic detergent bottle thoroughly cleaned and washed out, will invariably do just as well), a new supply of assorted spring washers, a set of new gaskets, and preferably a torque spanner, should be collected together.

9. REBUILDING THE ENGINE

1. Ensure that the crankcase is thoroughly clean and that all oilways are clear. A thin twist drill is useful for cleaning them out. If possible, blow them out with compressed air. Treat the crankshaft in the same fashion, and then inject engine oil into the crankshaft oilways. Commence work on rebuilding the engine by replacing the crankshaft and main bearings:-

2. If the old main bearing shells are to be replaced, (a false economy unless they are virtually as new), fit the three upper halves of the main bearing shells to their location in the crankcase, after wiping the locations clean.

3. If new bearings are being fitted, carefully clean away all traces of the protective grease with which they are coated.

4. Ensure that the thrust washers are fitted correctly to the side faces of the centre main bearing. These semi-circular washers have white metal thrust faces and these faces are easily recognised by the two vertical oil grooves cut across the white metal. The washers are fitted with their white metal thrust faces towards the crankshaft thrust faces.

5. Generously lubricate the crankshaft journals and the upper and lower main bearing shells and carefully place the crankshaft in position.

6. Place the lower halves of the main bearing shells into the caps and fit into position with the main bearing bolts. Ensure that the right shell goes into the right cap if the old bearings are being refitted. The mating surface must be spotlessly clean or the caps will not seat properly.

7. Test the crankshaft for freedom of rotation. Should it be very stiff to turn or possess high spots a most careful inspection must be made, preferably by a qualified mechanic with a micrometer to get to the root of the trouble. It is very seldom that any trouble of this nature will be experienced when fitting the crankshaft.

8. Check carefully that the machined front face of the front main bearing cap is in alignment with the machined face of the cylinder block as seen in Fig. 1. 6.

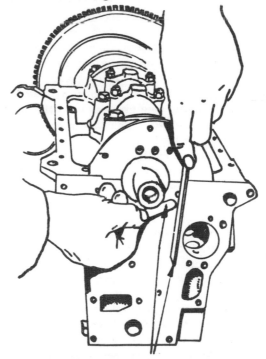

Fig. 1.6. Checking the front main bearing cap alignment with straight edge and 0.015 inch feeler gauge.

9. Tighten down the main bearing bolts to a torque of 50/60 lbs/ft., and then check the crankshaft end float with a feeler gauge 0.002 in. minimum and 0.004 in. maximum, as shown in Fig. 1.7.

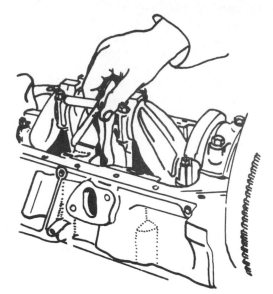

Fig. 1.7. Checking the crankshaft end float at the centre main bearing with a feeler gauge.

10. Should the piston rings require replacing the following procedure should be followed:-
11. Check that the piston ring grooves and oil-ways are thoroughly clean and unblocked. Piston rings must always be fitted over the head of the piston and never from the bottom. The easiest method to use when fitting rings is to wrap a .020 feeler gauge round the top of the piston and place the rings one at a time, starting with the bottom oil control ring, over the feeler gauge. The feeler gauge, complete with ring, can then be slid down the piston over the other piston ring grooves until the correct groove is reached. The piston ring is then slid gently off the feeler gauge into the groove. An alternative method is to fit the rings by holding them slightly open with the thumbs and both of your index fingers. This method requires a steady hand and great care as it is easy to open the ring too much and break it.
12. The pistons, complete with connecting rods, can be fitted to the cylinder bores in the following sequence:-
13. With a wad of clean rag wipe the cylinder bores clean.
14. The pistons, complete with connecting rods, are fitted to their bores from above.
15. As each piston is inserted into its bore ensure that it is the correct piston/connecting rod assembly for that particular bore and that the connecting rod is the right way round, and that the front of the piston is towards the front

of the bore, i.e. towards the front of the engine.
16. The piston will only slide into the bore as far as the oil control ring. (See photo). It is

then necessary to compress the piston rings into a clamp and to gently tap the piston into the cylinder bore with a wooden or plastic hammer. If a proper piston ring clamp is not available then a suitable jubilee clip does the job very well, or even a piece of flexible tin. (See photo).

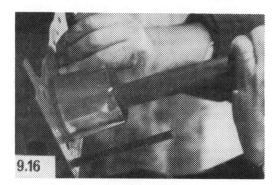

17. With each piston in position the engine is turned on its side in order to assemble the connecting rod big end bearings.
18. Wipe the connecting rod half of the big end bearing cap and the underside of the shell bearing clean, and fit the shell bearing in position with its locating tongue engaged with the corresponding groove in the connecting rod.
19. If the old bearings are nearly new and are being refitted then ensure they are replaced in their correct locations on the correct rods.
20. Generously lubricate the crankpin journals with engine oil, and turn the crankshaft so that the crankpin is in the most advantageous position for the connecting rod to be drawn onto it.
21. Wipe the connecting rod bearing cap and back of the shell bearing clean and fit the shell bearing in position ensuring that the locating tongue at the back of the bearing engages with the locating groove in connecting rod cap, (see

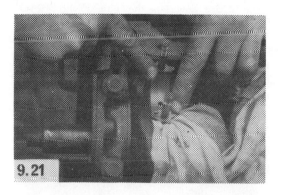

9.21

22. Generously lubricate the shell bearing and offer up the connecting rod bearing cap to the connecting rod. (See photo).

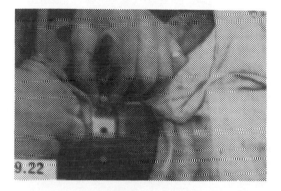

9.22

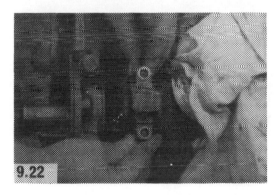

9.22

23. Fit the self locking nuts into position and if they can be screwed any distance down the bolt threads with the fingers, they should be discarded and new nuts fitted, as they will not securely grip the bolts under torque.

24. Each nut must be tightened to a torque of 24 lb/ft. The bolts will be either $\frac{5}{16}$ UNF or $\frac{11}{32}$ UNF.

25. When replacing nuts, note that where the nuts are $\frac{11}{32}$ inch x 24 threads per inch UNF take care to ensure that $\frac{3}{8}$ inch x 24 threads per inch UNF nuts which are used on some other Rootes Group engines are not fitted as replacement nuts. These larger nuts, having

the same number of threads per inch can in fact be screwed onto the $\frac{11}{32}$ in. bolts, but they will strip when tightened to 12 lbs/ft. torque. This means that they cannot be tightened correctly, and therefore will come adrift during the engine service life.

26. With all piston assemblies in position the crankshaft should be turned over by hand several times to ensure that everything is moving correctly and that there is no obstruction, such as would be the case if one shell liner had not been placed in position correctly.

27. The timing gears and chains can now be refitted in the following manner:-

28. When refitting the timing wheels, set Nos.1 and 4 pistons to top dead centre, so that the key is to the TOP of the crankshaft. (See photo).

9.28

29. Push the crankshaft (small) wheel onto the shaft until it is about $1\frac{1}{2}$ ins. from the shoulder of the shaft.

30. Now make sure that the crankshaft wheel dot and the similar dot on the camshaft (large) wheel are in line. (See photo).

9.30

31. Turn the camshaft until the key lines up with the keyway in the camshaft wheel.

32. With the camshaft wheel in the correct position, pull the camshaft wheel onto the camshaft end by using a bolt screwed into the camshaft end with a flat washer. (See photo).

33. Do not attempt to drive the camshaft sprocket onto the camshaft because this will

9.32

force the camshaft towards the rear and so displace the sealing disc at the outer rear end of the rear camshaft bearing.

34. Drive the crankshaft wheel onto the crankshaft with a brass drift.

35. Fit the camshaft wheel fixing bolt and lockwasher, and knock over the tab on the lockwasher. (See photo).

9.35

9.35

36. Replace the crankshaft oil thrower and refit the chain tensioner, and cover, making sure that the tensioner blade is in contact with the chain and pressing against it.

37. Note that the timing case is bolted to a pedestal bolt, and the free end of the tensioner blade rests on the inside of the timing case.

38. Generously oil the chain and gearwheels.

39. Place a new gasket in position on the timing case, and before securing the bolts around the outer edge of the case, make certain that the cover is centralised around the crankshaft pulley, (see photo). This can be done with the aid of a centralising tool placed over the end of the crankshaft. The securing bolts are then tightened using a socket spanner.

9.39

40. Drive the crankshaft pulley into position over the key. Fit the lockwasher with its projection in the keyhole and secure with the large nut. Remember to knock up the tabs on the lockwasher after replacing the nut. (See photo).

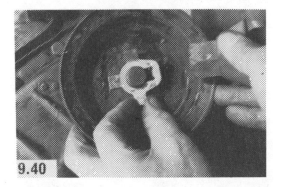
9.40

41. Turning to the other end of the engine; now fit the flywheel squarely on the end of the crankshaft. If the dowel has come away with the flywheel, tap it out of the flywheel and replace in the crankshaft flange. Refit the four setbolts with the tabwashers.

42. Tighten the setbolts to 37 - 43 lbs/ft., and then check the run-out at the outer edge of the clutch facing, if a clock gauge is available. This should not exceed 0.003 in.

43. Lock the four setbolts by bending over the tabs of the lockwashers.

44. Before replacing the oil pump it is advisable to check it for wear in the following way.

45. The pump must be held with the bottom facing upwards to prevent the rotor units from sliding out. Remove the filter if this has not already been taken away, and then unscrew the four setscrews securing the shroud and the pump base plate, and lift these off. Take care

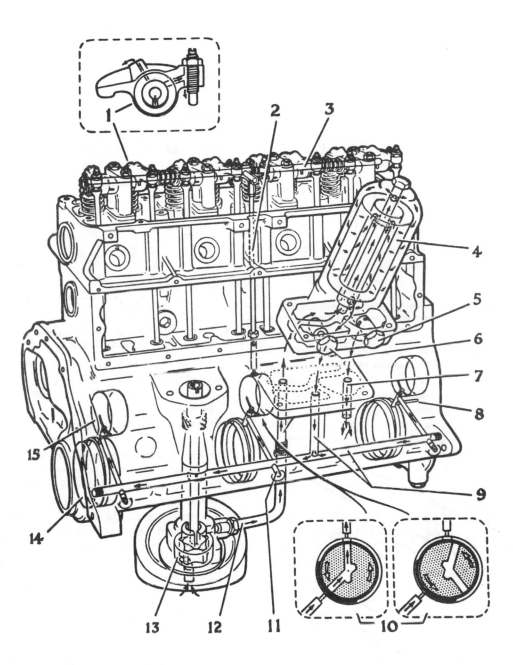

Fig. 1.8. EXPLODED VIEW OF THE ENGINE LUBRICATION SYSTEM.

1 Valve rocker oilways. 2 Oil feed pipe. 3 Oil feed to rocker shaft. 4 Full flow oil filter. 5 Oil pressure relief valve. 6 Filter by-pass valve. 7 Oil pressure relief valve discharge hole. 8 Oil feed to timing chain oil feed pipe. 9 Oil gallery and feed from filter. 10 Cross section through camshaft centre journal showing drilling in journal used to control oil feed to rocker gear. 11 Connection point for oil warning light switch or oil pressure gauge. 12 Oil feed from oil pump to filter. 13 Oil pump. 14 Main bearings. 15 Camshaft bearings.

not to drop the base plate otherwise this may crack.

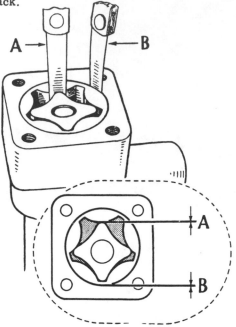

Fig. 1.9. Checking the rotor lip and outer rotor clearance in the pump body. Maximum clearance allowed at 'A' is .006 inch and at 'B' .008 inch.

46. The clearances on the ring and rotor can then be checked as shown in Fig.1.9 and 1.10 and if they are greater than those given, the parts must be replaced as a complete set. Maximum clearance at 'A' should be .006 in. and at 'B' 008 in. In Fig.1.10 the maximum and minimum clearances are .003 in. and .001 inch respectively.

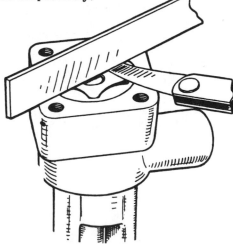

Fig. 1.10. Checking the rotor end clearance which have a maximum of .003 inch and a minimum of .001 inch.

47. The ignition distributor takes its drive from the helical drive on the oil pump shaft axially, through an off-set tongue and slot type coupling which can only be coupled one way.

It is essential that the oil pump helical gear is meshed to the corresponding gear on the camshaft so that the driving slot in the end of the gear is timed in correct relationship to the camshaft.

48. The pump is refitted in the following sequence. Make sure that number one piston is at top dead centre and that both valves of this cylinder are closed. This means that the cams nearest the front of the engine are pointing downwards, if the cylinder head has not been refitted.

49. With the supply pipe in position, push the pump into its bore in the crankcase, while holding the slot in a position shown in Fig.1.11

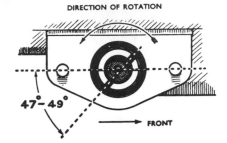

Fig. 1.11. The oil pump drive in the correct position with No. cylinder at T.D.C. firing.

50. Bolt the pump flange into position with the securing bolts, and replace the supply pipe union, making sure that both ends of the pipe are tightened.

51. One method which can be used to locate and check the slot in the oil pump when the pump is pushed fully home is to make up a cardboard template. This requires two holes punched to fit neatly over the ignition distributor securing studs, and a hole cut in the centre.

52. Draw a straight line across the two stud holes, and then at a point $1\frac{1}{8}$ in. from the centre of the stud nearest the front of the engine, construct a line at 48° to the horizontal line as shown in Fig.1.11. above.

53. When this template is placed over the studs as shown, (see photo), the angle line should about pass through the slot, with number 1 cy-

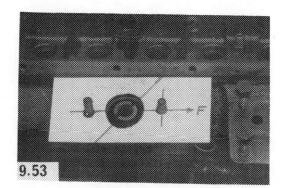

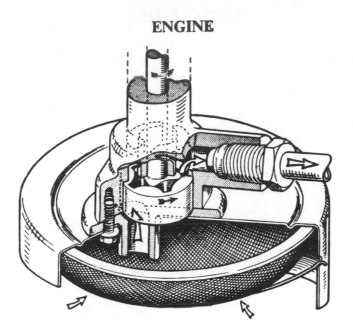

Fig. 1.12. Cut away view of the oil pump. The white arrows show the direction of oil flow and the black arrows the rotation of the pump

linder on its firing stroke and at T. D. C. The allowance is from 47° to 49° so that the slot may not quite pass through the centre, but will show if the pump is fitted one tooth or more out, and this can be corrected before the pump is actually bolted up.

54. At this point the oil sump can be replaced carefully following the procedure detailed below.

55. Thoroughly wash out the sump with petrol and then inspect the cork packings in the semicircular crankshaft seal housings. If these are at all flattened new ones should be fitted.

56. After the sump has been thoroughly cleaned, scrape all traces of the old sump gasket from the sump flange.

57. Wipe down the inside of the crankcase, including the crankshaft bearing surfaces, clean. Thoroughly clean and scrape the crankcase to sump flange.

58. With a new gasket held lightly in position the sump is then offered up to the crankcase and the centre bolts fitted first, all bolts being tightened progressively to ensure that the sump is secured all round.

59. At this stage in rebuilding the engine, it is a matter of choice whether the main block assembly is returned to the car or not. Because of the overall weight of the engine this may be considered the better procedure, leaving the refitting of the cylinder head, water pump, manifolds, ignition system and fuel pump, to be undertaken in the actual car, rather than having the additional weight to lift.

60. The cylinder head can now be replaced. First check that both the cylinder block and the cylinder head mating surfaces are clean, and then pour some engine oil into each cylinder. Fit oil feed pipe. (See photo).

61. Always use a new cylinder head gasket, because the old one will have been compressed and not capable of providing a sound gas and water tight seal. Fit the gasket with TOP uppermost.

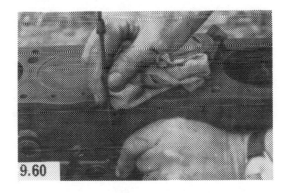

62. It is not a sound policy to apply any jointing compound to a new gasket, because if the mating surfaces are clean and true, such a compound is unnecessary, and becomes a liability when the head has to be removed in the future.

63. Never smear grease on either side of the gasket as when the engine heats up the grease will melt and may allow a compression leak to develop.

64. Lower the head into position, (see photo) and place the cylinder head bolts in position, together with their washers.

9.64

65. It is most important that the cylinder head is aligned so as to correctly position the machined location for the tappet cover in relation to the corresponding machined face on the cylinder block before tightening the cylinder head bolts.

66. The cylinder head bolts are tightened to the sequence shown in Fig. 1.4. to a torque of 48 lbs/ft. (See photo).

9.66

67. With the cylinder head in position fit the valve pushrods in the same order in which they were removed.

68. Refit the valve tappet cover to the side of the engine, and tighten the cover screws around the edges.

69. Replace the valve rockers, which are in two parts, making sure that the oil feed pipe is fitted up in the centre union before the rocker pedestals are secured. (See photo) Place the

9.69

bolts in the pedestals and tighten these down. turning the engine over in order to ease the pressure on the valves as the rockers are pulled down.

70. Check carefully that the pushrod ends are located in each tappet end. (See photo). With the pedestal bolts secured, the valve tappets can be adjusted initially.

9.70

10. ENGINE REPLACEMENT

1. Replacement of the engine in the car is basically the reverse of the sequence of operations for removal, the actual series of operations depending on whether the main block is returned to the car before the final assembly of the cylinder head and accessories (see note on Page 35.).

2. When returning the engine, take care to align the cylinder block and the bellhousing faces, if the gearbox has been left in the car, before attempting to slide the clutch centre plate splines onto the splines of the gearbox stem wheel shaft. The engine can be turned by using a spanner on the starting dog nut in order to relate the splines.

3. On engines fitted with a torque reaction restrictor, the bracket on the cylinder head must be positioned as shown in Fig. 1.13. The importance of the clearances lies in the fact that if these are too small this will restrict engine movement on the flexible mountings, and the engine will appear to run rough at low speeds.

4. On models fitted with a steering column gear change, the action of this should be checked after the linkage is reassembled. The correct method of adjustment is given in Chapter 6, Gearbox.

11 WORK THAT CAN BE DONE WITHOUT ENGINE REMOVAL

1. An engine needs to be tuned at regular intervals if it is to produce the best results in performance and economy. Tuning consists

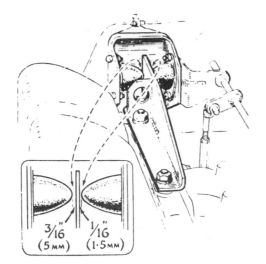

Fig. 1.13. Correct tolerances on the engine torque reaction restrictor (where fitted).

of adjusting relevant settings to their correct values and correcting small defects.

2. When tuning an engine it is essential first of all to determine the condition of the inside of each cylinder, otherwise any other tuning operation will be a waste of time. This can be accomplished with the aid of a compression gauge.

3. The compression test measures the ability of the pistons and rings to form an efficient seal with the cylinder walls, and the efficiency with which the valves are sealing.

4. The operation is performed by first warming up the engine to operating temperatures and then removing the sparking plugs. The compression gauge is fitted into each sparking plug hole in turn.

5. Each cylinder should be allowed about 12 piston compression strokes, and the pressure obtained should be recorded.

6. Test all cylinders in sequence. The recorded pressures should be within 5 to 10 lbs. If all readings are low, this will indicate that the pistons, rings and valves require attention. The correct compression pressures for your particular engine can be found in the specifications at the beginning of this chapter.

7. If the readings of two adjacent cylinders are low then suspect a leaking cylinder head gasket.

8. To determine whether the pistons and rings or the valves need attention, squirt some medium engine oil into each cylinder, turn the engine over several times to allow the oil to work round the rings, and then test each cylinder with the compression gauge.

9. If the readings produced, when compared with the initial readings, are normal this will indicate that the oil has temporarily blocked up the rings and that these need attention.

10. But if the valves are in poor condition, then the readings obtained, even with the oil sealing will not vary appreciably from the first set obtained.

11. If the compression readings are only partly improved this will indicate that both the rings and the valves need attention.

12. It should be noted that, after new rings have been fitted, a compression test may not show any marked improvement until the engine has been run for 200 or 300 miles, by which time the new parts will have bedded down.

13. However, after a valve regrind has been completed and the engine reassembled, a compression test should show a marked improvement.

14. If, during initial testing, one cylinder only shows a poor reading, this will indicate that only this cylinder requires attention, and this may be due either to a burned out valve, or a valve with a bent stem. These should be checked before dismantling the engine. Similarly, if a valve has collected a covering of sludge over the stem, this may be causing it to stick, and this in turn will show up by a poor compression reading.

15. Provided that the compression pressures are satisfactory the following checks can be carried out.

16. Run the engine up to operating temperatures and check the contact breaker points gap. Check the state of the battery charge. Clean and replace the air filter if necessary. Check the tightening of the cylinder head nuts together with the tightness of the intake and exhaust manifolds. Adjust the valve tappet clearances, and check the condition of the rocker cover gasket for oil leaking. Where necessary check and adjust the carburetter settings. Details of these settings can be found in Chapter 3.

17. The radiator and water pump removal are covered in Chapter 2 and the carburetter removal in Chapter 3. All these tasks can be carried out without removing the engine from the car.

18. To remove the timing cover and the timing wheels and chain the following procedure should be followed.

19. Drain and remove the radiator, slacken the generator mounting screws and remove the fan belt, unscrew the crankshaft jaw nut and pull off the crankshaft pulley. This is done by inserting two threaded bolts into two tapped holes provided and screwing these in evenly until the pulley is freed from the crankshaft.

20. Remove all the screws securing the timing

cover to the cylinder block and withdraw the cover. When the cover is refitted it must be centralised around the crankshaft pulley before the securing bolts are fully tightened.

21. The timing wheels and timing chain can be removed with the engine in the vehicle provided the radiator and fan belt are removed. The procedure is first to remove the split pin and plain washer from the tensioner pivot and lift off the chain tensioner blade. With a screwdriver, remove the setscrew, tab washer and plain washer from the front of the camshaft. Prise off the oil thrower in front of the crankshaft wheel, and then pull or lever off both camshaft and crankshaft wheels at the same time. Remove the woodruff key from the crankshaft with a pair of pliers, and drop into a tin or jar for safety.

22. The cylinder head is removed in the following manner. Unscrew the securing bolts and lift off the air cleaner or cleaners, and unscrew the nuts securing the rocker cover and lift this away together with the gasket.

23. Disconnect the water temperature lead by gripping the rubber sleeve at the end of the lead and pulling out the snap connector.

24. If a heater pipe is fitted, disconnect this at the hose clip and then carefully unscrew the union of the oil feed pipe at the rocker shaft.

25. On early models unscrew the series of screws securing the tappet side covers where these are secured to the cylinder head. If the side cover gasket of these models is damaged during removal, the cover will have to be removed completely and a new joint fitted when reassembling.

26. Disconnect the petrol supply pipe and the carburetter controls, and remove the nuts securing the exhaust pipe flange to the exhaust manifold flange. Drop the exhaust pipe clear of the engine.

27. The carburetter can be removed at this stage by unbolting the nuts securing the flange of the carburetter to the intake manifold, or can be left in position and lifted away with the cylinder head.

28. Unscrew the rocker pedestal nuts (eight) by unscrewing these evenly since the rocker shaft will be under some pressure from the valve springs. Lift off the rocker shaft as an assembly.

29. The pushrods are then removed, and these should be kept in their correct order by placing in a series of holes made in a strip of stiff cardboard, with the pushrod nearest the front of the engine in number one hole.

30. With a socket spanner, unscrew the nuts and bolts securing the cylinder head to the block, in the order indicated in Fig. 1.4. If the cylinder head will not lift away reasonably easily, replace the sparking plugs and turn the engine over as smartly as possible in order to generate a degree of compression inside the cylinders which may well loosen the head, especially if this has been previously fitted with the aid of a sealing solution on both sides of the gasket.

31. An alternative method is to use a wooden mallet to rap the corners of the cylinder head smartly while having the head pulled upwards, but under no circumstances should a metal headed hammer be used as this will crack the cast material of the head.

32. Any attempt to force a screwdriver between the head and block will probably damage the surface of the block and/or cylinder head so that it will no longer be gas or water tight.

33. Once the head has been loosened it should be lifted off and placed on the bench for subsequent overhaul.

34. Decarbonisation of the cylinder head can be carried out with the engine either in or out of the car. With the cylinder head off carefully remove with a wire brush and blunt scraper all traces of carbon deposits from the combustion spaces and the ports. The valve head stems and valve guides should also be freed from any carbon deposits. Wash the combustion spaces and ports down with petrol and scrape the cylinder head surface free of any foreign matter with the side of a steel rule, or a similar article.

35. Clean the pistons and top of the cylinder bores. If the pistons are still in the block then it is essential that great care is taken to ensure that no carbon gets into the cylinder bores as this could scratch the cylinder walls or cause damage to the pistons and rings. To ensure this does not happen, first turn the crankshaft so that two of the pistons are at the top of their bores. Stuff rag into the other two bores or seal them off with paper and masking tape. The waterways should also be covered with small pieces of masking tape to prevent particles of carbon entering the cooling system and damaging the water pump.

36. There are two schools of thought as to how much carbon should be removed from the piston crown. One school recommends that a ring of carbon should be left round the edge of the piston and on the cylinder bore wall as an aid to low oil consumption. Although this is probably true for early engines with worn bores, on later engines the thought of the second school can be applied; which is that for effective decarbonisation all traces of carbon should be

Fig. 1.14. CYLINDER HEAD REMOVED WITH ENGINE IN CAR SHOWING:-
Oil supply pipe to rocker shaft. 2 Distributor tied up away from the engine. 3 Camshaft followers.   4 Small bore water pipe left in position when head is removed.

removed.

37. If all traces of carbon are to be removed, press a little grease into the gap between the cylinder walls and the two pistons which are to be worked on. With a blunt scraper carefully scrape away the carbon from the piston crown, taking great care not to scratch the aluminium. Also scrape away the carbon from the surrounding lip of the cylinder wall. When all carbon has been removed, scrape away the grease which will now be contaminated with carbon particles, taking care not to press any into the bores. To assist prevention of carbon build-up the piston crown can be polished with a metal polish such as Brasso. Remove the rags or masking tape from the other two cylinders and turn the crankshaft so that the two pistons which were at the bottom are now at the top. Place rag or masking tape in the cylinders which have been decarbonised and proceed as just described.

38. If a ring of carbon is going to be left round the piston then this can be helped by inserting an old piston ring into the top of the bore to rest on the piston and ensure that carbon is not accidentally removed. Check that there are

no particles of carbon in the cylinder bores. Decarbonising is now complete.

39. The valves can be removed from the cylinder head by the following method:- Compress each spring in turn with a valve spring compressor until the two halves of the cotters can be removed. Release the compressor and remove the spring, shroud, and valve. (See photos).

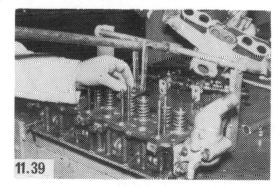

11.39

40. If, when the valve spring compressor is screwed down, the valve spring retaining cap refuses to free and expose the split cotter, do not continue to screw down on the compressor

11.39

as there is a likelihood of damaging it. Gently tap the top of the tool directly over the cap with a light hammer. This will free the cap. To avoid the compressor jumping off the valve spring retaining cap when it is tapped, hold the compressor firmly in position with one hand. (See photo).

11.40

41. It is essential that the valves are kept in their correct sequence unless they are so badly worn that they are to be renewed. If they are going to be kept and used again, place them in a sheet of card having eight holes numbered 1 to 8 corresponding with the relative positions the valves were in when fitted. Also keep the valve springs, washers, etc, in the correct order.

Fig. 1.15.   View of the valve springs, valve spring cup and cotters.

42. Examine the heads of the valves for pitting and burning, especially the heads of the exhaust valves. The valve seatings should be examined at the same time. If the pitting on valve and seat is very slight the marks can be removed by grinding the seats and valves together with coarse, and then fine, valve grinding paste. Where bad pitting has occured to the valve seats it will be necessary to recut them and fit new valves. If the valve seats are so worn that they cannot be recut, then it will be necessary to fit new valve seat inserts. These latter two jobs should be entrusted to the local Rootes agent or engineering works. In practice it is very seldom that the seats are so badly worn that they require renewal. Normally, it is the valve that is too badly worn for replacement, and the owner can easily purchase a new set of valves and match them to the seats by valve grinding.

43. Valve grinding is carried out as follows:-

Smear a trace of coarse carborundum paste on the seat face and apply a suction grinder tool to the valve head. With a semi-rotary motion, grind the valve head to its seat, lifting the valve occasionally to redistribute the grinding paste. When a dull matt even surface finish is produced on both the valve seat and the valve, then wipe off the paste and repeat the process with fine carborundum paste, lifting and turning the valve to redistribute the paste as before. A light spring placed under the valve head will greatly ease this operation. When a smooth unbroken ring of light grey matt finish is produced, on both valve and valve seat faces, the grinding operation is completed.   (See photo).

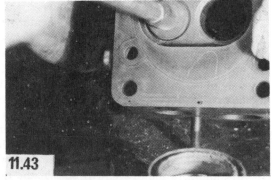

11.43

44. Scrape away all carbon from the valve head and the valve stem. Carefully clean away every trace of grinding compound, taking great care to leave none in the ports or in the valve guides. (See photos). Clean the valves and valve seats with a paraffin soaked rag then with a clean rag, and finally, if an air line is available, blow the valves, valve guides and

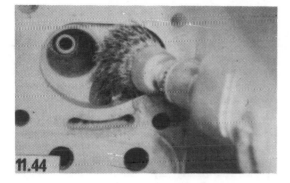

45. Examine the v a l v e guides internally for wear. If the valves are a very loose fit in the guides and there is the slightest suspicion of lateral rocking, then new guides will have to be fitted. If the valve guides have been removed compare them internally by visual inspection with a new guide as well as testing them for rocking with the valves.

46. The valve guides are a press fit into the head and as these require the use of a special drawing tool for both removal and replacement the head should be taken to your local Rootes dealer who will have this equipment.

47. The piston assemblies can be removed from the engine while this is in the car, but in general, unless a pit is available, this work is more satisfactorily done with the engine out of the car, largely because if a big end bearing or a crankshaft main bearing has disintegrated the crankshaft will need some attention.

valve p o r t s clean. See photo showing valve; before and after cleaning.

Fig. 1.16. The connecting rod oilways are cleared by using a pipe cleaner as shown.

FAULT FINDING CHART

Cause	Trouble	Remedy
SYMPTOM:	**ENGINE FAILS TO TURN OVER WHEN STARTER BUTTON PULLED**	
No current at starter motor	Flat or defective battery Loose battery leads Defective starter solenoid or switch or broken wiring Engine earth strap disconnected	Charge or replace battery. Push-start car. Tighten both terminals and earth ends of earth lead. Run a wire direct from the battery to the starter motor or by-pass the solenoid. Check and retighten strap.
Current at starter motor	Jammed starter motor drive pinion Defective starter motor	Place car in gear and rock from side to side. Alternatively, free exposed square end of shaft with spanner. Remove and recondition.
SYMPTOM:	**ENGINE TURNS OVER BUT WILL NOT START**	
No spark at sparking plug	Ignition damp or wet Ignition leads to spark plugs loose Shorted or disconnected low tension leads Dirty, incorrectly set, or pitted contact breaker points Faulty condenser Defective ignition switch Ignition leads connected wrong way round Faulty coil Contact breaker point spring earthed or broken	Wipe dry the distributor cap and ignition leads. Check and tighten at both spark plug and distributor cap ends. Check the wiring on the CB and SW terminals of the coil and to the distributor. Clean, file smooth, and adjust. Check contact breaker points for arcing, remove and fit new. By-pass switch with wire. Remove and replace leads to spark plugs in correct order. Remove and fit new coil. Check spring is not touching metal part of distributor. Check insulator washers are correctly placed. Renew points if the spring is broken.
No fuel at carburettor float chamber or at jets	No petrol in petrol tank Vapour lock in fuel line (In hot conditions or at high altitude) Blocked float chamber needle valve Fuel pump filter blocked Choked or blocked carburettor jets Faulty fuel pump	Refill tank! Blow into petrol tank, allow engine to cool, or apply a cold wet rag to the fuel line. Remove, clean, and replace. Remove, clean, and replace. Dismantle and clean. Remove, overhaul, and replace. Check CB points on S.U. pumps.
Excess of petrol in cylinder or carburettor flooding	Too much choke allowing too rich a mixture to wet plugs Float damaged or leaking or needle not seating Float lever incorrectly adjusted	Remove and dry sparking plugs or with wide open throttle, push-start the car. Remove, examine, clean and replace float and needle valve as necessary. Remove and adjust correctly.
SYMPTOM:	**ENGINE STALLS & WILL NOT START**	
No spark at sparking plug	Ignition failure - Sudden Ignition failure - Misfiring precludes total stoppage Ignition failure - In severe rain or after traversing water splash	Check over low and high tension circuits for breaks in wiring Check contact breaker points, clean and adjust. Renew condenser if faulty. Dry out ignition leads and distributor cap.
No fuel at jets	No petrol in petrol tank Petrol tank breather choked Sudden obstruction in carburettor(s) Water in fuel system	Refill tank. Remove petrol cap and clean out breather hole or pipe. Check jets, filter, and needle valve in float chamber for blockage Drain tank and blow out fuel lines

ENGINE FAULT FINDING CHART

Cause	Trouble	Remedy
SYMPTOM:	ENGINE MISFIRES OR IDLES UNEVENLY	
Intermittent sparking at sparking plug	Ignition leads loose	Check and tighten as necessary at spark plug and distributor cap ends.
	Battery leads loose on terminals	Check and tighten terminal leads.
	Battery earth strap loose on body attachment point	Check and tighten earth lead to body attachment point.
	Engine earth lead loose	Tighten lead.
	Low tension leads to SW and CB terminals on coil loose	Check and tighten leads if found loose.
	Low tension lead from CB terminal side to distributor loose	Check and tighten if found loose.
	Dirty, or incorrectly gapped plugs	Remove, clean, and regap.
	Dirty, incorrectly set, or pitted contact breaker points	Clean, file smooth, and adjust.
	Tracking across inside of distributor cover	Remove and fit new cover.
	Ignition too retarded	Check and adjust ignition timing.
	Faulty coil	Remove and fit new coil.
Fuel shortage at engine	Mixture too weak	Check jets, float chamber needle valve, and filters for obstruction. Clean as necessary. Carburettor(s) incorrectly adjusted.
	Air leak in carburettor(s)	Remove and overhaul carburettor.
	Air leak at inlet manifold to cylinder head, or inlet manifold to carburettor	Test by pouring oil along joints. Bubbles indicate leak. Renew manifold gasket as appropriate.
Mechanical wear	Incorrect valve clearances	Adjust rocker arms to take up wear.
	Burnt out exhaust valves	Remove cylinder head and renew defective valves.
	Sticking or leaking valves	Remove cylinder head, clean, check and renew valves as necessary.
	Weak or broken valve springs	Check and renew as necessary.
	Worn valve guides or stems	Renew valve guides and valves.
	Worn pistons and piston rings	Dismantle engine, renew pistons and rings.
SYMPTOM:	LACK OF POWER & POOR COMPRESSION	
Fuel/air mixture leaking from cylinder	Burnt out exhaust valves	Remove cylinder head, renew defective valves.
	Sticking or leaking valves	Remove cylinder head, clean, check, and renew valves as necessary.
	Worn valve guides and stems	Remove cylinder head and renew valves and valve guides.
	Weak or broken valve springs	Remove cylinder head, renew defective springs.
	Blown cylinder head gasket (Accompanied by increase in noise)	Remove cylinder head and fit new gasket.
	Worn pistons and piston rings	Dismantle engine, renew pistons and rings.
	Worn or scored cylinder bores	Dismantle engine, rebore, renew pistons & rings.
Incorrect Adjustments	Ignition timing wrongly set. Too advanced or retarded	Check and reset ignition timing.
	Contact breaker points incorrectly gapped	Check and reset contact breaker points.
	Incorrect valve clearances	Check and reset rocker arm to valve stem gap.
	Incorrectly set sparking plugs	Remove, clean and regap.
	Carburation too rich or too weak	Tune carburettor(s) for optimum performance.
Carburation and ignition faults	Dirty contact breaker points	Remove, clean, and replace.
	Fuel filters blocked causing top end fuel starvation	Dismantle, inspect, clean, and replace all fuel filters.
	Distributor automatic balance weights or vacuum advance and retard mechanisms not functioning correctly	Overhaul distributor.
	Faulty fuel pump giving top end fuel starvation	Remove, overhaul, or fit exchange reconditioned fuel pump.

Cause	Trouble	Remedy
SYMPTOM:	EXCESSIVE OIL CONSUMPTION	
Oil being burnt by engine	Badly worn, perished or missing valve stem oil seals	Remove, fit new oil seals to valve stems.
	Excessively worn valve stems and valve guides	Remove cylinder head and fit new valves and valve guides.
	Worn piston rings	Fit oil control rings to existing pistons or purchase new pistons.
	Worn pistons and cylinder bores	Fit new pistons and rings, rebore cylinders.
	Excessive piston ring gap allowing blow-by	Fit new piston rings and set gap correctly.
	Piston oil return holes choked	Decarbonise engine and pistons.
Oil being lost due to leaks	Leaking oil filter gasket	Inspect and fit new gasket as necessary.
	Leaking rocker cover gasket	" " " " " " "
	Leaking tappet chest gasket	" " " " " " "
	Leaking timing case gasket	" " " " " " "
	Leaking sump gasket	" " " " " " "
	Loose sump plug	Tighten, fit new gasket if necessary.
SYMPTOM:	UNUSUAL NOISES FROM ENGINE	
Excessive clearances due to mechanical wear	Worn valve gear (Noisy tapping from rocker box)	Inspect and renew rocker shaft, rocker arms, and ball pins as necessary.
	Worn big end bearing (Regular heavy knocking)	Drop sump, if bearings broken up clean out oil pump and oilways, fit new bearings. If bearings not broken but worn fit bearing shells.
	Worn timing chain and gears (Rattling from front of engine)	Remove timing cover, fit new timing wheels and timing chain.
	Worn main bearings (Rumbling and vibration)	Drop sump, remove crankshaft, if bearings worn but not broken up, renew. If broken up strip oil pump and clean out oilways.
	Worn crankshaft (Knocking, rumbling and vibration)	Regrind crankshaft, fit new main and big end bearings.

CHAPTER TWO

COOLING SYSTEM

CONTENTS

SPECIFICATIONS

Type of system	Centrifugal pump and fan
Fan - Number of blades	4
- Diameter	14.5 in.
ype of radiator	3 two grilled tube
Drain taps - Radiator	In bottom water pipe
- Cylinder block	Left-hand side
Thermostat setting (bellows type) ...	Opens at 170°F (76.7°C)
	Fully open at 185°F (85°C)
(wax type)	Opens at 185°F (85°C)
	Fully open at 200°F (93.3°C)
Radiator cap relief pressure	7 p. s. i.
Drive of pump and fan..	'V' belt from crankshaft
Capacity of cooling system	$13\frac{1}{4}$ pints with heater
	(Minx I to IIIC, Husky I & II)
	$12\frac{1}{2}$ pints
	(Minx V, Husky III)

GENERAL DESCRIPTION

Cooling water is circulated by an impeller type pump mounted on the front of the cylinder block, and the system is pressurised. This is to prevent undue loss of water down the radiator overflow pipe and also to prevent boiling of the water in adverse conditions. If the pressure exceeds that quoted in the specification above the pressure in the system forces the internal part of the cap off its seat, thus exposing the overflow pipe down which the steam from the boiling water escapes thus relieving the pressure. It is, therefore, important to check that the radiator cap is in good condition and that the spring behind the sealing washer has not weakened. Most garages have a special machine in which radiator caps can be tested.

The cooling system comprises the radiator, top and bottom water hoses, the thermostat and impeller pump and two drain taps and also a fan which is driven by a Vee belt from the crankshaft. This belt also drives the generator. Water is drawn from the lower radiator tank through the bottom water hose and delivered into the cylinder block passing round each cylinder barrel. From the cylinder block the water passes into the cylinder head through four brass jets. These cause the water to flow around the valve seats before leaving the cylinder head via the thermostat and top water tank hose into the upper water tank of the radiator.

This action of the cooling system is not required to come into full operation until the water has attained its normal working temperature and it is desirable that this should be brought about as quickly as possible after the engine is started from cold. To accomplish this, a thermostatic valve is located in a cast iron body located at the front of the cylinder head. The body which forms part of the hot water outlet pipe is connected to the radiator top tank by a rubber hose. The thermostat valve remains closed when the engine is cold, and when the engine is started, thus allowing the impeller pump to turn, water returns to the pump intake through a small by-pass pipe which connects the pump intake pipe with the engine side of the thermostat. Once the engine is running the water will heat up rapidly, but actual circulation does not commence until the temperature of about 170°F (77°C) (according to model) has been reached in the cylinder head and cylinder block water jackets. At this temperature the thermostat valve opens and the water commences to flow through the radiator.

2. DRAINING THE COOLING SYSTEM
1. If the engine is cold remove the filler cap from the radiator by turning the cap anti-clockwise. If the engine is hot having just been run, then turn the filler cap very slightly until the pressure in the system has had time to disperse. Use a rag over the cap to protect your hand from escaping steam. If, with the engine very hot, the cap is released suddenly the drop in pressure can result in the water boiling. With the pressure released the cap can be removed.
2. If anti-freeze is in the radiator drain it into a clean bucket or bowl for re-use.
3. Open the two drain taps which are located at the base of the radiator and on the left-hand side of the cylinder block. A short length of rubber tubing over the radiator drain tap nozzle will assist draining the coolant into a container without splashing.

4. When the water has finished running, probe the drain tap orifices with a short piece of wire to dislodge any particles of rust or sediment which may be blocking the taps and preventing all the water draining out.

3. FLUSHING THE COOLING SYSTEM
1. With time the cooling system will gradually lose its efficiency as the radiator becomes choked with rust scales, deposits from the water, and other sediment. To clean the system out, remove the radiator cap and the drain tap and leave a hose running in the radiator cap orifice for ten to fifteen minutes.
2. In very bad cases the radiator should be reverse flushed. This can be done with the radiator in position. The cylinder block tap is closed and a hose placed over the open radiator drain tap. Water, under pressure, is then forced up through the radiator and out of the header tank filler orifice.
3. The hose is then removed and placed in the filler orifice and the radiator washed out in the usual fashion.

4. FILLING THE COOLING SYSTEM
1. Close the two drain taps.
2. Fill the system slowly to ensure that no air locks develop. If a heater unit is fitted, check that the valve to the heater unit is open, otherwise an air lock may form in the heater. The best type of water to use in the cooling system is rain water, so use this whenever possible.
3. Do not fill the system higher than within ½ in. of the filler orifice. Overfilling will merely result in wastage which is especially to be avoided when anti-freeze is in use.
4. Only use anti-freeze mixture with a glycerine or ethylene base.
5. Replace the filler cap and turn it firmly clockwise to lock it into position.

5. RADIATOR REMOVAL & REPLACEMENT
1. To remove the radiator drain the cooling system, disconnect the top and bottom hoses, remove six bolts which secure the radiator baffle plates, and then lift the radiator out of the car.
2. When replacing the radiator, give the securing bolts and the caged nuts a liberal supply of grease to prevent the rusting up of the threads.

6. THERMOSTAT REMOVAL & TESTING
1. To remove the thermostat partly drain the cooling system, (four or five pints should be enough), loosen the upper radiator hose at the engine end and pull the hose away. Unscrew

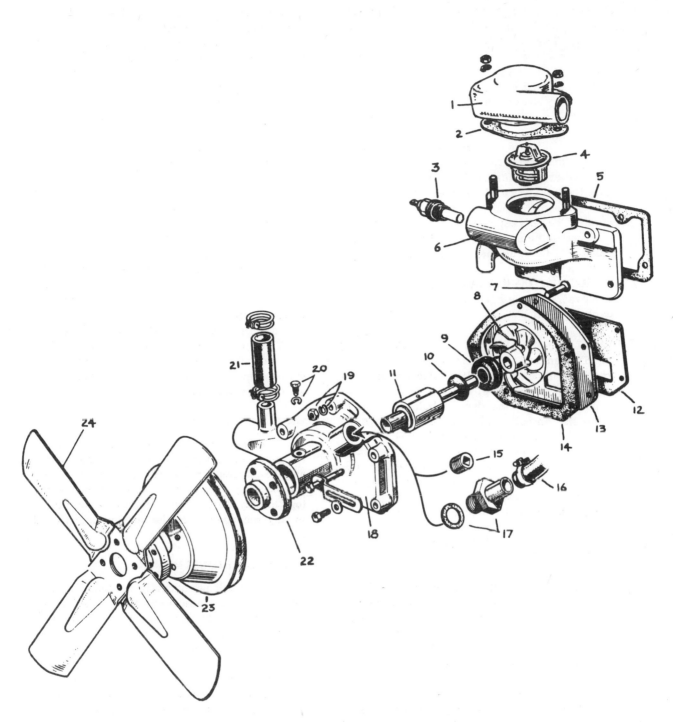

Fig. 2.1. EXPLODED VIEW OF THE WATER PUMP.

1 Water outlet pipe. 2 Gasket. 3 Thermometer element. 4 Thermostat. 5 Gasket. 6 Thermostat housing. 7 Cover plate screw. 8 Impellor. 9 Seal unit. 10 Thrower. 11 Bearing unit. 12 Gasket. 13 Cover plate. 14 Gasket. 15 Plug (cars without heater). 16 Heater hose. 17 Heater hose connector. 18 Body. 19 Cover plate nut and washer. 20 Bearing screw and washer. 21 By-pass hose. 22 Fan pulley centre. 23 Fan pulley and distance piece. 24 Fan blades.

the screws securing the housing to the cylinder head, lift the housing away together with a paper gasket. The thermostat can now be lifted out.

2. Examination of the thermostat may show that even though it is cold, the large area valve has not closed down, and if this is the case, throw away the old unit and replace with a new one. Thermostats are sealed units and cannot be repaired.

3. If the valve is seating down, test for opening by immersing in a saucepan of water, and have a thermometer handy. Heat the water and note the reading of the thermometer at the point where the thermostat valve begins to open. The correct opening temperatures can be found in the specifications at the start of the chapter. Continue heating until the valve is fully open.

4. Refitting the thermostat is the reverse to removal, and it is advisable always to fit a new paper gasket.

7. **WATER PUMP REMOVAL & REPLACEMENT**

1. To remove the water pump, remove the radiator as detailed earlier, slacken the hoses connected to the pump, remove the thermostat housing, slacken the dynamo bolts in order to allow the fan belt to be removed. Remove the fan belt, then remove the fan blades, disconnect heater hoses on models where these are connected to the pump. Unscrew the four securing bolts and lift the water pump away together with the gasket.

2. Reassembly is the reverse order.

8. **WATER PUMP DISMANTLING**

1. The construction of the water pump is seen in Fig. 2.1. and it should be noted that both the impeller and fan pulley are press fits onto the centre spindle. The pump spindle forms an assembly with the bearing unit and cannot be removed without first extracting the impeller and removing the bearing location screw.

2. The only special tool required is a drawer type puller for removal of the fan pulley hub and the impeller.

3. To overhaul the pump the method is as follows:- CAUTION do not wash out the complete pump unit in paraffin, petrol or other cleaning fluid because the pump bearing assembly is of the sealed lubricated type and cannot be lubricated in service.

4. Remove the nut and countersunk bolt securing the cover plate to the body, and lift off the cover plate and washer.

5. Remove the impeller with a suitable puller, and then remove the centre bearing screw from the top of the pump body and from the impeller end push out the spindle complete with the fan hub. A light tap will ensure the removal of the spindle and hub from the bearing once the bearing screw has been removed.

6. The fan hub is removed from the bearing unit spindle with the puller tool, and the rubber seal is pushed rearwards from the housing.

7. If the bearing unit shows signs of wear or is rough then it should be replaced as a unit.

8. Reassembly of the water pump and replacement is the reverse of the above sequence. The following points should be noted.

9. When pressing the larger diameter of the spindle into the fan hub press on slowly until the centre of the pulley is located as shown at dimension in Fig. 2.2. in order to ensure correct alignment with the crankshaft pulley.

10. The special rubber seal on the smaller diameter of the spindle must be assembled with the metal support of the seal facing toward the pulley end of the pump.

9. **WATER TEMPERATURE GAUGE**

This instrument is electrically operated, the gauge being fitted on the instrument panel and the element or transmitter in the thermostat housing. These two units are connected together by a single wire and the temperature is only recorded when the ignition is switched on.

10. **FAN BELT ADJUSTMENT**

The fan belt is correctly tensioned when a total of $\frac{5}{8}$ in. movement can be obtained on the longest run of the belt. To adjust the belt tension, slacken the mounting bolts at the front and rear of the generator, the strap pivot bolt and the screw through the strap slot. Move the generator about its mounting bolts with the aid of a long screwdriver or tyre lever if the generator is stiff to move, until the correct movement is obtained. Do not overtighten the tension as this leads to excessive wear on the generator front bearing, as well as unnecessarily stretching the fan belt. Retighten all the bolts securely once the correct tension has been obtained.

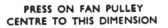

**PRESS ON FAN PULLEY
CENTRE TO THIS DIMENSION**

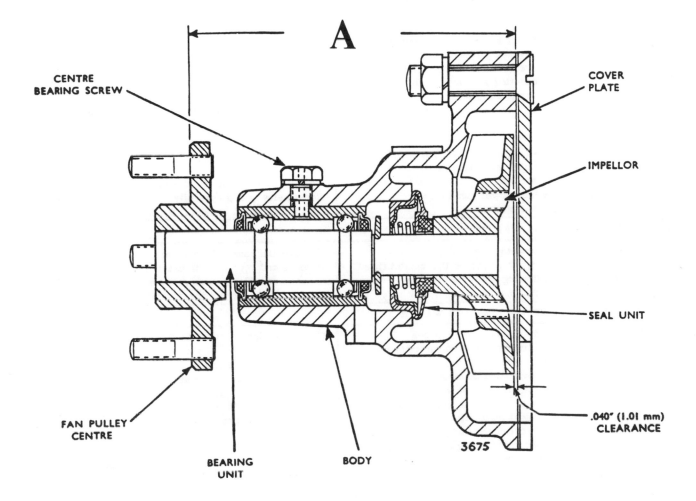

A

CENTRE
BEARING SCREW

COVER
PLATE

IMPELLOR

SEAL UNIT

FAN PULLEY
CENTRE

.040" (1.01 mm)
CLEARANCE

3675

BEARING
UNIT

BODY

Fig. 2.2. Sectional view of water pump assembly. Dimensions at 'A'. Early models 4.00 to 4.01 in. later models 4.865 to 4.875 in.

FAULT FINDING CHART

Cause	Trouble	Remedy
SYMPTOM:	OVERHEATING	
Heat generated in cylinder not being successfully disposed of by radiator	Insufficient water in cooling system	Top up radiator
	Fan belt slipping (Accompanied by a shrieking noise on rapid engine acceleration	Tighten fan belt to recommended tension or replace if worn.
	Radiator core blocked or radiator grill restricted	Reverse flush radiator, remove obstructions.
	Bottom water hose collapsed, impeding flow	Remove and fit new hose.
	Thermostat not opening properly	Remove and fit new thermostat.
	Ignition advance and retard incorrectly set (Accompanied by loss of power, and perhaps, misfiring)	Check and reset ignition timing.
	Carburettor(s) incorrectly adjusted (mixture too weak)	Tune carburettor(s).
	Exhaust system partially blocked	Check exhaust pipe for constrictive dents and blockages.
	Oil level in sump too low	Top up sump to full mark on dipstick.
	Blown cylinder head gasket (Water/steam being forced down the radiator overflow pipe under pressure)	Remove cylinder head, fit new gasket.
	Engine not yet run-in	Run-in slowly and carefully.
	Brakes binding	Check and adjust brakes if necessary.
SYMPTOM:	UNDERHEATING	
Too much heat being dispersed by radiator	Thermostat jammed open	Remove and renew thermostat.
	Incorrect grade of thermostat fitted allowing premature opening of valve	Remove and replace with new thermostat which opens at a higher temperature.
	Thermostat missing	Check and fit correct thermostat.
SYMPTOM	LOSS OF COOLING WATER	
Leaks in system	Loose clips on water hoses	Check and tighten clips if necessary.
	Top, bottom, or by-pass water hoses perished and leaking	Check and replace any faulty hoses.
	Radiator core leaking	Remove radiator and repair.
	Thermostat gasket leaking	Inspect and renew gasket.
	Radiator pressure cap spring worn or seal ineffective	Renew radiator pressure cap.
	Blown cylinder head gasket (Pressure in system forcing water/steam down overflow pipe	Remove cylinder head and fit new gasket.
	Cylinder wall or head cracked	Dismantle engine, dispatch to engineering works for repair.

CHAPTER THREE
FUEL SYSTEM AND CARBURATION

CONTENTS

SPECIFICATIONS

Fuel Pump.

Type	Mechanical
Location	Right-hand side
Operation	Lever by eccentric on camshaft

Carburetter ... ...   Series I and III special from Chassis No. A1986736

Make	Zenith 30VI or 30 VM8
Type	Down draught

Settings. (up to 4,000 ft.)

Venturi (choke)	22 mm.
Main jet	80 (77 on Series III special)
Compensation jet	75
Fast idle gap	1.3 mm.
Slow running jet	55
Needle valve seat	1.5 mm.

Carburetter ... ...   Series II & Series III DeLuxe & special up to Chassis No. A1986735

Make	Zenith 30VM8
Type	Down draught

Settings (up to 4,000 ft.)

Venturi	25 mm.
Main jet	87 (Series II - 90)
Compensator jet	90
Fast idle gap	1.3 mm.
Slow running jet	50
Needle valve seat	1.5 mm.

CHAPTER THREE

Carburetter	Series IIIA
Make	Zenith 30 VIG
Type	Down draught

Settings (up to 4,000 ft.)

Venturi (choke	26 mm.
Main jet	70
Compensator jet	100
Fast idle gap	1.1 mm.
Slow running jet	50
Needle valve seat	1.5 mm.
Pump jet	50

Carburetter	Series IIIC & V (manual gearbox)
Make	Zenith 30 VN
Type	Down draught

Settings (up to 4,000 ft.)

Venturi (choke	23 mm. (with extra bar)
Main jet	77
Compensator jet	70
Fast idle gap	1.1 mm.
Slow running jet	50
Capacity vent	2.0
Pump jet	50

Carburetter	Series V (automatic gearbox)
Make	Solex 33 PSE1
Type	Down draught

Settings (up to 4,000 ft.)

Venturi (choke)...	25 mm.
Main jet	112.5
Compensator jet	160 air correction
Fast idle gap	1.2
Slow running jet	60
Capacity vent	-
Pump jet	60

Carburetter	Husky I
Make	Zenith 30 VM8
Type	Down draught

Settings (up to 4,000 ft.)

Venturi (choke)...	22 mm.
Main jet	77
Compensator jet	75
Fast idle gap	1.3 mm.
Slow running jet	55
Needle valve seat	1.5 mm.

Carburetter	Husky Series I from chassis No. A 2824858 and ea
	Series II models
Make	Zenith 30 VIG
Type	Down draught

Settings (up to 4,000 ft.)

| Venturi (choke)... ... ... | 26 mm. |

Main jet	70
Compensator jet	100
Fast idle gap	1.3 mm.
Slow running jet	50
Needle valve seat	1.5 mm.
Pump jet	50

Carburetter...	Husky II (later models)
Make...	Zenith 26 VME
Type...	Down draught

Settings (up to 4.000 ft.)

Venturi (choke)..	21 mm.
Main jet	50
Compensator jet	92
Fast idle gap	1.1 mm.
Slow running jet	50
Needle valve seat	1.5 mm.

Carburetter...	Husky III
Make...	Zenith 30 VNN
Type...	Down draught

Settings (up to 4,000 ft.)

Venturi (choke)..	21 mm. (with single bar)
Main jet	55
Compensator jet	92
Slow running air bleed	50
Slow running jet	50
Ventilator screw	2.2
Progression hole	0.9
Emulsion block	4.5 x 4

Air Cleaner Types: Minx I to IIIA ...	Gauze or oil bath
Minx IIIB, IIIC & V	Gauze or paper element
Husky I & II ...	Gauze or oil bath
Husky III	Gauze or paper element

Fuel Pipe Size (all models)..	3/16 in. (4.7 mm.)internal diameter

1. GENERAL DESCRIPTION

1. The various types of carburetters employed on the range of Rootes engines are designed to suit the characteristics of the engine to which they are fitted. Fuel is drawn from the fuel tank by a mechanically operated diaphragm type of petrol pump mounted on the camshaft side of the engine and driven by a lever bearing on an eccentric on the camshaft. An electrically operated petrol gauge mounted on the instrument panel indicates the proportional amount of fuel in the tank. Paper element air cleaners and silencers are standard fitting, but in some cases an oil wetted cleaner unit is fitted.

AIR CLEANERS

1. To clean the paper element or gauze type of air cleaner remove the complete silencer by unscrewing one of the clips securing the cleaner to the carburetter.

2. In the case of paper element cleaners, do not wet either the element or the inside of the case, but blow out all dust from inside, and also from the element.

3. In the case of gauze types, wet the gauze by dipping the open end into a bowl of clean paraffin. Allow to drain thoroughly and redip the gauze in clean engine oil. Drain and wipe off all surplus oil and refit.

4. The intervals at which the A.C. oil bath air cleaner needs to be serviced will vary according to the conditions. For town areas every 3,000 miles can be taken as a guide. To clean and re-oil this type of cleaner, undo the top clip to release a flexible hose connecting the

cleaner to the top of the carburetter. Unscrew the wing nut in the centre of the cleaner and lift away the top.

5. Wash the element in clean paraffin and blow dry or hang it up to drain thoroughly. It is not necessary to re-oil the element as this is done automatically by the passage of air when the engine is running.

6. Clean out the oil bath and refill with clean engine oil to the level mark. Do not overfill.

7. Reassemble the filter element, refit the air cleaner to the engine, and tighten up the flexible hose clip at the carburetter.

3.   A.C. FUEL PUMP DESCRIPTION

1. The A.C. mechanically operated pump is mounted on the right-hand side of the engine toward the front and is operated by an eccentric on the camshaft.

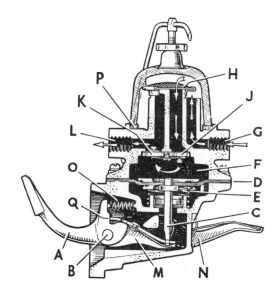

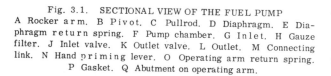

Fig. 3.1. SECTIONAL VIEW OF THE FUEL PUMP
A Rocker arm. B Pivot. C Pullrod. D Diaphragm. E Diaphragm return spring. F Pump chamber. G Inlet. H Gauze filter. J Inlet valve. K Outlet valve. L Outlet. M Connecting link. N Hand priming lever. O Operating arm return spring. P Gasket. Q Abutment on operating arm.

2. As the engine camshaft revolves, an eccentric actuates the rocker arm (A) Fig. 3.1. pivoted at (B) which moves the pull rod (C) together with the diaphragm (D) downwards against spring pressure (E) thus creating a depression in the pump chamber (F). Fuel is drawn from the tank and enters the pump at (G), passing through the filter gauze (H) and the inlet valve (J) into the pump chamber (F).

3. On the return stroke, pressure of the spring (E) pushes the diaphragm (D) upwards

forcing fuel from the chamber through the outlet valve (K) to the outlet union (L) and so to the carburetter float chamber.

4. When the carburetter bowl is full the float will shut off the needle valve, and thus prevent any flow of fuel from the pump chamber. This will force the diaphragm (D) down against the spring (E) and it will remain there until the carburetter requires more fuel.

5. To enable this action to take place the rocker arm (A) operates a connecting link (M) by making contact at (Q) and this construction allows an idling action of the rocker arm when there is no fuel movement. The spring (O) keeps the rocker arm (A) in constant contact with the eccentric to eliminate any noise.

6. On models having a hand priming lever (N) this lever operates a cam which bears on top of the connecting link, so that by lifting the lever the link will be forced down and this in turn operates the diaphragm rod.

4.   FUEL PUMP FILTER

The cleaning of the gauze at the top of the pump can be done by unscrewing the retaining clip hand screw so that the bowl clip can be pushed to one side. The bowl is lifted off and the filter is lifted upwards from the neck of the pump. Wash well with clean petrol. When replacing the bowl, press down carefully to ensure that an air-tight joint is made with the cork gasket, and tighten the retaining screw finger tight only.

5.   FUEL SHORTAGE AT THE CARBURETTER

If the pump does not appear to force a supply of fuel to the carburetter check the following points:-

1. Make sure that there is fuel in the tank.

2. Make sure that the pipe unions from the tank to the pump are tight by checking that they are not wet. If leakage is suspected this should be repaired because there is the chance that air is being drawn in rather than fuel.

3. Check that the fuel filter is clean. This can be seen through the glass cover.

4. Remove the delivery pipe union at the carburetter and with someone to operate the starter with the engine switched off, check that fuel is in fact being pumped out of this delivery pipe.

5. A well defined spurt of fuel should be discharged at each working stroke of the pump, which is in fact once every two revolutions of the engine.

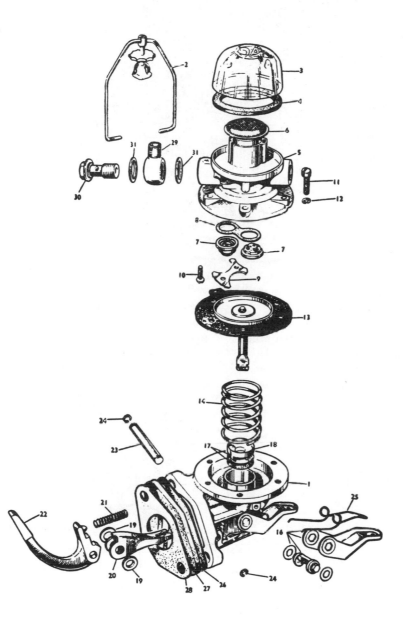

Fig. 3.2. EXPLODED VIEW OF THE FUEL PUMP.

1 Body. 2 Retainer—glass cover. 3 Glass bowl. 4 Gasket—bowl. 5 Cover. 6 Filter gauze. 7 Valve. 8 Gasket—valve. 9 Retaining plate—valve. 10 Screw—valve retainer. 11 Screw No. 10 UNF. 12 Washer ⁵/₁₆ inch spring. 13 Pull rod and diaphragm. 14 Spring—diaphragm. 16 Priming lever. 17 Washer—oil seal. 18 Retainer—oil seal. 19 Washer—rocker pin. 20 Link. 21 Return spring rocker arm. 22 Rocker arm. 23 Pin—rocker arm. 24 Circlip—rocker arm pin. 25 Primer spring. 26 Joint pump to insulator. 27 Heat insulator. 28 Joint—insulator to cylinder block. 29 Outlet union. 30 Banjo bolt. 31 Fibre washer.

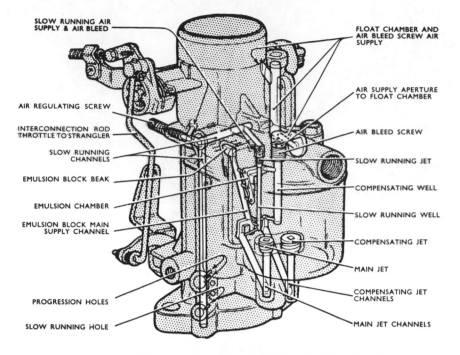

SLOW RUNNING AIR SUPPLY & AIR BLEED

AIR REGULATING SCREW

INTERCONNECTION ROD THROTTLE TO STRANGLER

SLOW RUNNING CHANNELS

EMULSION BLOCK BEAK

EMULSION CHAMBER

EMULSION BLOCK MAIN SUPPLY CHANNEL

PROGRESSION HOLES

SLOW RUNNING HOLE

FLOAT CHAMBER AND AIR BLEED SCREW AIR SUPPLY

AIR SUPPLY APERTURE TO FLOAT CHAMBER

AIR BLEED SCREW

SLOW RUNNING JET

COMPENSATING WELL

SLOW RUNNING WELL

COMPENSATING JET

MAIN JET

COMPENSATING JET CHANNELS

MAIN JET CHANNELS

Fig. 3.3. Jet positions and channel layout of the Zenith 30 VI carburetter.

6. CARBURETTERS, ZENITH 30VI & 30VM8

Zenith 30VI and Zenith 30VM8 carburetters are fitted to the majority of Hillman Minx engines, both being downdraught types and have throttle bore sizes of 30 mm. Details of models fitting these carburetters can be found in the specifications at the start of this chapter. The names of the various parts, jet positions and internal passages for the 30VI and 30VM8 carburetter are illustrated in Fig. 3.5. there being only very slight differences between the two models.

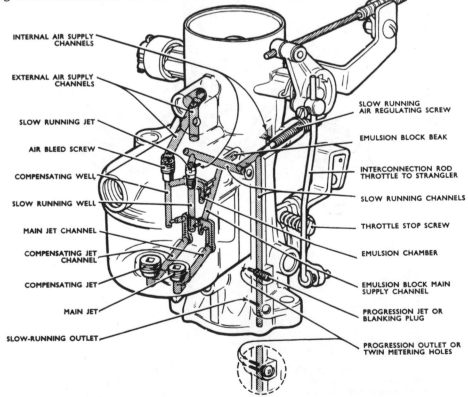

INTERNAL AIR SUPPLY CHANNELS

EXTERNAL AIR SUPPLY CHANNELS

SLOW RUNNING JET

AIR BLEED SCREW

COMPENSATING WELL

SLOW RUNNING WELL

MAIN JET CHANNEL

COMPENSATING JET CHANNEL

COMPENSATING JET

MAIN JET

SLOW-RUNNING OUTLET

SLOW RUNNING AIR REGULATING SCREW

EMULSION BLOCK BEAK

INTERCONNECTION ROD THROTTLE TO STRANGLER

SLOW RUNNING CHANNELS

THROTTLE STOP SCREW

EMULSION CHAMBER

EMULSION BLOCK MAIN SUPPLY CHANNEL

PROGRESSION JET OR BLANKING PLUG

PROGRESSION OUTLET OR TWIN METERING HOLES

Fig. 3.4. Jet positions and channel layout of the Zenith 30VM8 carburetter.

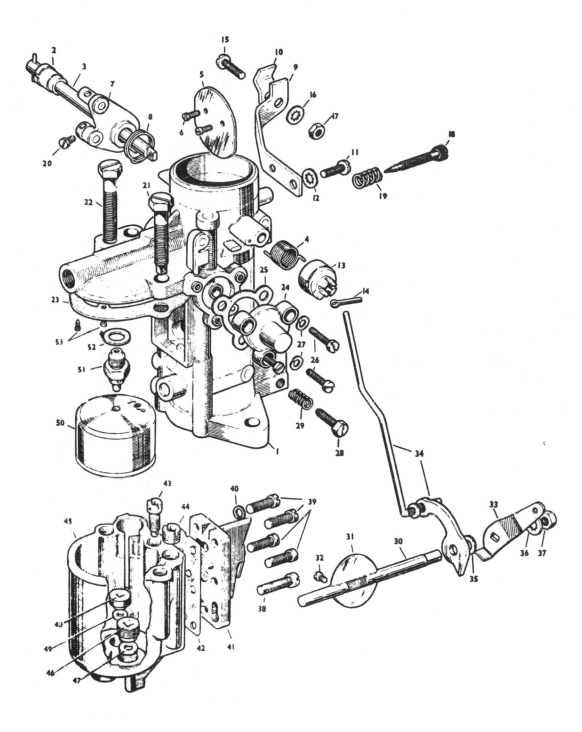

Fig. 3.5. EXPLODED VIEW OF THE ZENITH 30VI CARBURETTER

1 Main body. **2** Bearing—strangler lever. **3** Strangler spindle. **4** Spring—strangler spindle. **5** Flap—strangler. **6** Screw—flap to spindle. **7** Strangler lever. **8** Spring—strangler lever. **9** Bracket—strangler control. **10** Clip—strangler control. **11** Screw. **12** Washer, $\frac{3}{16}$ inch shakeproof. **13** Carrier—spring. **14** Split pin for strangler spindle. **15** Screw. **16** Washer, $\frac{3}{16}$ inch shakeproof. **17** Nut, 2BA. **18** Air regulating screw. **19** Spring—regulating screw. **20** Screw—interconnection swivel. **21** Screw (jet key). **22** Screw, plain. **23** Gasket. **24** Blanking cover. **25** Gasket. **26** Screw, cheese head (long). **27** Washer, $\frac{5}{32}$ inch spring. **28** Throttle stop screw. **29** Spring—stop screw. **30** Throttle spindle. **31** Throttle butterfly. **32** Screw—butterfly to spindle. **33** Throttle lever. **34** Floating lever and connection rod. **35** Washer—throttle to spindle. **36** Washer. **37** Nut. **38** Screw, cheese head (long). **39** Screw, cheese head (short). **40** Washer, special. **41** Emulsion block. **42** Gasket—emulsion block. **43** Slow running jet. **44** Screw—capacity well. **45** Float chamber. **46** Compensating jet. **47** Washer—compensating jet. **48** Main jet. **49** Washer—main jet. **50** Float. **51** Needle seating—float. **52** Washer—needle seating. **53** Drive screw—gasket.

7. CARBURETTER ADJUSTMENTS

1. The following items must be checked before making any slow running adjustments.

a) Sparking plug condition and gap.
b) Contact breaker point gap.
c) Ignition timing.
d) Valve tappet clearances.
e) Cylinder compression pressures.
f) Throttle pull off spring operating to return throttle hard onto stop screw.

2. The throttle stop screw limits the closing of the throttle valve, and thus fixes the idling speed of the engine. The air regulating screw allows the richness of the fuel/air mixture to be regulated. By turning the screw in a clockwise direction the mixture is made richer, while by turning in an anti-clockwise direction, the mixture is weakened, and when this condition is reached it can be recognised by irregular firing of the engine and a tendency to stall.

3. Normally this adjustment should be carried out when the engine has been brought up to normal working temperature.

4. Set the throttle adjusting screw until the idling speed is slightly on the fast side.

5. Screw in the air regulating screw until the engine begins to "hunt" (runs very irregularly/ nearly stalls then recovers).

6. Unscrew the air regulating screw very slowly until the hunting of the engine disappears.

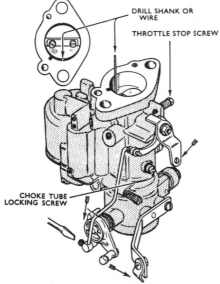

Fig. 3.6. Method of adjusting the fast idle gap on the Zenith 30VI and 30 VM 8 carburetters.

7. If the engine speed is too high, reset the throttle adjusting screw to slow the engine to an idling speed. If this causes a degree of hunting, slightly adjust the air regulating control screw in an anti-clockwise direction.

8. To reset the fast idle gap the carburetter must first be removed from the manifold.

9. Insert a drill shank or piece of wire of the size indicated in the specifications at the beginning of this Section between the throttle flap and the body in line with the flange mounting stud holes as shown in Fig. 3.6.

10. Close the strangler (choke) flap and then set the interconnecting rod so that the flap closes lightly on the drill shank, and tighten the clamping screw.

8. CARBURETTER DISMANTLING & CLEANING

1. To remove the float bowl, unscrew the two fixing bolts. One of these has a squared end which is employed to remove the main and compensating jets from the bottom of the bowl. See Fig. 3.7.

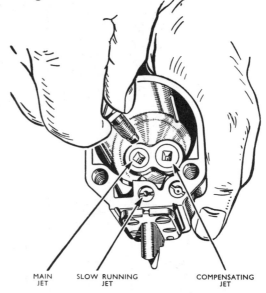

Fig. 3.7. Jet positions in the Zenith 30VM 8 carburetter.

2. The compensating jet is the larger of the two jets, so that incorrect reassembly is impossible.

3. All jets must be checked for blockage by washing in clean petrol and blowing through with air pressure. DO NOT PASS WIRE THROUGH THESE JETS BECAUSE AS THEY ARE ACCURATELY CALIBRATED ANY SLIGHT ALTERATION IN SHAPE OR SIZE WILL AFFECT THE FLOW THROUGH THEM.

4. The needle valve assembly is screwed into the float chamber cover and is fitted with a 1 mm. aluminium washer which must be either

replaced or renewed.

5. The emulsion block is secured to the body with five screws, the three lower ones being fitted with aluminium washers since they are below the petrol level.

6. To dismantle the strangler, remove the split pin on the end of the spindle and release the spring and carrier. Unscrew the two flap screws, pull out the flap and withdraw the spindle.

7. Reassembly is in the reverse order. Note that the lobe adjacent to the split pin slots on the spring carrier should be at 8 o'clock with the spring under tension and the strangler flap open. This will wind the spring up about half a turn.

8. When replacing the main and compensating jets, make sure that the fibre washers are fitted, and that they are not broken. Replace the float with the word 'Top' uppermost.

9. On models having a drain pipe fitted in the inlet manifold, it is essential that this pipe be kept clear of any obstruction. If carbon or gum deposits collect in this pipe, fuel will flood into the manifold and the engine will be very difficult to start.

10. Unscrew the brass union nut and remove the pipe periodically, and particularly if the engine has been decarbonised. Blow through the pipe to ensure that the small hole in the jet at the bottom end of the pipe is clear.

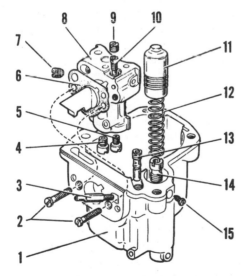

Fig. 3.8. EXPLODED VIEW OF THE FLOAT CHAMBER ASSEMBLY OF THE ZENITH 30VN CARBURETTER.

1 Float chamber. 2 Emulsion block securing screws. 3 Accelerator pump jet. 4 Main jet. 5 Compensating jet. 6 Emulsion block gasket. 7 Compensating well air bleed. 8 Emulsion block. 9 Slow running air bleed. 10 Slow running jet. 11 Accelerator pump piston. 12 Piston return spring. 13 Pump delivery ball valve. 14 Pump suction ball valve. 15 Pump piston retaining screw.

9. ZENITH 30VN CARBURETTER

1. The Zenith 30VN carburetter has a slow-running jet, compensating jet (5) main jet (4) and accelerator pump discharge jet (3) which are screwed into an emulsion block (8). (See Fig. 3.8.)

2. The compensating jet (5) can be identified by chamfered edges on the head of the jet, and by different threads to those of the main jet.

3. The accelerator pump (11) is operated by two levers mounted on a common pivot, and connected by a pull-type spring. One lever is connected to the throttle shaft and the other to the accelerator pump piston push rod.

4. An economy device consisting of a diaphragm and flat valve, operated by inlet manifold vacuum is used to give increased air bleed to the emulsion block in order to improve the fuel consumption under part open throttle conditions.

5. This economy device, fitted on one side of the carburetter body consists of a flexible diaphragm with a flat valve mounted in the centre, one side being spring loaded, the valve being in direct communication with the engine side of the throttle.

6. When the engine is running at part throttle, the valve and diaphragm are lifted from the seating and against a force exerted by the spring. This allows air to be sucked into the compensating well air bleed (7) which controls the air entering the emulsion block when the economy valve is off its seat.

7. Carburetter adjustment must be carried out when the engine is at its normal running temperature, and the slow running adjustment is made by means of the throttle stop screw seen in Fig. 3.9. which determines the throttle opening position for idling. To increase the engine idling the idling screw is turned in the clockwise direction

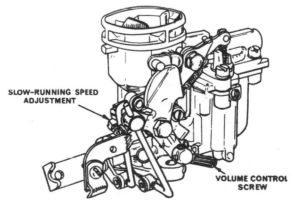

SLOW-RUNNING SPEED ADJUSTMENT

VOLUME CONTROL SCREW

Fig. 3.9. Adjusting screws on the Zenith 30VN carburetter.

8. If the engine tends to run unevenly as the idling speed is reduced this indicates that the fuel mixture is too rich, and it should be weakened by slowly turning the volume control screw in a clockwise direction.

9. In addition to these two adjustments the pump stroke length is controlled by means of a square block located on top of the pump rod, which is kept in position by a spring.

10. If this block is turned so that the projection on one corner can be brought into contact with the pump operating arm, then as the throttle is depressed, the pump travel will be limited, a particularly useful point during the summer weather when excessive injection of fuel is not required.

11. To reset the fast idle gap the carburetter must be unbolted and removed from the inlet manifold.

12. The method is to insert a drill shank or piece of wire of 1.1 mm. diameter between the throttle butterfly and the carburetter body in line with the flange mounting stud holes. Close the choke flap and then set the interconnecting rod so that the throttle butterfly closes lightly on the drill or wire. Then tighten the clamping screw. This will ensure a satisfactory relationship between the throttle flap and the choke control when the latter is pulled up.

13. Dismantling and cleaning of Zenith 30VN carburetter. Since the jets are contained in the emulsion block, it is necessary to first remove the four screws securing the chamber to the body of the carburetter, and then pull out the float lever from the forward edge of the chamber, noting that this lever is stamped 'Top' and that the lugs of the lever hinge are towards the top face. The float is then removed. The jets are shown in Fig. 3.8. the slow running jet (10) being screwed into the top face of the block (8) below the slow-running air bleed (9), which must be taken out before the jet (10) can be unscrewed.

14. Access to the main jet (4) and compensating jet (5) is obtained by removing the two screws (2) which secure the emulsion block to the body. The compensating jet has a chamfered top and a smaller thread than the main jet.

15. Once the jets have been blown through to clear any sediment or blockage, they are replaced securely in the block, and the block is positioned and secured to the body, taking care that the gasket (6) is in sound condition.

16. The accelerator pump piston (11) should be checked for easy movement in the bore, but without excessive looseness. If there are any brown sticky patches on the pistons, these should be removed with a rag soaked in petrol.

Do not use a woolly rag for this as the fluffy threads which may be left behind will find their way into the passages and jets.

10. CARBURETTER, SOLEX 33 PSEI

1. The 33 mm. Solex PSEI carburetter incorporates a hand operated strangler, an Econostat system and a mechanically operated accelerator pump unit.

2. A reverse flow main jet is used and is identified by two angular grooves around the head of the jet as well as by its size. Note particularly that an ungrooved jet of similar size must not be used as a replacement.

11. ADJUSTMENTS TO SOLEX 33 PSEI

1. The adjustments which may need some attention are:-
a) Slow running.
b) Choke control cable.
c) Throttle pedal adjustment.
d) Fast idle throttle position for cold starting.

2. Slow running adjustment requires that the engine shall be brought up to its normal running temperature, and then the slow running screw should be adjusted to give a fairly fast idling speed. Next slacken the volume control adjusting screw until the engine begins to hunt, indicating a rich mixture, and then screw in very slowly until the hunting just disappears.

3. If the idling speed is too high, reset the slow running screw so that the throttle closes to give the correct idling speed of between 500 and 550 rpm. This may cause a slight resumption of the hunting and if this happens, turn the volume control screw gently in a clockwise direction until the engine runs steadily.

4. If the idling speed is too low, once the adjustments have been completed, the engine may stop when the clutch pedal is depressed, with the throttle not being touched by the foot.

5. The sequence of operations for choke control adjustment is to remove the air cleaner body top, and then pull out the choke control knob ½ inch and then push it back to within ⅛ inch of the face of the dashboard. Now loosen off the strangler wire securing screw.

6. Tighten the wire securing screw on the spindle lever once the lever is pushed hard against its stop. Now pull out the choke control and check in the top of the carburetter that the choke valve is fully closed.

7. If it is found that this valve is not completely closed, adjust the operating lever by the set screw until it is.

8. If the control wire does not hold the valve in the closed position when the control is pulled

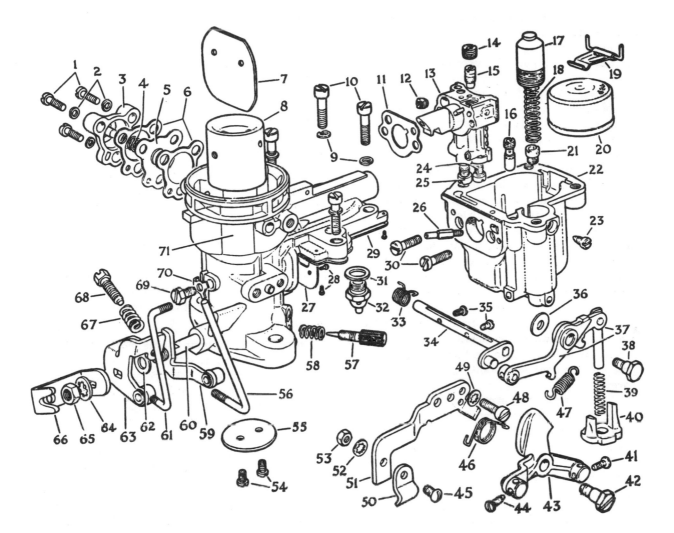

Fig. 3.10. EXPLODED VIEW OF THE ZENITH 30VN CARBURETTER

1 Diaphragm cover fixing screw. 2 Spring washer. 3 Diaphragm cover. 4 Diaphragm return spring. 5 Diaphragm. 6 Gaskets. 7 Strangler flap valve. 8 Venturi (choke tube). 9 Spring washers. 10 Float chamber securing screws. 11 Emulsion block gasket. 12 Ventilation screw for capacity well. 13 Emulsion block. 14 Slow running jet air bleed. 15 Slow running jet. 16 Accelerator pump discharge valve. 17 Accelerator pump piston. 18 Piston return spring. 19 Float lever. 20 Float. 21 Accelerator pump check (suction) valve. 22 Float chamber bowl. 23 Piston retaining screw. 24 Compensating jet. 25 Main jet. 26 Accelerator pump discharge jet. 27 Gasket—float chamber vertical face. 28 Parker screws. 29 Gasket—float chamber cover. 30 Emulsion block fixing screws. 31 Float needle seat washer. 32 Float needle and seat. 33 Spring—controlling automatic action of strangler valve. 34 Strangler valve spindle and lever. 35 Strangler valve securing screws. 36 Pivot screw washer. 37 Accelerator pump operating linkage. 38 Pivot screw. 39 Spring for pump operating rod. 40 Accelerator pump stop. 41 Screw for interconnection swivel. 42 Strangler operating lever and cam pivot screw. 43 Strangler operating lever and cam. 44 Cable securing screw. 45 Screw. 46 Strangler operating lever return spring. 47 Accelerator pump follow up spring. 48 Screw—strangler control bracket. 49 Shakeproof washer. 50 Control cable clip. 51 Strangler control bracket. 52 Shakeproof washer. 53 Nut. 54 Throttle securing screws. 55 Throttle. 56 Interconnection rod—throttle to strangler lever. 57 Slow running volume control screw. 58 Volume control screw spring. 59 Floating lever. 60 Throttle spindle. 61 Pump link. 62 Washer. 63 Throttle stop. 64 Shakeproof washer. 65 Nut. 66 Throttle lever. 67 Spring—slow running speed adjusting screw. 68 Slow running speed adjustment screw. 69 Screw—Venturi locating. 70 Lockwasher. 71 Carburetter main body.

out, then the inner wire should be removed and slightly bent in order to provide the necessary stiffness.

9. Accelerator pedal adjustment. It will be seen that an adjustable rod is provided between the accelerator shaft and the lever on the rear end of the throttle shaft. This rod needs to be adjusted so that when the throttle is fully open, the accelerator pedal pad is one inch from the floor.

10. Fast idle. Throttle cold starting setting. This adjustment can be carried out with the carburetter either removed from the engine or with the carburetter in position.

11. When the adjustment is correct it ensures that a fast idling speed, useful during initial warming up can be obtained when the choke control is pulled out $\frac{1}{2}$ inch. With the carburetter removed, tie the strangler lever in its full over position, and slacken the connecting rod screw. Insert a drill shank of a 1.0 mm. drill between the throttle edge and the throttle bore, and while holding the throttle in this position against the shank, tighten the set screw.

12. Now release the strangler lever and re-check that, when the strangler lever is pulled fully over, the throttle is just at a position where the drill shank can be entered easily.

13. To carry out the same adjustment with the carburetter in position, slacken off the set screw securing the strangler lever rod, remove the slow running speed adjusting screw completely and take away the coil spring, and then replace the screw without the spring. Hold the throttle in the closed position and screw in the adjustment screw until it just touches the abutment, and then turn another $3\frac{1}{2}$ turns.

14. Pull the choke control fully out, tighten the connecting rod screw making sure that the floating arm is in light contact with the circular shoulder on the throttle abutment plate, and then push in the choke control. Remove the slow running adjusting screw and replace the coil spring. Once this adjustment has been completed, carry out the slow running adjustment detailed above.

12. DISMANTLING & CLEANING OF SOLEX 33-PSEI

1. To dismantle and clean out the carburetter it is not necessary to remove the unit from the intake manifold.

2. Detach the air cleaner and disconnect the fuel pipe at the carburetter. Remove the screws and spring washers (1) and lift off the top cover (2) and gasket (53).

3. Lift out the spindle (7), float lever (8) and float (11). Unscrew the plug (16) with its aluminium washer (15) and with a long shank screwdriver unscrew the main jet (14).

4. Unscrew the pilot jet (47) and the air correction jet and emulsion tube (52) from the body (48). Remove the valve (12) and the plunger (13) and then detach the accelerator pump nozzle (51) and lift out the ball valve (49) from underneath.

5. Note particularly that this ball valve (49) has no spring underneath it, and it cannot be lifted with a magnet. To remove, blank off the carburetter intake with a rag and then operate the accelerator pump, catching the ball as it is lifted from its seat. Never operate the accelerator pump with the pump jet removed without taking precautions to prevent the possible entry of the ball valve into the inlet manifold.

6. The sequence for reassembly is as follows. Refit the main jet (14) washer (15) and plug (16), the pilot jet (47) air correction jet and emulsion tube jet (52) non-return valve (49) and accelerator pump nozzle (51) with its washer (50).

7. Fit the float (11), lever (8) and spindle (7). Locate a new gasket (53) on the carburetter body and then hold the strangler butterfly open while replacing the top cover (2) and securing in position with the screws and spring washers (1).

8. Reconnect the fuel supply pipe and refit the air cleaner.

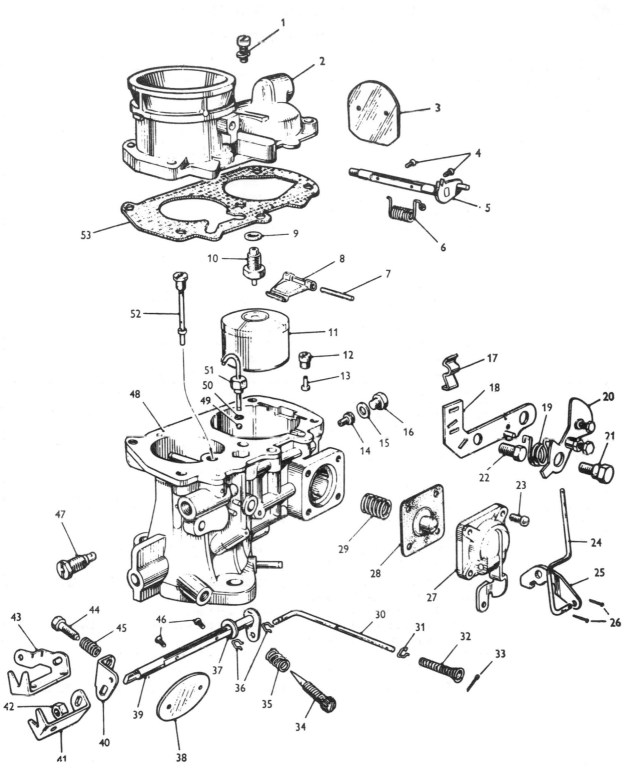

Fig. 3.11. EXPLODED VIEW OF THE SOLEX 33 PSE1 CARBURETTER

1 Top body screw. 2 Top body. 3 Strangler valve. 4 Strangler valve retaining screws. 5 Strangler spindle. 6 Strangler valve return spring. 7 Float lever pivot pin. 8 Float lever. 9 Needle seat washer. 10 Needle seat. 11 Float. 12 Accelerator pump breather valve body. 13 Accelerator pump breather valve. 14 Main jet. 15 Main jet access plug washer. 16 Main jet access plug. 17 Strangler cable clip. 18 Strangler cable bracket. 19 Strangler cam return spring. 20 Strangler cam. 21 Pivot bolt. 22 Bolt. 23 Screw. 24 Connecting rod–throttle to strangler. 25 Connecting rod operating lever. 26 Split pins. 27 Accelerator pump cover. 28 Accelerator pump diaphragm. 29 Accelerator pump return spring. 30 Accelerator pump operating rod. 31 Circlip. 32 Coil spring. 33 Split pin. 34 Slow running mixture control screw. 35 Coil spring. 36 Circlips. 37 Washer. 38 Throttle valve. 39 Throttle spindle. 40 Throttle abutment plate. 41 Throttle lever. 42 Throttle spindle nut. 43 Throttle lever (used with 35 automatic transmission). 44 Slow running speed adjusting screw. 45 Coil spring. 46 Throttle valve fixing screws. 47 Pilot jet. 48 Carburetter main body. 49 Ball valve. 50 Sealing washer. 51 Accelerator pump jet. 52 Air connection jet and emulsion tube. 53 Gasket.

FUEL SYSTEM AND CARBURATION

FAULT FINDING CHART

Cause	Trouble	Remedy
SYMPTOM:	FUEL CONSUMPTION EXCESSIVE	
Carburation and ignition faults	Air cleaner choked and dirty giving rich mixture	Remove, clean and replace air cleaner.
	Fuel leaking from carburettor(s), fuel pumps, or fuel lines	Check for and eliminate all fuel leaks. Tighten fuel line union nuts.
	Float chamber flooding	Check and adjust float level.
	Generally worn carburettor(s)	Remove, overhaul and replace.
	Distributor condenser faulty	Remove, and fit new unit.
	Balance weights or vacuum advance mechanism in distributor faulty	Remove, and overhaul distributor.
Incorrect adjustment	Carburettor(s) incorrectly adjusted mixture too rich	Tune and adjust carburettor(s).
	Idling speed too high	Adjust idling speed.
	Contact breaker gap incorrect	Check and reset gap.
	Valve clearances incorrect	Check rocker arm to valve stem clearances and adjust as necessary.
	Incorrectly set sparking plugs	Remove, clean, and regap.
	Tyres under-inflated	Check tyre pressures and inflate if necessary.
	Wrong sparking plugs fitted	Remove and replace with correct units.
	Brakes dragging	Check and adjust brakes.
SYMPTOM:	INSUFFICIENT FUEL DELIVERY OR WEAK MIXTURE DUE TO AIR LEAKS	
Dirt in system	Petrol tank air vent restricted	Remove petrol cap and clean out air vent.
	Partially clogged filters in pump and carburettor(s)	Remove and clean filters.
	Dirt lodged in float chamber needle housing	Remove and clean out float chamber and needle valve assembly.
	Incorrectly seating valves in fuel pump	Remove, dismantle, and clean out fuel pump.
Fuel pump faults	Fuel pump diaphragm leaking or damaged	Remove, and overhaul fuel pump.
	Gasket in fuel pump damaged	Remove, and overhaul fuel pump.
	Fuel pump valves sticking due to petrol gumming	Remove, and thoroughly clean fuel pump.
Air leaks	Too little fuel in fuel tank (Prevalent when climbing steep hills)	Refill fuel tank.
	Union joints on pipe connections loose	Tighten joints and check for air leaks.
	Split in fuel pipe on suction side of fuel pump	Examine, locate, and repair.
	Inlet manifold to block or inlet manifold to carburettor(s) gasket leaking	Test by pouring oil along joints - bubbles indicate leak. Renew gasket as appropriate.

CHAPTER FOUR
IGNITION SYSTEM

CONTENTS

SPECIFICATIONS

Distributor : Rotation	Anti-clockwise viewed from above
: Make	Lucas
: Makers numbers	DM/P4S94; D2A4; DM2/PAS94; DM2; 25D4
Contact breaker gap.	.015 in.
Sparking Plugs : Make	K. L. G.
: Type	Minx I & II, Husky I FE.50 Minx III on, Husky II on FE.70A
: Gaps	.025 in. (0.63 mm.)
Firing order	1 - 3 - 4 - 2
Static ignition settings	B.T.D.C.
Series I & II H.C.	$4^o - 6^o$
L.C.	4°
Series III (all) H.C.	$9^o - 11^o$
L.C.	$10^o - 12^o$
Series V	$6^o - 10^o$

1. **GENERAL DESCRIPTION**

In order that the engine can run correctly it is necessary for an electrical spark to ignite the fuel/air mixture in the combustion chamber at exactly the right moment in relation to engine speed and load. The ignition system is based on feeding low tension voltage from the battery to the coil where it is converted to high tension voltage. The high tension voltage is powerful enough to jump the sparking plug gap in the cylinders many times a second under high compression pressures, providing that the system is in good condition and that all adjustments are correct.

The ignition system is divided into two circuits. The low tension circuit and the high tension circuit.

The low tension (sometimes known as the primary) circuit consists of the battery, lead to the control box, lead to the ignition switch, lead from the ignition switch to the low tension or primary coil windings (terminal SW), and the lead from the low tension coil windings (coil terminal CB) to the contact breaker points and condenser in the distributor.

The high tension circuit consists of the high tension or secondary coil windings, the heavy ignition lead from the centre of the coil to the centre of the distributor cap, the rotor arm, and the sparking plug leads and sparking plugs.

The system functions in the following manner. Low tension voltage is changed in the coil into high tension voltage by the opening and closing of the contact breaker points in the low tension circuit. High tension voltage is then fed via the carbon brush in the centre of the distributor cap to the rotor arm of the distributor. The rotor arm revolves inside the distributor cap, and each time it comes in line with one of the four metal segments in the cap, which are connected to the sparking plug leads, the opening and closing of the contact breaker points causes the high tension voltage to build up, jump the gap from the rotor arm to the appropriate metal segment and so via the sparking plug lead to the sparking plug, where it finally jumps the spark plug gap before going to earth.

The ignition is advanced and retarded automatically, to ensure the spark occurs at just the right instant for the particular load at the prevailing engine speed.

The ignition advance is controlled both mechanically and by a vacuum operated system. The mechanical governor mechanism comprises two lead weights, which move out from the distributor shaft as the engine speed rises due to centrifugal force. As they move outwards they rotate the cam relative to the distributor shaft, and so advance the spark, The weights are held in position by two light springs and it is the tension of the springs which is largely responsible for correct spark advancement.

The vacuum control consists of a diaphragm, one side of which is connected via a small bore tube to the carburetter, and the other side to the contact breaker plate. Depression in the inlet manifold and carburetter, which varies with engine speed and throttle opening, causes the diaphragm to move, so moving the contact breaker plate, and advanc-ing or retarding the spark. A fine degree of control is achieved by a spring in the vacuum assembly.

2. CONTACT BREAKER ADJUSTMENT

1. To adjust the contact breaker points to the correct gap, first pull off the two clips securing the distributor cap to the distributor body, and lift away the cap. Clean the cap inside and out with a dry cloth. It is unlikely that the four segments will be badly burned or scored, but if they are the cap will have to be renewed.

2. Push in the carbon brush located in the top of the cap once or twice, to make sure that it moves freely.

3. Gently prise the contact breaker points open to examine the condition of their faces. If they are rough, pitted or dirty, it will be necessary to remove them for resurfacing, or for replacement points to be fitted.

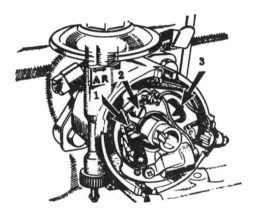

Fig. 4.1. The DM2 distributor with the cover and rotor arm removed showing 1 Contact breaker points. 2 Securing screw 3 Slot for screwdriver to vary point gap.

4. Presuming the points are satisfactory, or that they have been cleaned and replaced, measure the gap between the points by turning the engine over until the contact breaker arm is on the peak of one of the four cam lobes. A 0.015 in. feeler gauge should now just fit between the points.

5. If the gap varies from this amount, slacken the contact plate securing screw, and adjust the contact gap by inserting a screwdriver in the notched hole at the end of the plate. Turning clockwise to decrease and anti-clockwise to increase the gap. Tighten the securing screw and check the gap again.

6. Replace the rotor arm and distributor cap and clip the spring blade retainers into position.

3. REMOVING & REPLACING CONTACT BREAKER POINTS

1. If the contact breaker points are burned, pitted or badly worn, they must be removed and either replaced, or their faces must be filed smooth.

2. To remove the points unscrew the terminal nut and remove it together with the steel washer under its head. Remove the flanged nylon bush and then the condenser lead and the low tension lead from the terminal pin. Lift off the contact breaker arm and then remove the large fibre washer from the terminal pin.

3. The adjustable contact breaker plate is removed by unscrewing the one holding down screw and removing it, complete with spring and flat washer.

4. To reface the points, rub their faces on a fine carborundum stone, or on fine emery paper. It is important that the faces are rubbed flat and parallel to each other so that there will be complete face to face contact when the points are closed. One of the points will be pitted and the other will have deposits on it.

5. It is necessary to completely remove the built-up deposits, but not necessary to rub the pitted point right down to the stage where all the pitting has disappeared, though obviously if this is done it will prolong the time before the operation of refacing the points has to be repeated.

6. To replace the points, first position the adjustable contact breaker plate, and secure it with its screw spring and flat washer. Fit the fibre washer to the terminal pin, and fit the contact breaker arm over it. Insert the flanged nylon bush with the condenser lead immediately under its head, and the low tension lead under that, over the terminal pin. Fit the steel washer and screw on the securing nut.

7. The points are now reassembled and the gap should be set as detailed in the previous section.

4. CONDENSER REMOVAL, TESTING & REPLACEMENT

1. The purpose of the condenser, (sometimes known as a capacitor) is to ensure that when the contact breaker points open there is no sparking across them which would waste voltage.

2. The condenser is fitted in parallel with the contact breaker points, and if it develops a short circuit, will cause ignition failure as the points will be prevented from interrupting the low tension circuit.

3. If the engine becomes very difficult to start or begins to miss after several miles running and the breaker points show signs of excessive burning, then the condition of the condenser must be suspect. A further test can be made by separating the points by hand with the ignition switched on. If this is accompanied by a flash it is indicative that the condenser has failed.

4. Without special test equipment the only sure way to diagnose condenser trouble is to replace a suspected unit with a new one and note if there is any improvement.

5. To remove the condenser from the distributor, remove the distributor cap and the rotor arm. Unscrew the contact breaker arm terminal nut, and remove the nut, washer, and flanged nylon bush and release the condenser lead from the bush. Unscrew the condenser retaining screw from the breaker plate and remove the condenser. Replacement of the condenser is simply a reversal of the removal process. Take particular care that the condenser lead does not short circuit against any portion of the breaker plate.

5. DISTRIBUTOR LUBRICATION

1. It is important that the distributor cam is lubricated with petroleum jelly at the specified mileages, and that the breaker arm, governor weights, and cam spindle, are lubricated with engine oil once every 1,000 miles. In practice it will be found that lubrication every 3,000 miles is adequate, although this is not recommended by the factory.

2. Great care should be taken not to use too much lubricant, as any excess that might find its way onto the contact breaker points could cause burning and misfiring.

3. To gain access to the cam spindle, lift away the rotor arm. Drop no more than two drops of engine oil onto the screw head. This will run down the spindle when the engine is hot and lubricate the bearings. No more than ONE drop of oil should be applied to the pivot post.

6. DISTRIBUTOR REMOVAL & REPLACEMENT

1. To remove the distributor from the engine, start by pulling the terminals off each of the sparking plugs. Release the nut securing the low tension lead to the terminal on the side of the distributor and unscrew the high tension lead retaining cap from the coil and remove the lead.

2. Unscrew the union holding the vacuum tube to the distributor vacuum housing.

3. Remove the distributor body clamp bolts which hold the distributor clamp plate to the

engine and remove the distributor. NOTE if it is not wished to disturb the timing then under no circumstances should the clamp pinch bolt, which secures the distributor in its relative position in the clamp, be loosened. Providing the distributor is removed without the clamp being loosened from the distributor body, the timing will not be lost.

4. Replacement is a reversal of the above process providing that the engine has not been turned in the meantime. If the engine has been turned it will be best to retime the ignition. This will also be necessary if the clamp pinch bolt has been loosened.

7. DISTRIBUTOR DISMANTLING

1. With the distributor removed from the car and on the bench, remove the distributor cap and lift off the rotor arm. If very tight, lever it off gently with a screwdriver.

2. Remove the points from the distributor as

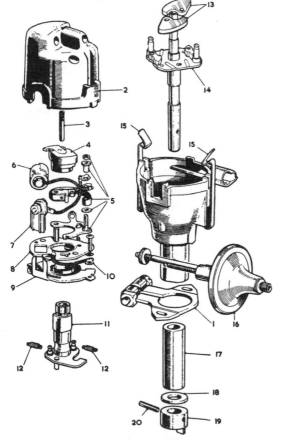

detailed in the section 'Removing and replacing contact breaker points' on page 67.

3. Remove the condenser from the contact breaker plate by releasing its securing screw.

4. Unhook the vacuum unit spring from its mounting pin on the moving contact breaker plate.

5. Remove the contact breaker plate.

6. Unscrew the two screws and lockwasher which hold the contact breaker base plate in position and remove the earth lead from the relevant screw. Remember to replace this lead on reassembly.

7. Lift out the contact breaker base plate.

8. NOTE the position of the slot in the rotor arm drive in relation to the offset drive dog at the opposite end of the distributor. It is essential that this is reassembled correctly as otherwise the timing may be 180° out.

9. Unscrew the cam spindle retaining screw, which is located in the centre of the rotor arm drive, and remove the cam spindle.

10. Lift out the centrifugal weights together with their springs.

11. To remove the vacuum unit, spring off the small circlip which secures the advance adjustment nut which should then be unscrewed. With the micrometer adjusting nut removed, release the spring and the micrometer adjusting nut lock spring clip. This is the clip that is responsible for the 'clicks' when the micrometer adjuster is turned, and it is small and easily lost as is the circlip, so put them in a safe place. Do not forget to replace the lock spring clip on reassembly.

12. It is only necessary to remove the distributor drive shaft or spindle if it is thought to be excessively worn. With a thin punch drive out the retaining pin from the driving tongue collar on the bottom end of the distributor drive shaft. The shaft can then be removed. The distributor is now completely dismantled.

8. DISTRIBUTOR INSPECTION & REPAIR

1. Check the points as has already been detailed on page 67. Check the distributor cap for signs of tracking, indicated by a thin black line between the segments. Replace the cap if any signs of tracking are found.

2. If the metal portion of the rotor arm is badly burned or loose, renew the arm. If slightly burnt clean the arm with a fine file.

3. Check that the carbon brush moves freely in the centre of the distributor cover.

4. Examine the fit of the breaker plate on the bearing plate and also check the breaker arm pivot for looseness or wear and renew as necessary.

Fig. 4.2. EXPLODED VIEW OF THE DISTRIBUTOR SHOWING THE COMPONENT PARTS

1 Clamping plate 2 Moulded cap. 3 Brush and spring 4 Rotor arm 5 Contact (set). 6 Capacitor. 7 Terminal and lead (low tension). 8 Moving contact breaker plate. 9 Contact breaker base plate. 10 Earth lead. 11 Cam. 12 Automatic advance springs. 13 Weight assembly. 14 Shaft and action plate. 15 Cap-retaining clips. 16 Vacuum unit. 17 Bush. 18 Thrust washer. 19 Driving dog. 20 Parallel pin.

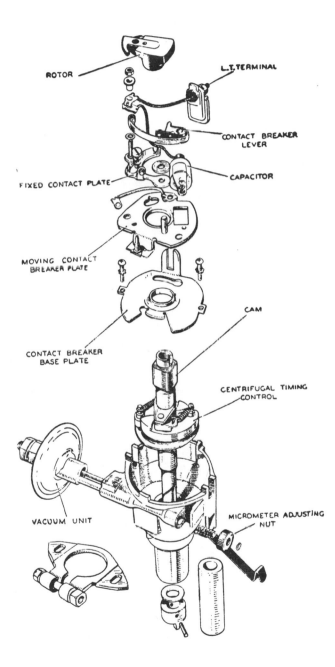

ROTOR

L.T. TERMINAL

CONTACT BREAKER
LEVER

FIXED CONTACT PLATE

CAPACITOR

MOVING CONTACT
BREAKER PLATE

CONTACT BREAKER
BASE PLATE

CAM

CENTRIFUGAL TIMING
CONTROL

VACUUM UNIT

MICROMETER ADJUSTING
NUT

Fig. 4.3. An exploded view of the DM2 distributor showing the centrifugal timing control in the assembled position

69

5. Examine the balance weights and pivot pins for wear, and renew the weights or cam assembly if a degree of wear is found.

6. Examine the shaft and the fit of the cam assembly on the shaft. If the clearance is excessive compare the items with new units, and renew either, or both, if they show excessive wear.

7. If the shaft is a loose fit in the distributor bushes and can be seen to be worn, it will be necessary to fit a new shaft and bushes. The old bushes in the early distributor, or the single bush in later ones, are simply pressed out. NOTE that before inserting new bushes they should be stood in engine oil for 24 hours.

8. Examine the length of the balance weight springs and compare them with new springs. If they have stretched they must be renewed.

9. DISTRIBUTOR REASSEMBLY

1. Reassembly is a straight forward reversal of the dismantling process, but there are several points which should be noted in addition to those already given in the section on dismantling.

2. Lubricate with S.A.E. 20 engine oil the balance weights and other parts of the mechanical advance mechanism, the distributor shaft, and the portion of the shaft on which the cam bears, during assembly. Do not oil excessively but ensure these parts are adequately lubricated.

3. On reassembling the cam driving pins with the centrifugal weights, check that they are in the correct position so that when viewed from above, the rotor arm should be at the six o'clock position, and the small offset on the driving dog must be on the right.

4. Check the action of the weights in the fully advanced and fully retarded positions and ensure they are not binding.

5. Tighten the micrometer adjusting nut to the middle position on the timing scale.

6. Finally, set the contact breaker gap to the correct clearance of .015 in.

10. IGNITION TIMING

1. On earlier models there are three means of adjusting timing. (1) A clamp screw mounted horizontally. When slackened, the body of the distributor is turned relative to the mounting plate. (2) Slotted holes provided in the mounting plate to allow the complete distributor to be turned through a small angle when the securing nuts have been loosened. (3) The vernier control. (Fig. 4.4. refers).

2. On later models two adjustments are provided (1) a clamp screw mounted horizontally which is a coarse adjustment and (2) a vernier control.

3. On earlier models the timing mark is a pointer on the crankshaft pulley which must be lined up with a pointer on the timing cover in order to give T.D.C. for numbers 1 and 4 cylinders. (Fig. 4.5. refers).

4. The distributor vernier should be set so that only one division can be seen on the scale, the distributor cap is then removed and a 12 volt bulb connected between the L.T. terminal of the distributor and a good earth point.

5. With the ignition switched on, this bulb should light immediately the contact points open.

6. Slacken the distributor clamp screw and turn the body of the distributor in the anti-clockwise direction as far as it will go. Switch on the ignition again and slowly turn the distributor body until the bulb just lights.

7. The clamp screw should now be tightened. The setting is now checked by turning the crankshaft two turns, noting that the bulb lights up at the same time as the crankshaft

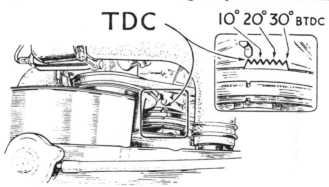

Fig. 4.5. Early models No.1 and No.4 cylinder TDC pointers - Inset shows TDC up to 30° BTDC pointers fitted to later models.

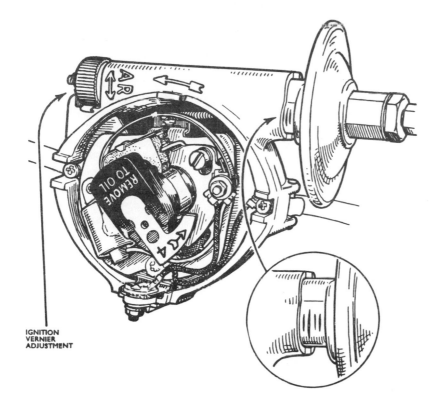

IGNITION
VERNIER
ADJUSTMENT

REMOVE TO OIL

Fig. 4.4. The vernier control on the distributor for timing adjustment

pulley mark lines up with the pointer on the timing case.

8. At this setting the engine is now firing at T.D.C, and can be advanced by the vernier adjustment to give the correct static timing. One division of the vernier represents four degrees, and one turn of the knurled nut corresponds to three degrees.

9. If a stroboscopic timing light is being used, clean and mark the pointer and pulley mark with white chalk to make them easier to see, connect the leads according to the maker's instructions and run the engine at an idling speed of between 400 and 500 r.p.m. This is below the speed at which the centrifugal advance mechanism starts to operate.

10. If the light shows a dimple in the pulley wheel to the right of the timing marks, the ignition will be too far advanced, while if the dimple appears to the left, then the ignition will be too retarded, and adjustment can be effected either by a small degree of turn being applied to the distributor body, or by adjusting the vernier.

11. SPARKING PLUG & LEADS

1. The correct functioning of the sparking plugs are vital for the correct running and efficiency of the engine.

2. At intervals of 6,000 miles the plugs should be removed, examined, cleaned and if worn excessively, replaced. The condition of the sparking plug will also tell much about the overall condition of the engine.

3. If the insulator nose of the sparking plug is clean and white, with no deposits, this is indicative of a weak mixture, or too hot a plug (A hot plug transfers heat away from the electrodes slowly - a cold plug transfers it away quickly).

4. The plugs fitted as standard are the KLG FE50 or 70A types. If the tip and insulator nose is covered with hard black-looking deposits, then this is indicative that the mixture is too rich. Should the plug be black and oily, then it is likely that the engine is fairly worn, as well as the mixture being too rich.

5. If the insulator nose is covered with light tan to greyish brown deposits, then the mixture is correct and it is likely that the engine is in good condition.

6. If there are any traces of long brown tapering stains on the outside of the white portion of the plug, then the plug will have to be renewed, as this shows that there is a faulty joint between the plug body and the insulator, and compression is being allowed to leak away.

7. Plugs should be cleaned by a sand blasting

machine, which will free them from carbon more thoroughly than cleaning by hand. The machine will also test the condition of the plugs under compression. Any plug that fails to spark regularly at the recommended pressure should be renewed.

8. The sparking plug gap is of considerable importance, as if it is too large or too small, the size of the spark and its efficiency will be seriously impaired. The sparking plug gap should be set to 0.025 in. for the best results.

9. This is done by measuring the gap with a feeler gauge, and then bending open, or closed, the outer plug electrode until the correct gap is achieved. The centre electrode should never be bent as bending it will crack the insulation and cause plug failure if nothing worse.

10. When replacing the plugs, remember to use new plug washers, and replace the leads from the distributor in the correct firing order, which is 1, 3, 4, 2, No. 1 cylinder being the one nearest the radiator.

11. The plug leads require no routine attention other than being kept clean and wiped over regularly. Also at intervals of 6,000 miles, pull each lead off the plug in turn, and also remove them from the distributor by unscrewing the knurled moulded terminal knobs. Water can seep down into these joints giving rise to a white corrosive deposit, which must be carefully removed from the brass washer at the end of each cable, through which the ignition wires pass.

12. IGNITION SYSTEM FAULT - FINDING

By far the majority of breakdown and running troubles are caused by faults in the ignition system either in the low tension or high tension circuits.

13. IGNITION SYSTEM FAULT SYMPTOMS

There are two main symptoms indicating ignition faults. Either the engine will not start or fire, or the engine is difficult to start and misfires. If it is a regular misfire, so that the engine is only running on two or three cylinders, the fault will almost sure to be in the secondary, or high tension, circuit. If the misfiring is intermittent, the fault could be in either the high or low tension circuits. If the car stops suddenly, or will not start at all, it is likely that the fault is in the low tension circuit. Loss of power and overheating, apart from faulty carburation settings, are normally due to faults in the distributor or incorrect ignition timing.

14. FAULT DIAGNOSIS - ENGINE FAILS TO START

1. If the engine fails to start it is likely that the fault is in the low tension circuit. It will be known whether there is a good charge in the battery by the way the starter motor spins over. If the battery is evidently in good condition, then check the distributor.

2. Remove the distributor cap and rotor arm, and check that the contact points are not burnt, pitted or dirty. If the points are badly pitted, or burnt or dirty, clean and reset them as has already been detailed on page 67.

3. If the engine still refuses to fire check the low tension circuit further. Check the condition of the condenser as detailed under 'Condenser removal, testing and replacement' on page 67. Switch on the ignition and turn the crankshaft until the contact breaker points have fully opened. With either a voltmeter or bulb, and length of wire, connect the contact breaker plate terminal to earth on the engine. If the bulb lights, the low tension circuit is in order, and the fault is in the points. If the points have been cleaned and reset, and the bulb still lights, then the fault is in the high tension circuit.

4. If the bulb fails to light, connect it to the ignition coil terminal CB and earth. If it lights, it points to a damaged wire or loose connection in the cable from the CB terminal to the terminal on the contact breaker plate.

5. If the bulb fails to light, connect it between the ignition coil terminal SW and earth. If the bulb lights it indicates a fault in the primary winding of the coil, and it will be necessary to fit a replacement unit.

6. Should the bulb not light at this stage, then check the cable to SW for faults or a loose connection. Connect the bulb from the negative terminal of the battery to the SW terminal of the coil. If the bulb lights, then the fault is somewhere in the switch, or wiring and control box. Check further as follows:-

   a) Check the white cable leading from the fuse box A.3 terminal to the ignition switch. If the bulb fails to light, then this indicates that the cable is damaged, or one of the connections loose, or that there is a fault in the switch.

   b) Connect the bulb between the ignition switch white terminal cable and earth. If the bulb fails to light, this indicates a fault in the switch or in the wiring leading from the control box.

   c) Connect the bulb to the other ignition switch terminal and then to earth. If the bulb fails to light, this indicates a fault or loose connection in the wiring leading from the control box.

d) Connect the bulb between the lighting and ignition terminal in the control box, and then to earth. If the bulb fails to light this indicates a faulty control box.

e) Connect the bulb from the fuse unit terminal to earth. If the bulb fails to light this indicates a fault or loose connection in the wire leading from the starter solenoid to the control box.

f) Connect the bulb from the input terminal of the solenoid switch to earth. If the bulb fails to light then there is a fault in the cable from the battery to the solenoid switch, or the earth lead of the battery is not properly earthed, and the whole circuit is dead.

If the fault is not in the low tension circuit, check the high tension circuit. Disconnect each plug lead in turn at the sparking plug end, and hold the end of the cable about $\frac{3}{16}$ in. away from the cylinder block. Spin the engine on the starter motor by pressing the rubber button on the starter motor solenoid switch (under the bonnet). Sparking between the end of the cable and the block should be fairly strong with a regular blue spark. (Hold the lead with rubber to avoid electric shocks).

7. Should there be no spark at the end of the plug leads, disconnect the lead at the distributor cap, and hold the end of the lead about $\frac{1}{4}$ in. from the block. Spin the engine as before, when a rapid succession of blue sparks between the end of the lead and the block, indicate that the coil is in order, and that either the distributor cap is cracked, or the carbon brush is stuck or worn, or the rotor arm is faulty.

8. Check the cap for cracks and tracking, and the rotor arm for cracks or looseness of the metal portion and renew as necessary.

9. If there are no sparks from the end of the lead from the coil, then check the connections of the lead to the coil and distributor head, and if they are good, and the low tension side is without fault, then it will be necessary to fit a replacement coil.

15. FAULT DIAGNOSIS - ENGINE MISFIRES

1. If the engine misfires regularly, run it at a fast idling speed, and short out each of the plugs in turn by placing a short screwdriver across from the plug terminal to the cylinder.

Ensure that the screwdriver has a WOODEN or PLASTIC INSULATED HANDLE.

2. No difference in engine running will be noticed when the plug in the defective cylinder is short circuited. Short circuiting the working plugs will accentuate the misfire.

3. Remove the plug lead from the end of the defective plug and hold it about $\frac{3}{16}$ in. away from the block. Restart the engine. If the sparking is fairly strong and regular the fault must lie in the sparking plug.

4. The plug may be loose, the insulation may be cracked, or the points may have burnt away giving too wide a gap for the spark to jump. Worse still, one of the points may have broken off. Either renew the plug, or clean, cap, and test it.

5. If there is no spark at the end of the plug lead, or if it is weak and intermittent, check the ignition lead from the distributor to the plug. If the insulation is cracked or perished, renew the lead. Check the connections at the distributor cap.

6. If there is still no spark, examine the distributor cap carefully for tracking. This can be recognised by a very thin black line running between two or more electrodes, or between an electrode and some other part of the distributor. These lines are paths which now conduct electricity across the gap thus letting it run to earth. The only answer is a new distributor cap.

7. Apart from the ignition timing being incorrect, other causes of misfiring have already been dealt with under the section dealing with the failure of the engine to start. To recap - these are that:

a) The coil may be faulty giving an intermittent misfire.

b) There may be a damaged wire or loose connection in the low tension circuit.

c) The condenser may be short circuiting.

d) There may be a mechanical fault in the distributor (broken driving spindle or contact breaker spring).

8. If the ignition timing is too far retarded, it should be noted that the engine will tend to overheat, and there will be a quite noticeable drop in power. If the engine is overheating and the power is down, and the ignition timing is correct, then the carburetter should be checked, as it is likely that this is where the fault lies. See Chapter 3 for further details on this.

White deposits and damaged porcelain insulation indicating overheating

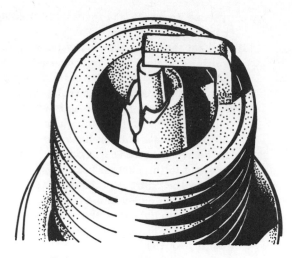

Broken porcelain insulation due to bent central electrode

Electrodes burnt away due to wrong heat value or chronic pre-ignition (pinking)

Excessive black deposits caused by over-rich mixture or wrong heat value

Mild white deposits and electrode burnt indicating too weak a fuel mixture

Plug in sound condition with light greyish brown deposits

CHAPTER FIVE
CLUTCH AND ACTUATING MECHANISM

CONTENTS

SPECIFICATIONS

Make...	Borg and Beck
Type	Single dry plate
Diameter: Hillman Series I & II	7¼ in.
Hillman other models	8 in.
Release bearing	MY3D carbon ring
Number of pressure springs	6
Colour: Series 1 & 11	Light blue
Other models	Cream/light green
Pedal free movement	3/32 in.
Damper springs: Series 1 & 11	4
Other models	6
Colour: Series 1 & 11	White/light green
Other models	Black/light green

1. **GENERAL DESCRIPTION**

Early models are fitted with a 7¼ in. diameter Borg and Beck dry plate clutch, while later models have an 8 in. diameter clutch of the same make and design.

The clutch assembly comprises a steel cover which is bolted and doweled to the rear face of the flywheel and contains the pressure plate, pressure plate springs, release levers, and clutch disc or driven plate.

The pressure plate, pressure springs, and release levers are all attached to the clutch assembly cover. The clutch disc is free to slide along the splined first motion shaft and is held in position between the flywheel and the pressure plate by the pressure of the pressure plate springs.

Friction lining material is riveted to the clutch disc and it has a spring cushioned hub to absorb transmission shocks and to help ensure a smooth take-off.

The clutch is actuated **hydraulically**. The

CHAPTER FIVE

pendant clutch pedal is connected to the clutch master cylinder and hydraulic fluid reservoir by a short push rod.

Depressing the clutch pedal moves the piston in the master cylinder forwards, so forcing hydraulic fluid through the clutch hydraulic pipe to the slave cylinder.

The piston in the slave cylinder moves forward on the entry of the fluid and actuates the clutch release arm by means of a short pushrod. The opposite end of the release arm is forked and is located behind the release bearing.

As this pivoted clutch release arm moves backwards it bears against the release bearing pushing it forwards to bear against the release bearing thrust plate and three clutch release levers. These levers are also pivoted so as to move the pressure plate backwards against the pressure of the pressure plate springs, in this way disengaging the pressure plate from the clutch disc.

When the clutch pedal is released, the pressure plate springs force the pressure plate into contact with the high friction linings on the clutch disc, at the same time forcing the clutch disc against the flywheel and so taking the drive up.

As the friction linings on the clutch disc wear, the pressure plate automatically moves closer to the disc to compensate. This makes the inner ends of the release levers travel further towards the gearbox which decreases the release bearing clearance but not the clutch free pedal travel, as unless the master cylinder has been disturbed this is automatically compensated for.

2. MAINTENANCE

1. Routine maintenance consists of checking the level of the hydraulic fluid in the master cylinder every 1,000 miles and topping up with the correct fluid if the level falls.
2. If it is noted that the level of the liquid has fallen then an immediate check should be made to determine the source of the leak.
3. Before checking the level of the fluid in the master cylinder reservoir, carefully clean the cap and body of the reservoir unit with clean rag so as to ensure that no dirt enters the system when the cap is removed. On no account should paraffin or any other cleaning solvent be used in case the hydraulic fluid becomes contaminated.
4. Check that the level of the hydraulic fluid is up to within $\frac{1}{2}$ in. of the filler neck and that the vent hole in the gap is clear. Do not overfill.

3. CLUTCH SYSTEM - BLEEDING

1. Gather together a clean jam jar, a 9 in. length of rubber tubing which fits tightly over the bleed nipple in the slave cylinder, a tin of hydraulic brake fluid, and a friend to help.
2. Check that the master cylinder is full and if not fill it, and cover the bottom inch of the jar with hydraulic fluid.
3. Remove the rubber dust cap from the bleed nipple on the slave cylinder and with a suitable spanner open the bleed nipple one turn.
4. Place one end of the tube securely over the nipple and insert the other end in the jam jar so that the tube orifice is below the level of the fluid.
5. The assistant should now pump the clutch pedal up and down slowly until air bubbles cease to emerge from the end of the tubing. He should also check the reservoir frequently to ensure that the hydraulic fluid does not disappear so letting air into the system.
6. When no more air bubbles appear, tighten the bleed nipple on the downstroke.
7. Replace the rubber dust cap over the bleed nipple. Allow the hydraulic fluid in the jar to stand for at least 24 hours before using it, to allow all the minute air bubbles to escape.

4. CLUTCH SLAVE CYLINDER - DISMANTLING EXAMINATION & REASSEMBLY

1. Unscrew the union nut retaining the pipe to the slave cylinder and remove the pipe. Catch the hydraulic fluid in a suitable clean container and plug the end of the pipe to ensure no dirt enters.
2. Free the clutch slave cylinder pushrod from the clutch release arm by pulling out the split pin from the end of the clevis pin, and removing the clevis pin.
3. Unscrew the two bolts and spring washers holding the clutch slave cylinder to the clutch housing and lift the slave cylinder away.
4. Clean the cylinder down externally with a clean rag until it is free from dirt.
5. Pull off the rubber boot or dust cap, remove the pushrod, and release the circlip with a pair of long-nosed pliers. Tap or shake out the piston, piston cup, cup filler and the small spring.
6. Clean all the components thoroughly with hydraulic fluid or alcohol and then dry them off.
7. Carefully examine the rubber components for signs of swelling, distortion, splitting or other wear, and check the piston and cylinder wall for wear and score marks. Replace any parts that are found faulty.
8. Reassembly is a straightforward reversal

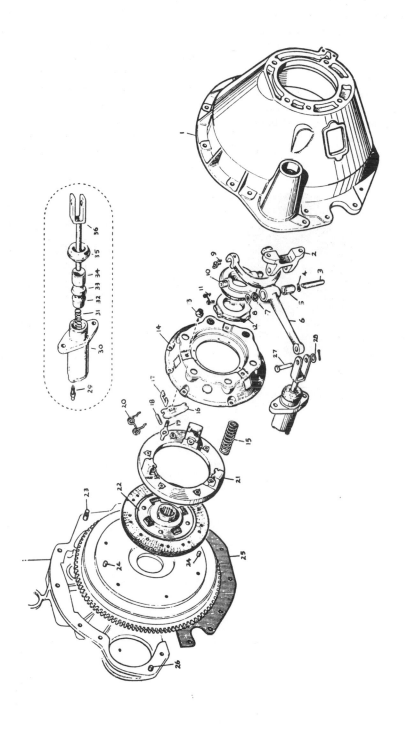

Fig. 5.1. EXPLODED VIEW OF THE CLUTCH AND CLUTCH SLAVE CYLINDER ASSEMBLIES.

1 Clutch bell housing. 2 Withdrawal lever bracket. 3 Fulcrum pin. 4 Washer. 5 Bush. 6 Withdrawal lever. 7 Felt washer. 8 Washer. 9 Release bearing retainer. 10 Release bearing and cup. 11 Release lever retainer. 12 Release lever plate. 13 Eyebolt nut. 14 Clutch cover. 15 Thrust spring. 16 Release lever. 17 Release lever strut. 18 Release lever pin. 19 Eyebolt. 20 Anti-rattle spring. 21 Pressure plate. 22 Driven plate. 23 Dowel bolt (bellhousing to cylinder block). 24 Dowel (clutch assembly to flywheel). 25 Clutch cover plate. 26 Dowel (bellhousing to cylinder block.) 27 Pin. 28 Washer. 29 Bleeder screw. 30 Slave cylinder body. 31 Spring. 32 Cup filler. 33 Cup. 34 Piston. 35 Rubber boot. 36 Push rod.

of the dismantling procedure, but NOTE the following points:-

a) As the component parts are refitted to the slave cylinder barrel smear them with hydraulic fluid.

b) On completion of reassembly, top up the reservoir tank with the correct grade of hydraulic fluid and bleed the system. It might also be necessary to bleed the brake system if the brake pedal was pressed with the reservoir empty.

5. MASTER CYLINDER

1. The master cylinder as seen in Fig. 5.2. incorporates a fluid reservoir and a master cylinder. Directly in front of the main rubber cup (8) is a by-pass port (X) which is provided to ensure that the system is full of fluid at all times.

extract the circlip (13). Withdraw the piston, washer (9) rubber cup (8) retainer (7) and return spring (6). Remove the secondary cup (11) with the fingers by stretching it over the end flange of the piston. Reassembly is the reverse of dismantling, and once the unit has been assembled, fill with clean Lockheed fluid and then test by pushing the piston inwards and allowing it to return unassisted. After several applications the fluid should flow from the outlet connection in the head of the cylinder.

4. The clutch can be removed either by lifting out the engine (see Chapter 1) or by withdrawing the gearbox (see Chapter 6). Remove the clutch assembly by unscrewing the six bolts securing the cover to the flywheel, unscrewing the bolts diagonally a turn at a time in order to release the pressure evenly. With all the bolts away the clutch can be lifted as a unit

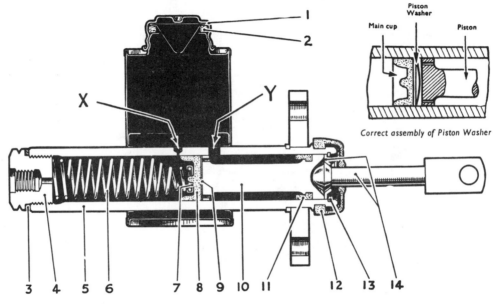

Fig. 5.2. SECTIONAL VIEW OF THE CLUTCH MASTER CYLINDER
1 Filler cup.   2 Washer.   3 Outlet plug washer.   4 Outlet plug.   5 Cylinder.   6 Return spring.   7 Spring retainer.   8 Main cup
9 Piston washer.   10 Piston.   11 Secondary cup.   12 Rubber boot.   13 Stop circlip.   14 Pushrod.   X By-pass port.   Y Main port

2. In order that the rubber cup is not drawn into the holes in the piston head a piston washer (9) is sandwiched between the two parts. It is essential that this washer be reassembled as shown in the illustration, Fig. 5.2.

3. To remove the master cylinder disconnect the pressure pipe (73) in the exploded view Fig. 5.3. from the barrel, and the clevis pin (71) from the pedal. Remove the fixing bolts and detach the cylinder and pushrod, and then unscrew the filler cap and drain the fluid into a clean container. To dismantle, push down piston (10 in Fig. 5.2.) in the bore in order to

from the flywheel.

6. CLUTCH REPLACEMENT

1. It is important that no oil or grease gets on the clutch disc friction linings, or the pressure plate and flywheel faces. It is advisable to replace the clutch with clean hands and to wipe down the pressure plate and flywheel faces with a clean dry rag before assembly begins.

2. Place the clutch disc against the flywheel with the shorter end of the hub, which is the end with the chamfered splines, facing the fly-

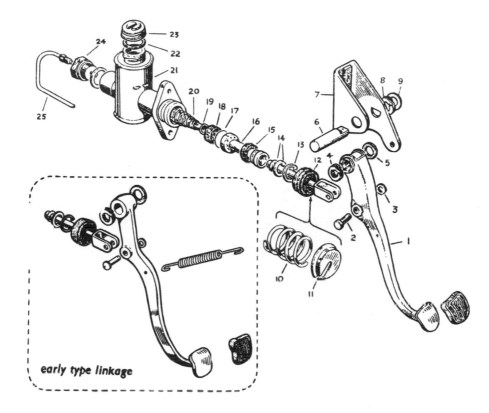

Fig. 5.3. EXPLODED VIEW OF THE CLUTCH MASTER CYLINDER AND PEDAL LINKAGES.
1 Pedal. 2 Clevis pin. 3 Washer. 4 Spring washer. 5 Fibre washer. 6 Pivot pin. 7 Bracket. 8 Spring washer. 9 Plain washer.
10 & 11 Pedal return spring and cap. 12 Rubber boot. 13 Circlip. 15 Piston collar. 16 Piston. 17 Piston washer. 18 Main cup.
19 Spring retainer. 20 Spring. 21 Reservoir. 22 Washer. 23 Filler cap. 24 Outlet plug. 25 Pressure pipe.

wheel. On no account should the clutch disc be replaced with the longer end of the centre hub facing the flywheel as on reassembly it will be found quite impossible to operate the clutch in this position.

3. Replace the clutch cover assembly loosely on the two dowels. Replace the six bolts and spring washers and tighten them finger-tight so that the clutch disc is gripped but can still be moved.

4. The clutch disc must now be centralised so that when the engine and gearbox are mated the gearbox input shaft splines will pass through the splines in the centre of the driven plate hub.

5. Centralisation can be carried out quite easily by inserting a round bar or long screwdriver through the hole in the centre of the clutch, so that the end of the bar rests in the small hole in the end of the crankshaft containing the input shaft bearing bush.

6. Using the input shaft bearing bush as a fulcrum, moving the bar sideways or up and down will move the clutch disc in whichever direction is necessary to achieve centralisation.

7. Centralisation is easily judged by removing the bar and viewing the driven plate hub in relation to the hole in the release bearing. When the hub appears exactly in the centre of the release bearing hole all is correct.

8. Tighten the clutch bolts in a diagonal sequence to ensure that the cover plate is pulled down evenly and without distortion of the flange.

9. Mate the engine and gearbox, and check that the clutch is operating properly.

7. CLUTCH DISMANTLING

It is not very often that it is necessary to dismantle the clutch cover assembly, and in the normal course of events clutch replacement is the term used for simply fitting a new clutch disc.

If a new clutch disc is being fitted it is a false economy not to renew the release bearing at the same time. This will preclude having to replace it at a later date when wear on the clutch linings is still very small.

It should be noted here that it is preferable to purchase an exchange clutch cover assembly unit, which has been built up by the manufacturers and properly balanced, rather than to dismantle and build up your existing clutch cover assembly. A special tool is necessary to ensure that the job is done properly.

Presuming that it is possible to borrow from your local Rootes agent, a clutch assembly tool proceed as follows:-

1. Mark the clutch cover, release levers, and pressure plate lugs so that they can be refitted in the same relative positions.

2. Unhook the springs from the release bearing thrust plate and remove the plate and spring.

3. Place the three correctly sized spacing washers provided with the clutch assembly tool on the tool base plate in the positions indicated by the chart (found inside the lid of the assembly tool container).

4. Place the clutch face down on the three spacing washers so that the washers are as close as possible to the release levers, with the six holes in the cover flange in line with the six holes in the base plate.

5. Insert the six bolts provided with the assembly tool through the six holes in the cover flange, and tighten the cover down diagonally onto the base plate.

6. With a suitable punch, tap back the three tab washers and then remove the three adjusting nuts and bearing plates from the pressure plate bolts on early models, and just unscrew the three adjusting nuts on later models.

7. Unscrew the six bolts holding the clutch cover to the base plate, diagonally, and a turn at a time, so as to release the cover evenly. Lift the cover off and extract the six pressure springs and the spring retaining cups.

8. CLUTCH INSPECTION

1. Examine the clutch disc friction linings for wear and loose rivets and the disc for rim distortion, cracks, broken hub springs, and worn splines.

2. It is always best to renew the clutch driven plate as an assembly to preclude further trouble, but, if it is wished to merely renew the linings, the rivets should be drilled out and not knocked out with a punch. The manufacturers do not advise that only the linings are renewed and personal experience dictates that it is far more satisfactory to renew the driven plate complete than to try and economise by only fitting new friction linings.

3. Check the machined faces of the flywheel and the pressure plate. If either are badly grooved they should be machined until smooth. If the pressure plate is cracked or split it must be renewed, also if the portion on the other side of the plate in contact with the three release lever tips are grooved.

4. Check the release bearing thrust plate for cracks and renew it if any are found.

5. Examine the tips of the release levers which bear against the thrust plate, and renew the levers if more than a small flat has been worn on them.

6. Renew any clutch pressure springs that are broken or shorter than standard.

7. Examine the depressions in the release levers which fit over the knife edge fulcrum and renew the levers if the metal appears badly worn.

8. Examine the clutch release bearing in the gearbox bellhousing and if it is worn to within $1/16$ in. of the rim of the metal cup, or if it is cracked or pitted, it must be removed and replaced.

9. Removal of the clutch release bearing is easily accomplished by pulling off the two retaining springs.

10. Also check the clutch withdrawal lever for slackness. If this is evident, withdraw the lever and renew the bush.

9. CLUTCH REASSEMBLY

1. During clutch reassembly ensure that the marked components are placed in their correct relative positions.

2. Place the three spacing washers on the clutch assembly tool base in the same position as for dismantling the clutch.

3. Place the clutch pressure plate face down on the three spacing washers.

4. Position the three release levers on the knife edge fulcrums (or release lever floating pins in the later clutches) and ensure that the anti-rattle springs are in place over the inner end of the levers.

5. Position the pressure springs on the pressure plate bosses.

6. Fit the flanged cups to the clutch cover and fit the cover over the pressure plate in the same relative positions as it was originally.

7. Insert the six assembly tool bolts through the six holes in the clutch cover flange and tighten the cover down, diagonally, a turn at a time.

8. Replace the three bearing plates, tag washers, and adjusting nuts over the pressure plate studs in the early units, and just screw the adjusting nuts into the eyebolts in the later models.

9. To correctly adjust the clutch release levers use the clutch assembly tool as detailed below:-

a) Screw the actuator into the base plate and settle the clutch mechanism by pumping the actuator handle up and down a dozen times. Unscrew the actuator.

b) Screw the tool pillar into the base plate and slide the correctly sized distance piece (as indicated in the chart in the tool's box) recessed side downwards, over the pillar.

c) Slip the height finger over the centre pillar, and turn the release lever adjusting nuts, until the height fingers, when rotated and held firmly down, just contact the highest part of the clutch release lever tips.

d) Remove the pillar, replace the actuator, and settle the clutch mechanism as in (a).

e) Refit the centre pillar and height finger and recheck the clutch release lever clearance, and adjust if not correct.

10. With the centre pillar removed, lock the adjusting nuts found on early clutches by bending up the tab washers.

11. Replace the release bearing thrust plate and fit the retaining springs over the thrust plate hooks.

12. Unscrew the six bolts holding the clutch cover to the base plate, diagonally, a turn at a time and assembly is now complete.

10. CLUTCH FAULTS

There are four main faults which the clutch and release mechanism are prone to. They may occur by themselves or in conjunction with any of the other faults. They are clutch squeal, slip, spin and judder.

11. CLUTCH SQUEAL - DIAGNOSIS & CURE

If on taking up the drive or when changing gear, the clutch squeals, this is a sure indication of a badly worn clutch release bearing. As well as regular wear due to normal use, wear of the clutch release bearing is much accentuated if the clutch is ridden, or held down for long periods in gear, with the engine running. To minimise wear of this component the car should always be taken out of gear at traffic lights and for similar hold-ups.

The clutch release bearing is not an expensive item, but it is difficult to get to, for to renew it, it is necessary to separate the engine from the gearbox. If the clutch is being overhauled it is a false economy not to renew the clutch release bearing at the same time.

12. CLUTCH SLIP - DIAGNOSIS & CURE

Clutch slip is a self-evident condition which occurs when the clutch friction plate is badly worn, the release arm free travel is insufficient, oil or grease have got onto the flywheel or pressure plate faces, or the pressure plate itself is faulty.

The reason for clutch slip is that, due to one of the faults just listed, there is either insufficient pressure from the pressure plate, or insufficient friction from the friction plate to ensure solid drive.

If small amounts of oil get onto the clutch, under the heat of clutch engagement it will be burnt off, in the process gradually darkening the linings. Excessive oil on the clutch will burn off leaving a carbon deposit which can cause quite bad slip, or fierceness, spin and judder.

If clutch slip is suspected, and confirmation of this condition is required, there are several tests which can be made.

1. With the engine in second or third gear and pulling lightly up a moderate incline, sudden depression of the accelerator pedal may cause the engine to increase its speed without any increase in road speed. Easing off on the accelerator will then give a definite drop in engine speed without the car slowing.

2. Drive the car at a steady speed in top gear and, braking with the left leg, try and maintain the same speed by pressing down on the accelerator. Providing the same speed is maintained a change in the speed of the engine confirms that slip is taking place.

3. In extreme cases of clutch slip the engine will race under normal acceleration conditions. If slip is due to oil or grease on the linings a temporary cure can sometimes be affected by squirting carbon tetrochloride into the clutch. The permanent cure, of course, is to renew the clutch driven plate and trace and rectify the oil leak.

13. CLUTCH SPIN - DIAGNOSIS & CURE

Clutch spin is a condition which occurs when there is a leak in the clutch hydraulic actuating mechanism where this system of actuation is used, the release arm free travel is excessive, there is an obstruction in the clutch either on the input gear splines, or in the release arm itself, or the oil may have partially burnt off the clutch linings and have left a resinous deposit which is causing the clutch disc to stick to the pressure plate or flywheel.

The reason for clutch spin is that due to any, or a combination of the faults just listed, the clutch pressure plate is not completely freeing from the centre plate even with the clutch pedal fully depressed.

If clutch spin is suspected, the condition can be confirmed by extreme difficulty in engaging first gear from rest, difficulty in changing gear, and very sudden take-up of the clutch drive at the fully depressed end of the clutch pedal travel as the clutch is released. If the clutch has just been stripped and rebuilt and is locked solid the clutch disc has been put in the wrong way round with the long portion of

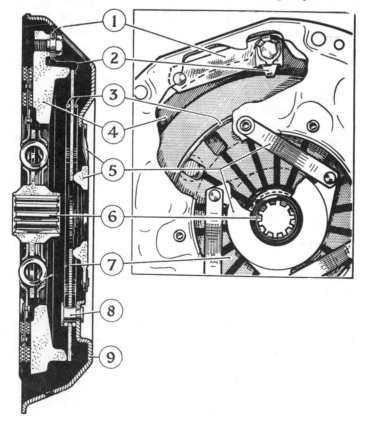

Fig. 5.4. SECTIONAL VIEW OF THE DIAPHRAGM CLUTCH.
1 Drive straps. 2 Retractor clips. 3 Fulcrum rings. 4 Pressure plate. 5 Release plate. 6 Driven plate. 7 Diaphragm spring. 8 Rivets. 9 Cover plate.

the hub facing forwards towards the flywheel.

Check the release arm free travel. If this is correct examine the clutch master and slave cylinders and the connecting hydraulic pipe for leaks. Fluid in one of the rubber boots fitted over the end of either the master or slave cylinders, where fitted, is a sure sign of a leaking piston seal.

If these points are checked and found to be in order then the fault lies internally in the release mechanism or the clutch, and it will be necessary to remove the clutch for examination.

14. CLUTCH JUDDER - DIAGNOSIS & CURE

Clutch judder is a self-evident condition which occurs when the gearbox or engine mountings are loose or too flexible, when there is oil on the faces of the clutch friction plate, or when the clutch pressure plate has been incorrectly adjusted.

The reason for clutch judder is that due to one of the faults just listed, the clutch pressure plate is not freeing smoothly from the friction disc, and is snatching.

Clutch judder normally occurs when the clutch pedal is released in first or reverse gears, and the whole car shudders as it moves backwards or forwards.

Remove the clutch assembly by unscrewing the six bolts holding the cover to the rear face of the flywheel. Unscrew the bolts diagonally half a turn at a time to prevent distortion to the cover flange.

With all the bolts and spring washers removed lift the clutch assembly off the two locating dowels. The driven plate or clutch disc will fall out at this stage as it is not attached to either the clutch cover assembly or the flywheel.

15. DIAPHRAGM SPRING TYPE CLUTCH

1. Later models are fitted with a single dry plate clutch having a diaphragm spring in place of the normal pressure springs.

2. Where these are fitted a copper impregnated graphite grease bearing is used and no attention is required to the lubrication of this bearing.

3. As can be seen in the illustration Fig. 5.4. the assembly consists of a pressed steel cover (9) and a pressure plate (4) which are linked together by three flat steel straps (1) and a large diameter diaphragm spring (7).

4. The cover assembly and driven plate is bolted to the flywheel, and the diaphragm spring then comes under load and is deflected from its shallow coned shape to a flat condition.

5. The clutch is operated hydraulically and no adjustment is provided. Details are the same as given earlier.

6. Removal of the clutch assembly and its replacement are the same as described earlier.

7. No servicing of the assembly should be attempted because the unit is carefully balanced when assembled, and when worn or damaged, must be replaced with a new clutch unit.

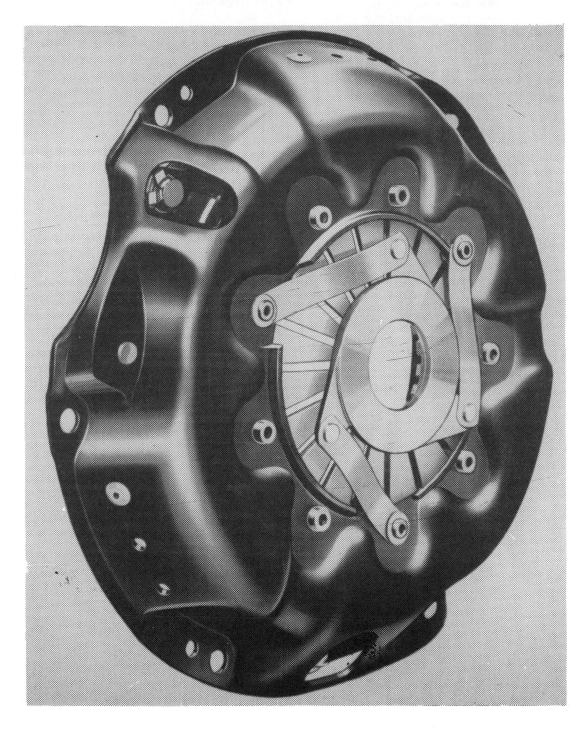

Fig. 5.5. Rear view of the diaphragm type clutch unit.

CLUTCH AND ACTUATING MECHANISM

Cause	Trouble	Remedy
Oil or air leaks	Engine backplate damaged or bent	Remove and straighten backplate.
	Air leaks in clutch hydraulic system, pipe unions loose	Trace and rectify leak, bleed hydraulic system.
	Clutch slave cylinder leaking	Overhaul slave cylinder and fit new rubbers.
	Clutch master cylinder leaking	Overhaul master cylinder and fit new rubbers.
	Hydraulic pipe from master cylinder to slave cylinder leaking	Fit new pipe.
	Centre plate linings covered in oil	Remove clutch, remedy oil leak, fit new centre plate.

SYMPTOM: CLUTCH JUDDER

Cause	Trouble	Remedy
General wear	Worn or partially sheared engine or gearbox rubber mountings	Fit new rubber mountings.
	Propellor shaft to differential bolts loose	Inspect and tighten bolts.
	Rear spring shackles worn	Fit new rear spring shackles.
	Excessive backlash in transmission	Inspect universal joints, rear axle, and mainshaft splines for wear. Replace as necessary.
	Rear springs weak or broken	Remove and fit reconditioned springs.
Damage or dirt	Pressure plate not parallel with flywheel face	Remove and overhaul pressure plate assembly.
	Clutch centre plate bent	Remove and fit new centre plate and linings.
	First motion shaft bent	Examine first motion shaft, straighten or fit new shaft.
	Engine backplate bent or distorted	Remove and straighten backplate.
Oil leaks	Oil on clutch centre plate linings	Remove clutch and fit new centre plate and linings. Rectify oil leak.

SYMPTOM: CLUTCH RATTLE

Cause	Trouble	Remedy
General wear	Clutch release bearing loose on clutch release fork	Separate engine and gearbox and check and rectify.
	Worn clutch release mechanism	Overhaul release mechanism and fit new parts as required.
	Excessive backlash in the transmission	Check universal joints, splines, and rear axle for wear. Renew component parts as necessary.

SYMPTOM: CLUTCH KNOCK

Cause	Trouble	Remedy
Components loose or worn	Clutch pressure plate not parallel with flywheel face	Remove and overhaul pressure plate assembly.
	Splines on first motion shaft or in centre plate hub badly worn	Inspect and renew first motion shaft or centre plate hub.
	First motion shaft bush badly worn	Extract old bush and fit new replacement.
	Flywheel bolts loose	Fit new tab washers and tighten bolts securely.

FAULT FINDING CHART

Cause	Trouble	Remedy
SYMPTOM:	CLUTCH SLIP	
General wear	Worn clutch linings Worn clutch release bearing Weak or broken thrust springs Weak anti-rattle springs	Remove clutch and fit new centre plate and linings. Fit new clutch release bearing. Remove clutch cover assembly, dismantle and fit new springs. Remove and overhaul clutch assembly.
Damage or dirt Oil or air leaks	Piston seized in clutch slave cylinder Engine backplate bent or distorted Air leak in clutch hydraulic actuating system Oil on clutch centre plate	Overhaul or replace clutch slave cylinder. Remove and straighten backplate. Trace and rectify leak. Bleed clutch system. Remove clutch and fit new centre plate and linings. Rectify oil leak.
SYMPTOM:	CLUTCH DRAG, SPIN, FIERCENESS OR SNATCH	
General wear	Worn centre plate linings Forward end of first motion shaft binding on spigot bush	Remove clutch and fit new centre plate. Examine bush and first motion shaft for wear and renew as necessary.
Damage or dirt	Dirt in clutch hydraulic system Centre plate hub binding on first motion shaft splines Clutch centre plate linings broken Clutch centre plate distorted or damaged Clutch pressure plate broken	Flush out, clean, and bleed system. Clean splines and check for obstruction. Remove clutch, and fit new clutch centre plate. Remove clutch, fit new clutch centre plate. Fit new pressure plate assembly.

CHAPTER SIX

GEARBOX

CONTENTS

SPECIFICATIONS

Type	Four speed forward and reverse				
Synchromesh	Top, 3rd and 2nd				
Gear ratios:	Top	Third	Second	First	Reverse
Minx I & II. Husky I (early models) ...	1.000:1	1.491:1	2.471:1	3.567:1	4.757:1
Husky I (later models)	1.000:1	1.516:1	2.331:1	3.644:1	4.615:1
Minx IIIA & IIIB. Husky II...	1.000:1	1.392:1	2.141:1	3.346:1	4.239:1
Minx IIIC & V. Husky II	1.000:1	1.392:1	2.141:1	3.746:1	4.994:1

with Zenith 26 VME carburetter
and Husky III

Layshaft bearings	Needle roller
Reverse gear bearings	Phospher bronze bush
Primary shaft stem wheel bearing	Ball bearing
Adjustment of mainshaft	None (end float controlled by ball race)
Layshaft end float	0.006 – 0.008 in.
Oil capacity	2¾ pints

Minx V has synchromesh on all forward speeds after September 1964.

TORQUE WRENCH SETTING

Mainshaft nuts ... ... 80 lb.ft.

---

1. GENERAL DESCRIPTION

The gearbox contains four forward speed ratios and reverse, with synchromesh on top, third and second ratios on earlier models and on all forward speeds on the 1600 Series.

2. GEARBOX REMOVAL

1. The gearbox can be removed as a unit with the engine, but for the owner it will generally be found to be more practical to remove it as a separate unit, largely because of the weights involved. The following sequences of operation will vary very slightly according to the model.

2. If the car can be placed over a pit, or lifted on a ramp, the work will be easier, otherwise the front end of the car should be very securely jacked up (see page 13) and firm solid ramps placed under the front wheels, while both sides of the rear wheels should be choked with blocks of wood or bricks. REMEMBER YOU HAVE TO WORK UNDERNEATH THE CAR, and you do not want the weight of the vehicle on your chest.

3. It is necessary to lower the rear end of the

engine in order to remove the gearbox, and this means that the battery should be disconnected and removed and then all the connections on the engine disconnected where these will obstruct the tilt. These include the top radiator hose, throttle and choke controls and exhaust pipe.

4. Next remove the propeller shaft rear coupling bolts, and remove the shaft rearwards.

5. Now jack up the rear of the engine to take the weight of the rear end, and at the same time, because of the weight of the gearbox, a jack should be used to support this unit. At least two people are required to move the gearbox rearwards, since the weight must not be allowed to rest on the drive shaft splines as the gearbox is moved towards the rear.

6. Disconnect the speedometer cable from the rear of the gearbox unit.

7. Disconnect the gear control operating mechanism at the gearbox, and then remove the bolts securing the rear mounting bracket to the chassis frame. (See Fig. 6.1.)

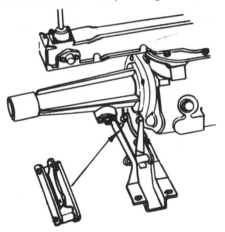

Fig. 6.1. Single point rear mounting behind the gearbox of later models.

8. At this point it will be found practical to carefully lower the jack under the rear of the engine and the jack under the gearbox together to allow the engine to tilt until the gearbox can clear the floor pressing.

9. The bolts around the clutch housing are then unscrewed to separate the gearbox from the rear of the engine. With these bolts released, it will be found that if one person is on one side of the car and another on the other, operating together at the crossmember, this will allow the gearbox to be drawn rearwards. This will tilt the jack over, and the gearbox is then lowered to the ground. KEEP THE FINGERS CLEAR OF THE UNDERSIDE OF THE GEARBOX. (See photo).

2.9

10. Having lifted the gearbox from the car it will be found an advantage to well clean down the outside of the casing before taking it inside for dismantling. This leaves all the oily dirt outside, rather than having a sticky mess to clear up from the bench and floor.

3. DISMANTLING THE GEARBOX

1. Removing the bellhousing. Unscrew the bolts and washers securing the clutch withdrawal lever bracket and lift out the lever and clutch release bearing. (See photo). Unscrew the remaining bolts and washers securing the bellhousing and lift away. (See photo).

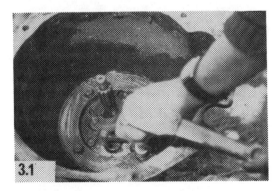

3.1

3.1

2. Removing the top cover. Lift out the oil dipstick, unscrew the bolts around the top cover and lift off the cover. (See photo). On

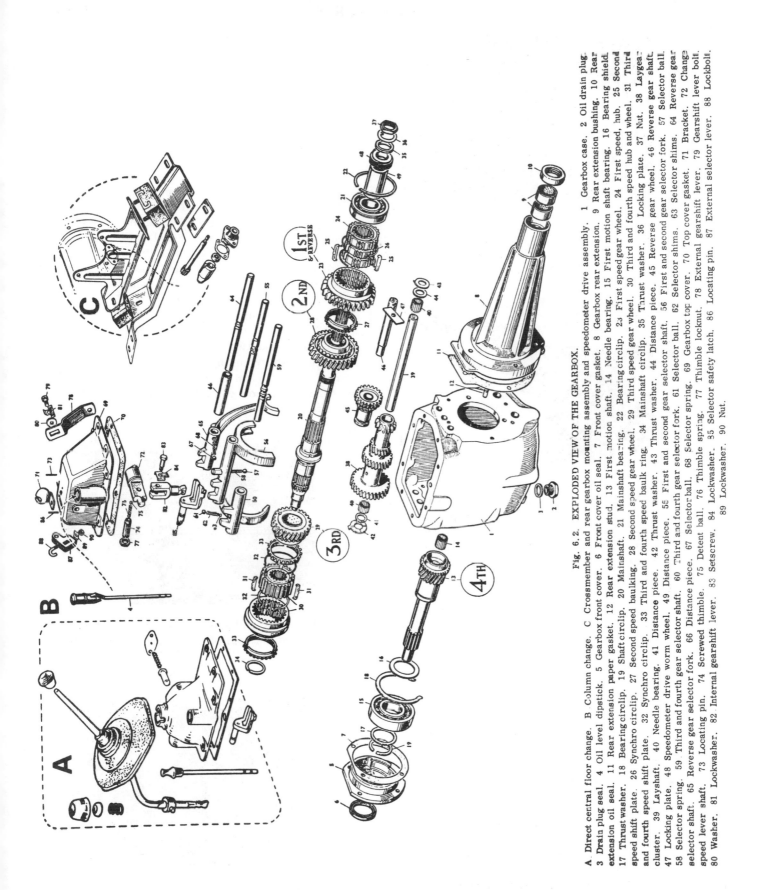

Fig. 6.2. EXPLODED VIEW OF THE GEARBOX.

A. Direct central floor change. B. Column change. C. Crossmember and rear gearbox mounting assembly and speedometer drive assembly. 1 Gearbox case. 2 Oil drain plug. 3 Drain plug seal. 4 Oil level dipstick. 5 Gearbox front cover. 6 Front cover oil seal. 7 Front cover gasket. 8 Gearbox rear extension. 9 Rear extension bushing. 10 Rear extension oil seal. 11 Rear extension paper gasket. 12 Rear extension stud. 13 First motion shaft. 14 Needle bearing. 15 First motion shaft bearing. 16 Bearing shield. 17 Thrust washer. 18 Bearing circlip. 19 Shaft circlip. 20 Mainshaft. 21 Mainshaft bearing. 22 Bearing circlip. 23 First speed gear wheel. 24 First speed, hub. 25 Second speed shift plate. 26 Synchro circlip. 27 Second speed baulking. 28 Second speed gear wheel. 29 Third speed gear wheel. 30 Third and fourth speed hub and wheel. 31 Third and fourth speed shift plate. 32 Synchro circlip. 33 Third and fourth speed baulk ring. 34 Mainshaft circlip. 35 Thrust washer. 36 Locking plate. 37 Nut. 38 Laygear cluster. 39 Layshaft. 40 Needle bearing. 41 Distance piece. 42 Thrust washer. 43 Thrust washer. 44 Distance piece. 45 Reverse gear wheel. 46 Reverse gear shaft. 47 Locking plate. 48 Speedometer drive worm wheel. 49 Distance piece. 55 First and second gear selector shaft. 56 First and second gear selector fork. 57 Selector ball. 58 Selector spring. 59 Third and fourth gear selector shaft. 60 Third and fourth gear selector fork. 61 Selector ball. 62 Selector shims. 63 Selector ball. 64 Reverse gear selector shaft. 65 Reverse gear selector fork. 66 Distance piece. 67 Selector ball. 68 Selector spring. 69 Gearbox top cover. 70 Top cover gasket. 71 Bracket. 72 Change speed lever shaft. 73 Locating pin. 74 Screwed thimble. 75 Detent ball. 76 Thimble spring. 77 Thimble locknut. 78 External gearshift lever. 79 Gearshift lever bolt. 80 Washer. 81 Lockwasher. 82 Internal gearshift lever. 83 Setscrew. 84 Lockwasher. 85 Selector safety latch. 86 Locating pin. 87 External selector lever. 88 Lockbolt. 89 Lockwasher. 90 Nut.

89

3.2

cars having a column change note that there is **a small** bracket held in position by two of the **top** cover bolts. (See photo).

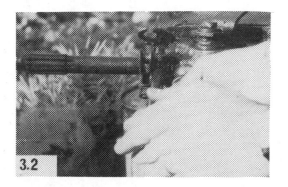

3.2

3. Unless the operation in the cover is **known** to be faulty, it is sound policy not to **dismantle the** unit. If it is necessary to **dismantle** in order to replace **worn** or broken parts, the sequence for dismantling is as follows. Numbers refer to Fig. 6.2.

4. Undo the lockwasher (81) and remove the bolt (79) with its **washer** (80) securing the external gear shift lever (78). Undo the lockwasher (89) and slacken the nut (90) releasing the selector lever (87).

5. Undo the lockwasher (84) on the internal gearchange lever (82), remove the setscrew (83) releasing lever (82).

6. Pay special attention to the detent mechanism, items 74 to 77 because these have two functions. First to locate the neutral position of the shaft (72) and second by the screwed thimble (74) which is bored eccentrically where it contains the spring (76) controlling the ball (75), the operating position of the shaft (72) can be adjusted axially by turning this thimble by means of its slotted head. This adjustment is provided for the initial adjustments during manufacture, and **must** not be disturbed in service.

7. The locating pin (73) is removed **with a** punch to allow the change speed lever shaft (72) to be pushed out from inside. Take care

not to lose the ball and spring (75, 76). Drive out the pin (86) and push the selector shaft (85) and lever (82) into the cover.

8. Reassembly is the **reverse**, but it is important that when tightening the bolt (83) this must not be over-tightened. The lever must swing freely on its shaft. When replacing the locating pins, the ends of these must be peened over.

9. The following **tools** will be found useful when dismantling and reassembling the gearbox. One dummy layshaft spindle $\frac{3}{4}$ in. diameter and $6\frac{1}{2}$ in. long. Three dummy selector shafts $\frac{7}{16}$ in. **diameter** and 2 in. long. A selector shaft loading test clamp.

10. With the gearbox on the workbench, start on the extension/rear cover assembly by first unbolting **the** speedometer pinion flange and lifting out the pinion and bush.

11. Next remove the two bolts and one nut from the rear mounting plate, and lift the cross-member and mounting plate away. Remove the remaining **bolts** securing the extension and withdraw the **casing** from **the** shaft. (See photo).

3.11

12. The three selector shafts must be tapped **out** toward the rear of the gearbox, (see photo) **starting** with the reverse selector shaft (64) which has a distance piece on the forward end.

3.12

13. Next tap out the **first** and second speed selector shaft (55) and then tap out the third and **fourth** speed selector shaft (59) noting

carefully the location of each shaft as it is removed. (See photo).

14. Lay the shafts in their correct relationship and then lift out the reverse selector fork, (see photo) and slide it onto its shaft for easy reassembly.

15. Now lift out the first and second selector fork and slide onto its shaft, and finally lift out the third and fourth selector fork, taking care that the ball (61) spring (62) and any shims which may be fitted (63) are not lost.

16. Front cover removal. NOTE that this can only be removed once the layshaft cluster (38) has been lowered into the bottom of the gearbox, and this is done by first removing the four screws (5) from the front cover. Remove the small setscrew at the rear of the cover which secures the flat lock plate (47). Slide this plate downwards to remove it, and then displace the layshaft (39) using the dummy layshaft from the rear of the box, pushing it forward until it is clear of the fixed thrust washer (43), so that the layshaft can be lowered into the bottom of the gearbox casing.

17. This will allow the front cover to be pulled forward, and in doing so the needle rollers (14) will be displaced from the mainshaft spigot.

18. Mainshaft assembly removal. At this point the mainshaft assembly can be removed by first releasing the lockwasher (36), (see photo) and undoing the large nut (37) and then by holding the front end of the gear cluster, drive the mainshaft forward with a mallet until it is free of the rear ball bearing (21).

19. By holding the second speed synchrohub assembly (23 to 26) the mainshaft is withdrawn through the hole in the front of the gearbox. (See photo). The second speed synchrohub is then lifted out of the top of the box.

20. With the mainshaft away, lift out the larger gears through the top of the gearbox. (See photo).

21. The layshaft can now be lifted up from the bottom of the gearbox and out through the forward hole complete with the dummy shaft retaining the needle bearings. (See photo).

4. GEARBOX REASSEMBLY

1. Where the gearbox has been completely dismantled the following is the sequence for reassembly.

2. It should be noted that, if the gearbox is not fitted with a paper gasket between the front cover and the casing, one should be obtained from a Rootes Service Agent, and fitted.

3. First assemble the reverse gear wheel and shaft, with the gears to the rear of the box.

4. Apply some thick grease to the bronze

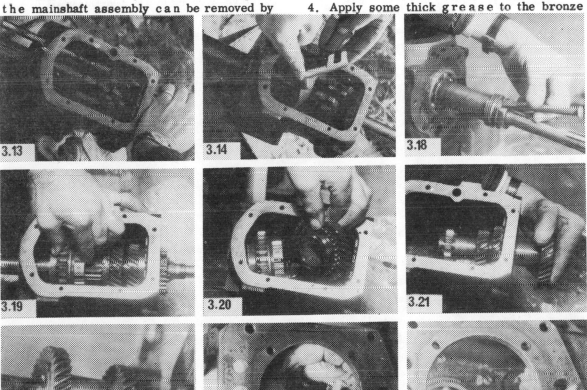

3.13   3.14   3.18

3.19   3.20   3.21

4.5   4.7   4.8

washers of the layshaft and place the large one to the front of the casing, holding in position with the grease.

5. Check that there are twenty seven needle rollers in each end of the layshaft cluster, and locate them in position with plenty of thick grease. Refitting the needle bearings is made easier by using the dummy shaft. (See photo).

6. Fit the abutment ring into the front of the cluster and lower the whole cluster, complete with the dummy shaft into the casing, and then fit the rear floating steel thrust washer.

7. Well coat the thrust washers with thick grease and locate them with the tab in the machined slot at the top of each bore. (See photo).

8. Fit the layshaft and dummy shaft into the gearbox, holding it and the washers temporarily in position with a thin rod. (See photo).

9. When assembling the synchrohub units, fit the three pads close up to one spring wire, and bring upwards to clip to the other spring wire. (See photo).

10. The pads can be retained more easily if a rubber band is fitted around the centre. (See photo).

11. This will slide off as the mating parts are brought together. (See photo).

12. We are now ready to reassemble and re-place the mainshaft unit. (See photo).

13. Pass the first and second synchrohub unit and the second speed wheel assembly through the top of the casing with the bevelled first speed teeth towards the rear, and enter the mainshaft unit through the front of the casing, passing it through the synchrohub assembly, and the bearing in the casing.

14. Fit the rear bearing and tap it right home, then fit the speedometer gear in position, with the spacer, locking washer and the nut.

15. Now make sure that there are twenty seven needle rollers in the end of the stemwheel, held in position with heavy grease. These are most easily assembled with the aid of a short length of round steel tube held in the centre while the needle rollers are inserted individually and guided into position with a piece of stiff, thin wire. (See photo).

16. Once the rollers are all in position, the dummy shaft is carefully withdrawn, and the grease will hold the set of rollers in position. Carefully enter the stemwheel assembly complete with the front cover which is then secured with the four screws and washers. A slight twist during fitting will ensure that the needle bearing is seated. (See photo).

17. Make sure that the fourth speed bronze baulking ring is in position before entering the

4.9   4.10   4.11
4.12   4.15   4.16
4.18   4.19   4.20

the stemwheel assembly, as this is a loose unit at the forward end of the synchrohub.

18. Now invert the whole gearbox and with the aid of the thin rod passing right through the centre of the dummy tube shaft locate the layshaft and the end washers in alignment with the layshaft spindle bores, and start the spindle from the rear of the box. As the spindle is driven in, the thin rod and the dummy layshaft tube will be driven out, leaving the needle bearings in their correct position. (See photo).

19. With the spindle pushed home, insert the locking plate at the back of the gearbox, and secure in position with the small bolt. (See photo).

20. Now turn the gearbox the right way up, and fit the selector forks, third and top fork first, first and second fork second, and reverse fork last. (See photo). The long distance piece on the reverse fork must go to the front of the shaft, when this is inserted.

21. Place the rear cover in position and secure. (See photo). At this stage revolve the gear

and make quite sure that they are moving freely, and then check each fork to ensure that the gears can be selected.

22. When the top cover is fitted, place all the forks in the neutral position and make sure that the selector in the cover is also in the neutral position. (See photo). Once the top

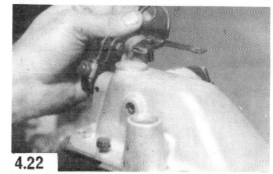

4.22

cover is bolted down, (see photo) check to make sure that the selector lever moves freely across the three slots in the three selector forks.

4.21

4.22

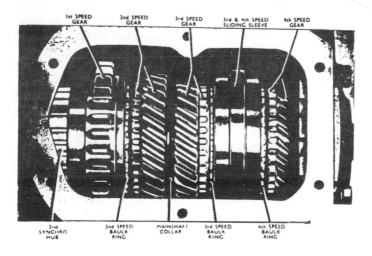

Fig. 6.3. View of the mainshaft correctly assembled in the gearbox casing.

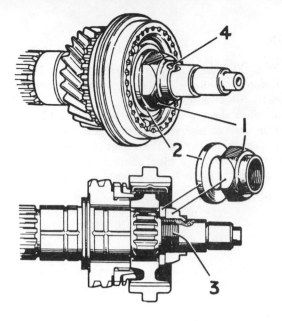

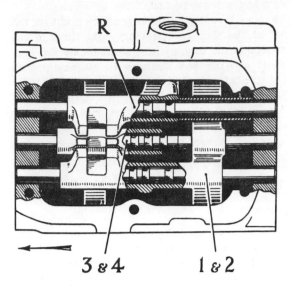

Fig. 6.4. VIEW OF THE MAINSHAFT NUT ASSEMBLY
1 Mainshaft nut. 2 Washer. 3 Mainshaft. 4 Nut flange.

Fig. 6.6. Layout of the selector shafts and forks on cars with column gear change.

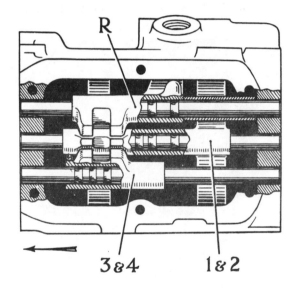

Fig. 6.5. Layout of the selector shafts and forks on cars with central floor gear change.

5. SELECTOR CONTROL CABLE ADJUSTMENT (COLUMN CHANGE)

1. With the gearbox returned to the car, the column control cable is adjusted by engaging the first gear position with the cable punch nut slackened.

2. Grip the inner cable with a pair of pliers and pull it upwards as far as it will go. The cable can be chalked, and then a pencil mark made at the point where it protrudes through the trunnion. Now push the cable right down and mark it again. Now pull the cable up, and mark the position mid way between the two previous marks, push the cable to this mark level with the top of the trunnion, and tighten the pinch nut, holding the trunnion with one spanner and tightening the nut with a second spanner to save kinking the inner cable.

3. Having carried out the above adjustment the gear lever should not come into contact with the steering column cowl when reverse gear is selected. If it does, then it can be adjusted by placing the lever in the neutral position, and the ball joint at the bottom of the gearchange actuating lever disconnected. This ball joint should be turned to lengthen the control rod until the lever assumes a position of 1 inch above the horizontal position. After completing the adjustment, check that there is a clearance between the column cowl and the lever when the lever is in the reverse position.

FAULT FINDING CHART

Cause	Trouble	Remedy
SYMPTOM:	**WEAK OR INEFFECTIVE SYNCHROMESH**	
General wear	Synchronising cones worn, split or damaged.	Dismantle and overhaul gearbox. Fit new gear wheels and synchronising cones.
	Baulk ring synchromesh dogs worn, or damaged	Dismantle and overhaul gearbox. Fit new baulk ring synchromesh.
SYMPTOM:	**JUMPS OUT OF GEAR**	
General wear or damage	Broken gearchange fork rod spring	Dismantle and replace spring.
	Gearbox coupling dogs badly worn	Dismantle gearbox. Fit new coupling dogs.
	Selector fork rod groove badly worn	Fit new selector fork rod.
	Selector fork rod securing screw and locknut loose	Remove side cover, tighten securing screw and locknut.
SYMPTOM:	**EXCESSIVE NOISE**	
Lack of maintenance	Incorrect grade of oil in gearbox or oil level too low	Drain, refill, or top up gearbox with correct grade of oil.
General wear	Bush or needle roller bearings worn or damaged	Dismantle and overhaul gearbox. Renew bearings.
	Gearteeth excessively worn or damaged	Dismantle, overhaul gearbox. Renew gearwheels.
	Laygear thrust washers worn allowing excessive end play	Dismantle and overhaul gearbox. Renew thrust washers.
SYMPTOM:	**EXCESSIVE DIFFICULTY IN ENGAGING GEAR**	
Clutch not fully disengaging	Clutch pedal adjustment incorrect	Adjust clutch pedal correctly.

CHAPTER SEVEN
PROPELLER SHAFT AND UNIVERSAL JOINTS

CONTENTS

1. GENERAL DESCRIPTION

Drive is transmitted from the gearbox to the rear axle by means of a finely balanced tubular propeller shaft. Fitted at each end of the shaft is a universal joint which allows for vertical movement of the rear axle. Each universal joint comprises a four legged centre spider, four needle roller bearings and two yokes.

Fore and aft movement of the rear axle is absorbed by a sliding spline in the front of the propeller shaft which slides over a mating spline on the rear of the gearbox mainshaft. A supply of oil through very small oil holes from the gearbox lubricates the splines, and a grease nipple is fitted to each universal joint so that the needle roller bearings can be lubricated. Access to the nipple at the front of the propeller shaft is usually through a hole, normally covered by a rubber plug, on the left-hand side of the propeller shaft tunnel, just behind the gearbox. The propeller shaft is a relatively simple component, and to overhaul and repair it is fairly easy.

2. PROPELLER SHAFT - REMOVAL & REPLACEMENT

1. Jack up the rear of the car, or position the rear of the car over a pit or on a ramp.
2. If the rear of the car is jacked up supplement the jack with support blocks so that danger is minimised should the jack collapse.
3. If the rear wheels are off the ground place the car in gear or put the handbrake on to ensure that the propeller shaft does not turn when an attempt is made to loosen the four nuts securing the propeller shaft to the rear axle.
4. Unscrew and remove the four self-locking nuts, bolts and securing washers which hold the flange on the propeller shaft to the flange on the rear axle.
5. The propeller shaft is carefully balanced to fine limits and it is important that it is replaced in exactly the same position it was in prior to its removal. Scratch a mark on the propeller shaft and rear axle flanges to ensure accurate mating when the time comes for reassembly.
6. Slightly push the shaft forward to separate the two flanges, and then lower the end of the shaft and pull it rearwards to disengage the gearbox mainshaft splines.
7. Place a large can or a tray under the rear of the gearbox extension to catch any oil which is likely to leak through the spline lubricating holes, when the propeller shaft is removed.
8. Replacement of the propeller shaft is a reversal of the above procedure. Ensure that the mating marks scratched on the propeller shaft and rear axle flanges line up.

3. UNIVERSAL JOINTS - INSPECTION & REPAIR

1. Wear in the needle roller bearings is characterised by vibration in the transmission, 'clonks' on taking up the drive, and in extreme cases of lack of lubrication, metallic squeaking, and ultimately grating and shrieking sounds as the bearings break up.
2. It is easy to check if the needle roller bearings are worn with the propeller shaft in position, by trying to turn the shaft with one hand,

the other hand holding the rear axle flange when the rear universal is being checked, and the front half coupling when the front universal is being checked. Any movement between the propeller shaft and the front and the rear half couplings is indicative of considerable wear. If worn, the old bearings and spiders will have to be discarded and a repair kit, comprising new universal joint spiders, bearings, oil seals, and retainers purchased. Check also by trying to lift the shaft and noticing any movement in the joints.

3. Examine the propeller shaft splines for wear. If worn it will be necessary to purchase a new front half coupling, or if the yokes are badly worn, an exchange propeller shaft. It is not possible to fit oversize bearings and journals to the trunnion bearing holes.

4. UNIVERSAL JOINTS - DISMANTLING

1. Clean away all traces of dirt and grease from circlips located on the ends of the spiders, and remove the clips by pressing their open ends together with a pair of pliers and lever them out with a screwdriver. NOTE if they are difficult to remove tap the bearing face resting on top of the spider with a mallet which will ease the pressure on the circlip.

2. Hold the propeller shaft in one hand and remove the bearing cups and needle rollers by

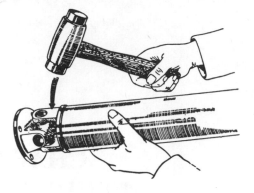

Fig. 7.1.   Tap the universal joint to free the bearing.

tapping the yoke at each bearing with a copper or hide faced hammer. As soon as the bearings start to emerge they can be drawn out with your fingers. If the bearing cup refuses to move then place a thin bar against the inside of the bearing and tap it gently until the cup starts to emerge.

3. With the bearings removed it is relatively easy to extract the spiders from their yokes. If the bearings and spider journals are thought to be badly worn this can easily be ascertained visually with the universal joints dismantled.

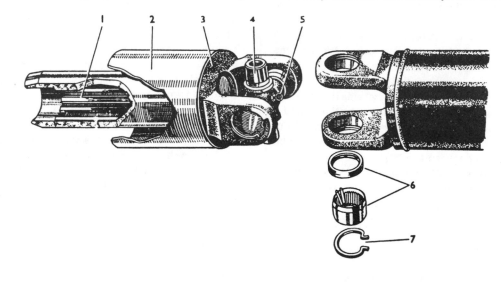

Fig. 7.3. EXPLODED VIEW OF THE FRONT UNIVERSAL JOINT.
1 Internal splined end of propeller shaft. 2 Dust cover. 3 Front half coupling. 4 Spider. 5 Lubricating nipple. 6 Needle bearing assembly. 7 Spring ring.

PROPELLER SHAFT AND UNIVERSAL JOINTS

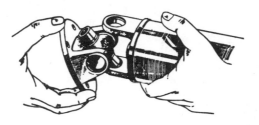

Fig. 7.2. Separating the universal joint.

5. UNIVERSAL JOINTS - REASSEMBLY

1. Thoroughly clean out the yokes and journals.

2. Fit new cork oil seals and retainers on the spider journals, place the spider on the propeller shaft yoke, and assemble the needle rollers in the bearing races with the assistance of some thin grease.

3. Refit the bearing cups on the spider and tap the bearings home so that they lie squarely in position.

4. Replace the circlips and lubricate the bearings well with a lithium based grease.

6. PROPELLER SHAFT - LATER MODELS

1. On later models the propeller shaft assembly will incorporate either a rubber bonded vibration damper at the rear axle end, as shown in Fig. 7.4. or the rear joint may be of the metal to rubber rear joint as seen in Fig. 7.5.

2. On models fitted with the vibration damper, remove the nuts from the rear axle coupling, and when refitting always fit new shakeproof washers.

3. On models fitted with the metal to rubber joint, two nuts and bolts are used to connect the shaft to the rear axle flange. NOTE particularly which way round the heads of the nuts are facing so as to ensure correct replacement.

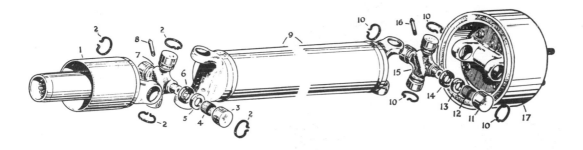

Fig. 7.4. EXPLODED VIEW OF THE PROPELLER SHAFT WITH VIBRATION DAMPER.
1 Sleeve yoke (dust shield not fitted to later models). 2 Snap ring. 3 Bearing cap. 4 Needle roller assembly. 5 Gasket. 6 Gasket retainer. 7 Journal. 8 Greaser (not fitted to sealed bearings). 9 Propeller shaft. 10 Snap ring. 11 Bearing cap. 12 Needle roller assembly. 13 Gasket. 14 Gasket retainer. 15 Journal. 16 Greaser (not fitted to sealed bearings). 17 Rear coupling and vibration damper.

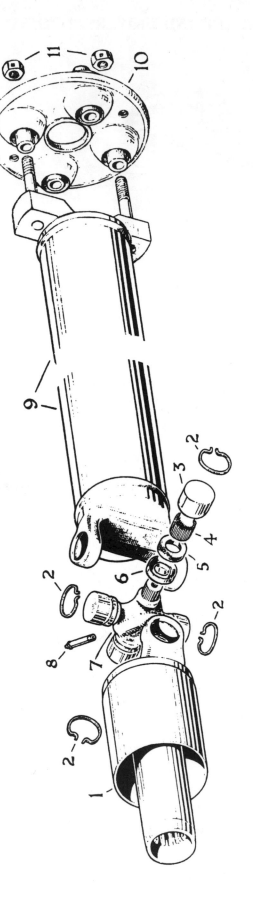

Fig. 7.5. EXPLODED VIEW OF THE PROPELLER SHAFT WITH METAL TO RUBBER REAR UNIVERSAL JOINT.

1 Sleeve yoke (dust shield not fitted to later models). 2 Snap ring. 3 Bearing cap. 4 Needle roller assembly. 5 Gasket. 6 Gasket retainer. 7 Journal. 8 Greaser (not fitted to sealed bearings). 9 Propeller shaft. 10 Rear universal joint. 11 Universal joint retaining nuts.

CHAPTER EIGHT

REAR AXLE

CONTENTS

SPECIFICATIONS

		Crown wheel	Pinion
Type	Semi-floating		
Final Drive - Early models	Spiral bevel		
- Later models	Hypoid		
Ratios & number of teeth on:-			
Minx I & II Saloon & convertible)			
Minx II, III & IIIA estate cars)	4.78 : 1	43	9
from Chassis No. A. 1820115)			
Husky I up to Chassis No. A. 2817457)			
Minx I & II estate car..	5.22 : 1	47	9
Minx III, IIIA saloon & convertible)	4.55 : 1	41	9
Husky I and early II)			
Minx IIIB (high compression))	4.44 : 1	40	9
Husky II (with hypoid axle))			
Minx IIIB (low compression)	4.86 : 1	34	7
Minx IIIC	4.22 : 1	38	9
Minx V	3.89 : 1	35	9
Husky II (with Zenith 26 UME carb))	4.22 : 1	38	9
Husky III)			
Bearings - Bevel pinion	Taper roller		
- Crown wheel assembly	Taper roller		

CHAPTER EIGHT

Bearings - Hub bearings..   ... ...   Ball
Adjustment - Bevel pinion   ... ...   Shims
         - Differential   ... ...   Shims
Backlash, crown wheel and pinion.. ...   0.005 - 0.009 in.

TORQUE WRENCH SETTINGS

Bevel pin nut ... ...   110 lb/ft.
Axle shaft.. ... ...   180 lb/ft.

1. GENERAL DESCRIPTION

Basically both the spiral bevel and hypoid types of axle assembly and repair procedures are the same, crown wheel adjustment being provided by the disposition of shims adjacent to the taper roller bearings carrying the housing and bevel pinion shaft. The complete differential assembly is detachable from the axle casing once the axle shafts have been withdrawn. The axle shafts are fully machined and supported at their outer ends on ball bearings. It should be noted that on various different models the relationship of the number of teeth on the crown wheel and on the pinion varies, as seen in the specifications above, and it is essential when replacing drive units that the replacement units are identical to those being replaced.

2. REPLACING THE BEVEL PINION HOUSING SEAL

1. If the rear axle oil leaks out of the bevel pinion housing just behind the propeller shaft flange, see fig. 8.1., the flange is unbolted to permit access to the bevel flange nut which is then unscrewed and the bevel flange pulled from the shaft.
2. The seal (25) is withdrawn, and the outside of the cage of the new seal should be well coated with a liquid jointing compound before the seal is pressed into position.
3. The seal operates in one direction only, and must be fitted with the lip and spring facing the rear axle.

3. HUB OIL SEALS

1. When the hub oil seals break down the method of fitting new seals is first to jack up the rear axle, remove the road wheel and clean away the dirt from the backplate.
2. Remove the set screw securing the brake drum, and pull off the drum, and remove the shoes.
3. Remove the shaft centre nut (48) and washer (47), and fit a suitable hub extractor tool over the wheel securing bolts. Tighten the extractor centre nut, give it a sharp blow with a hammer and lift off the hub and extractor.

4. Remove the three plain bolts and two dowel bolts passing through the oil catcher and seal housing. Hook out the oil seal (37) and fit the new seal in position. Take care when refitting the securing bolts to fit the dowel bolts into the reamed holes. Tighten the bolts only after the hub is right home, in order to centralise the seal. The rear hub is then reassembled and it will probably be necessary to re-adjust the brake shoes.

4. AXLE SHAFT REMOVAL

To remove the axle shaft after the road wheel has been removed and the brake drum taken away, it is essential to unbolt the backing plate and then fit an axle removing tool and its adaptor over the wheel studs and secure it with the wheel nuts. Operation of the removal tool will bring away the shaft complete with the backplate, oil seal, dust excluder and hub.

5. REMOVING THE DIFFERENTIAL FROM THE REAR AXLE

Removal of the differential unit is quite a straightforward operation. First drain the oil away, and then remove the two axle shafts. Unbolt the flanges of the propeller shaft from the rear coupling and then unbolt all the nuts securing the differential housing to the front of the axle casing.

6. REPLACING THE DIFFERENTIAL UNIT

When replacing the assembly the operations are the reverse of the above, noting the following important guides. New paper joints must be used, both faces of which should be well coated with jointing compound, to eliminate any oil leaks from the front of the axle. The hydraulic brakes must be bled, once the brake units are reassembled.

7. DISMANTLING THE DIFFERENTIAL

1. With the unit out of the casing and on the workshop bench, first unbolt the securing caps over the bearings supporting the assembly, (see photo), after first marking them to ensure correct reassembly. (See photo).
2. The differential is then lifted out complete

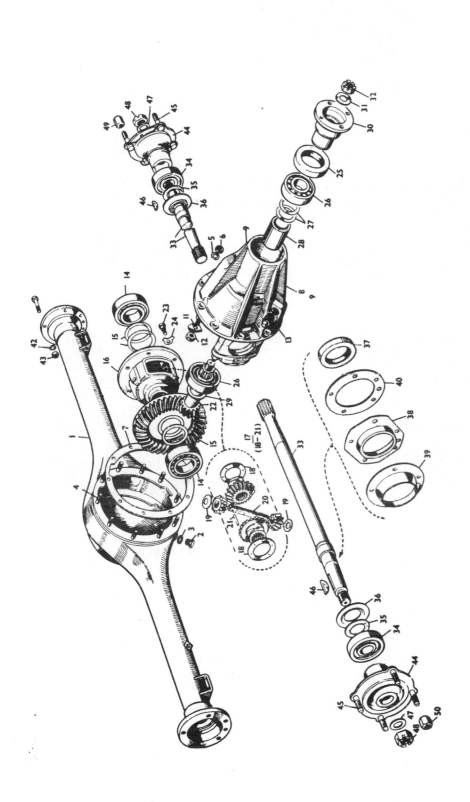

Fig. 8.1. EXPLODED VIEW OF THE REAR AXLE.

1 Axle casing. 2 Axle oil drain plug. 3 Drain plug washer. 5 Spring washer. 6 Nu. 7 Gasket. 8 Differential housing. 9 Differential assembly. 11 Lockwasher. 12 Nut. 13 Oil filler plug. 14 Side bearings. 15 Crown wheel. 16 Differential box. 17 Differential box gears (18-21). 18 Thrust washers. 19 Thrust washers. 20 Thrust washers. 20 Cross pin. 21 Tapered pin. 22 Pinion. 23 Setscrew. 24 Lockwasher. 25 Oil seal. 23 Pinion bearings. 27 Shims. 28 Distance piece. 29 Pinion spacer. 30 Drive coupling to propeller shaft. 31 Thrust washer. 32 Slotted nut. 33 Axle shafts. 34 Axle shafts. 35 Oil guard inner ring. 36 Oil guard outer ring. 37 Oil seal. 38 Oil seal housing. 39 Dust shield. 40 Gasket. 41 Bolt. 42 Spring washer. 43 Nut. 44 Hub. 45 Hub stud--to road wheel. 46 Key. 47 Flat washer. 48 Axle nut. 49 Wheel nut. 50 Wheel nut.

CHAPTER EIGHT

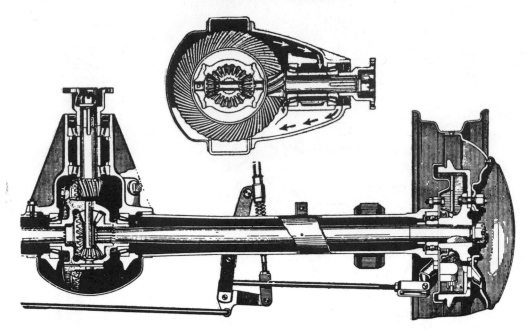

Fig. 8.2. Sectional view of the rear axle assembly

7.1

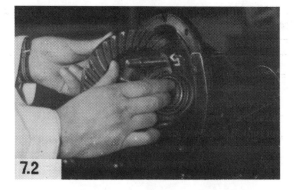

7.2

7.1

3. If the crown wheel is to be renewed, then this is removed by unscrewing the eight set screws (23) securing it to the differential unit, after the lockwashers (24) have been eased up.

4. If the differential pinions have to be renewed, knock out a taper pin (21) which will be found securing a cross pin (20) in the differential box (16), push out the cross pin, and the differential pinions complete with their thrust washers (18) can then be carried round in order to extract them through the wide openings in the differential box.

8. RENEWAL OF BEARINGS

When it is necessary to renew the ball bearing races on which the differential assembly is mounted, (14) it is necessary to draw the old inner races from the differential with the aid of a claw drawer tool. The whole race must be renewed, otherwise if only the outer

with the crown wheel and bearings. The outer races of the bearings will come away, so that it is important that these are kept to their correct sides. (See photo).

race and the ball cages are fitted, these will break down after a short service life, since they will be slack, and so allow wear to take place rapidly.

9. BEVEL PINION DISMANTLING

1. Clamp the bevel pinion unit in a vice, remove the split pin, nut and washer at the propeller shaft drive coupling flange, and with a brass drift, tap out the bevel pinion, taking care not to damage the threads. (See photo).

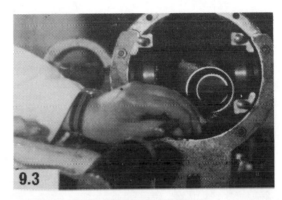

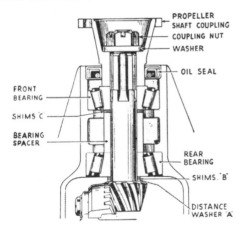

2. The inner race of the rear bearing will be found to have a distance washer (A in Fig. 8.3. together with shims (B and C in Fig. 8.3.) and these will become detached with the pinion shaft as it is withdrawn.

Fig. 8.3. Sectional view of bevel pinion assembly.

3. If the races have to be renewed, the inner race of the bevel pinion rear bearing will have to be removed in an arbor press because this is a press fit onto the shaft. (See photo). The outer races can be knocked out with a brass drift. (See photo).

4. The oil seal is prised from the nose of the housing, because subsequent pre-loading is checked without the oil seal in position.

10. REFITTING THE BEVEL PINION

1. It should be noted that since the object of pre-loading the bearings and indeed readjusting the differential unit is to ensure that the noise from the gears is kept to a minimum it means that special and generally expensive tools are required, which are not readily available to the owner, and would certainly not warrant purchasing.

2. Thus it is often more satisfactory to replace the worn and damaged parts of the differential with factory replacement units, which are ready to assemble into the casing, rather than attempt to strip down and completely rebuild each unit.

3. An example of the application of special equipment is seen in the reassembly of the pinion unit, where it is necessary to use a dummy pinion shaft between the inner half of the rear bearing and the bearing spacer and any shims previously removed. (See photo). Then the coupling nut is fitted and tightened fully, and if the shims are accurate, the bearings should be pre-loaded.

4. This pre-loading is tested by applying a suitable spring balance to the flange and pulling on this until the flange turns on the bearings, (see photo) noting the reading on the balance. This must be within the range of 5 to 9 lbs pull, if new bearings have been fitted.

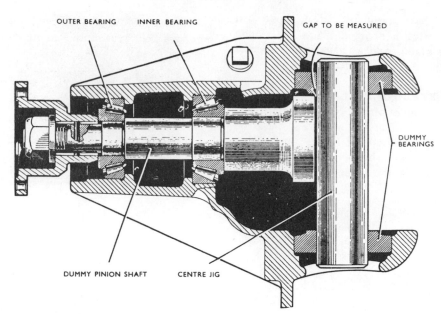

OUTER BEARING   INNER BEARING   GAP TO BE MEASURED

DUMMY BEARINGS

DUMMY PINION SHAFT   CENTRE JIG

Fig. 8.4. A view of the various special jigs and tools that can be used to determine the correct bevel pinion preload and bevel position relative to the crown wheel axis.

10.3

10.4

5. If the old bearings are still being used, then the reading on the balance must be between 3 and 7 lbs. ins.

6. This pull should normally be taken at 4 inches from the centre of the pinion shaft, and if leverage is needed to provide this distance

then a ring spanner can be used, applying this to the flange nut, this spanner pointing downwards, and the spring balance being pulled at right angles to it.

7. If the readings shown on the balance are outside those given above then it is necessary to add or remove shims from their location between the bearing spacer and the front bearing. Having established this pre-load, a centre jig tool is now fitted into the casing. It will be found that a gap exists between the end of the dummy pinion shaft and this centre jig.

8. Place the distance washer (A in Fig. 8.3.) in this gap and measure any remaining clearance with a feeler gauge in order to establish the actual thickness of shims (B) in Fig. 8.3. which will be needed on the pinion shaft when reassembling. (See photo).

10.8

9. However, in practice it will be found that as the bearing is pressed onto the pinion shaft during assembly, this length will be altered by

about 0.020 in. so that this amount must be subtracted from the shim thickness total which would be required to fill the gap.

10. Having established this essential data, the centre jig and the dummy pinion shaft are removed, and the bevel pinion shaft together with the distance washer which must have the chamfered edge towards the gear, and the shims and press the inner race of the rear bearing in position.

11. Place the bearing spacer and then the shims on the shaft and refit the unit into the housing.

12. Next refit a new oil seal after coating the outer cage with a quick drying jointing cement, taking care that the three openings in the rear face of the oil seal are so positioned that one of them is at the 12 o'clock position.

11. REFITTING THE DIFFERENTIAL UNIT

1. With the differential box bearings out of the way, fit dummy bearings without any shims and with their faces abutting the differential box.

2. Now place the differential assembly together with these dummy bearings in position in the housing, replace the bearing caps and lightly tighten the securing nuts. (See photo).

11.2

3. Now paint the teeth of the crown wheel with a thin paste of red lead and engine oil, or engineers blue marking paste, and rotate the crown wheel in order to obtain a clear impression between the crown wheel and pinion teeth. (See Fig. 8.7.)

4. The positions of the markings on each tooth are important because the area of contact between the teeth will determine the operation and the noise in the differential.

5. The bearing area is between the crown and base of the teeth but should be considerably nearer the toe, or inner end of the teeth, than the heel or outer end.

6. Adjustment is effected with the aid of a short length of steel tube. This is used to drive the appropriate dummy bearing inwards, in order to reposition the crown wheel to the correct position.

7. Having obtained a correct marking area, measure the gaps between the outer faces of the dummy bearings and the casing. (See photo)

11.7

These dummy bearings will be 0.812 in. thick, and by adding this thickness to each measurement obtained at the casing, this will provide the dimensions shown at C and D in Fig. 8.5.

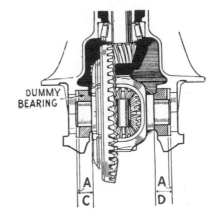

DUMMY BEARING

Fig. 8.5. Bearing measurements required to determine correct shim thickness.

8. Next measure the thickness of the actual bearings to be used, (see photo), and subtract

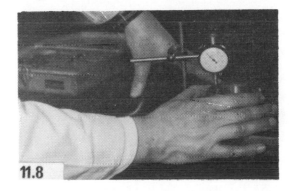

11.8

this from the totals shown at C and D. The result will give the thickness of shims needed on each side, adding a dimension of 0.002 in. to each side to provide a pre-load for the bearings.

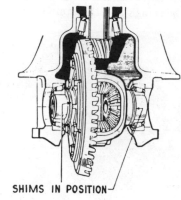

SHIMS IN POSITION

Fig. 8.6. Correct shims in position on reassembly of the bearings.

9. The result of these calculations should be noted down. Now lift out the differential unit, remove the dummy bearings, press on the new bearings after fitting the required shims in position as shown in Fig. 8.6. and refit the differential unit into the housing, complete with the bearing retaining caps.

10. It is of practical value to recheck the adjustment of the teeth after the differential unit has been assembled, and this is done by cleaning off all the previous marking compound, making sure that the teeth of both the crown wheel and pinion are clean, and then applying a small amount of the paste to the teeth. The crown wheel is then revolved by hand in both directions, and the actual contact areas can be checked. At the same time the backlash between the crown wheel and pinion should be checked in at least three positions, and this should be between 0.005 and 0.009 in. when checked with feeler gauges between the teeth.

12. REAR AXLE REMOVAL

1. If it becomes necessary to remove the complete rear axle from the car the procedure is as follows:-

2. Jack up the rear end of the car securely. Remove the road wheels.

3. Disconnect the propeller shaft at the rear drive coupling by unscrewing the securing bolts, after marking the two flanges with a file to ensure correct reassembly. Disconnect the shock absorber lower mountings. Disconnect the handbrake linkage cable.

4. Disconnect the rear brake flexible hoses at the union on the body brackets, taking care of the flow of fluid from these hoses. Block the openings to prevent entry of dirt. If the hoses are lifted upwards, and tied this will save much of the fluid from running away.

5. Unscrew the nuts securing the spring U bolts. With the U bolts lifted away, the axle can be withdrawn to one side from between the springs and lowered to the floor.

13. REAR AXLE REPLACEMENT

The series of operations to replace is the reverse of the above, but make sure that the U bolts are tightened, and that the hydraulic brakes are bled after reassembly of the flexible pipe, (See Chapter 9).

14. AXLE BREATHER

On later models there is a $\frac{3}{32}$ in. diameter drilling directly on the top of the right-hand side of the sleeve of the axle casing $14\frac{1}{4}$ in. from the centre of the banjo casing. This breather hole needs to be kept clear, and should be examined from time to time.

	Tooth Contact	Condition	Remedy
A	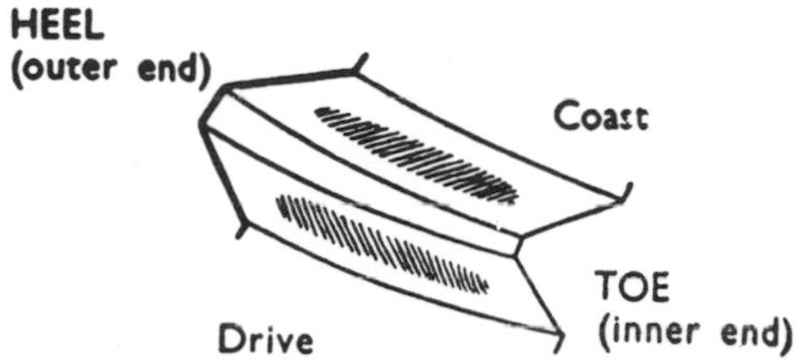 HEEL (outer end) / Coast / Drive / TOE (inner end)	IDEAL TOOTH CONTACT evenly spread over profile, nearer toe than heel.	
B	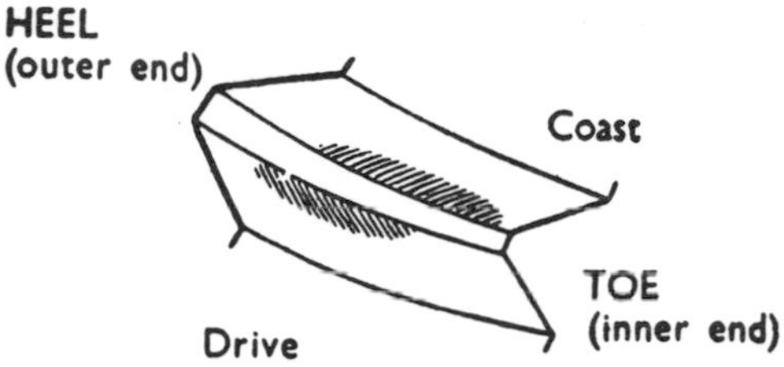 HEEL (outer end) / Coast / Drive / TOE (inner end)	HIGH TOOTH CONTACT heavy on the top of the drive gear tooth profile.	Move the Drive PINION DEEPER into MESH, *i.e.* Reduce the pinion cone setting.
C	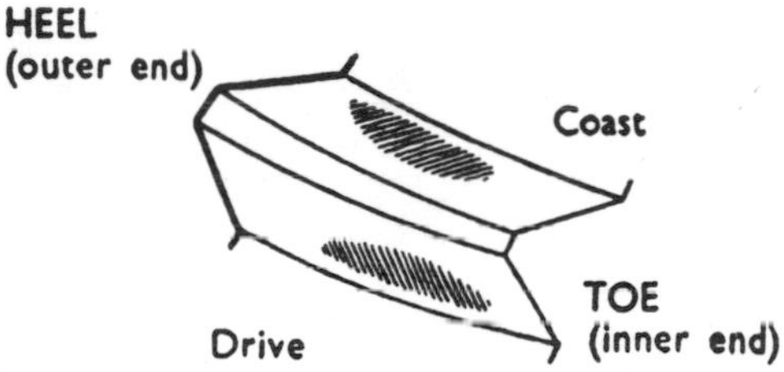 HEEL (outer end) / Coast / Drive / TOE (inner end)	LOW TOOTH CONTACT heavy in the root of the drive gear tooth profile.	Move the Drive PINION OUT of MESH, *i.e.* Increase the pinion cone setting.
D	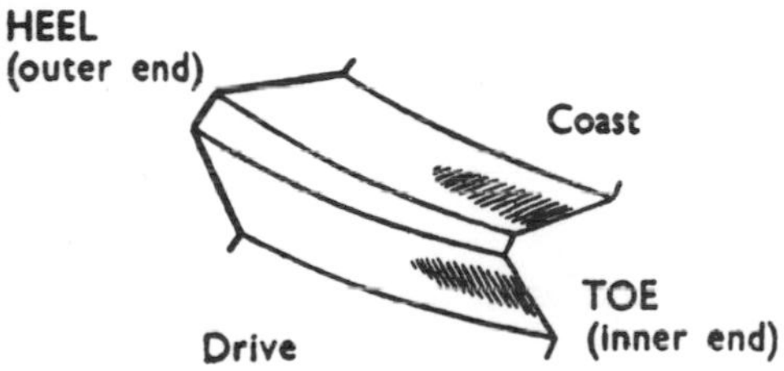 HEEL (outer end) / Coast / Drive / TOE (inner end)	TOE CONTACT hard on the small end of the drive gear tooth.	Move the Drive GEAR OUT of MESH, *i.e.* INCREASE BACKLASH.
E	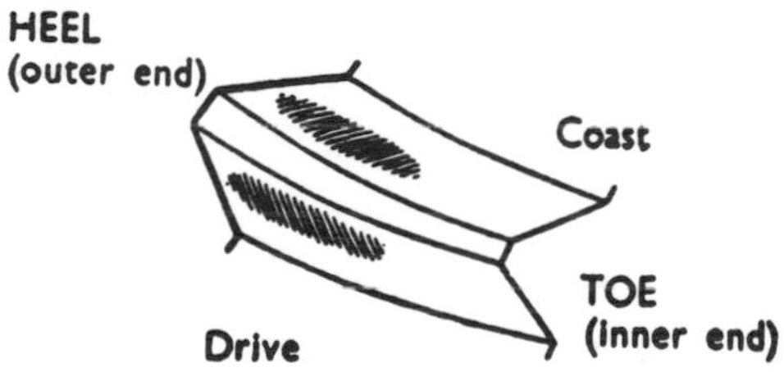 HEEL (outer end) / Coast / Drive / TOE (inner end)	HEEL CONTACT hard on the large end of the drive gear tooth.	Move the Drive GEAR INTO MESH, *i.e.* DECREASE BACKLASH *BUT* MAINTAIN MINIMUM BACKLASH.

Fig. 8.7. Tooth contact chart to obtain the correct meshing between the crown wheel and pinion.

CHAPTER NINE
BRAKING SYSTEM

CONTENTS

SPECIFICATIONS

Make & Type..	Lockheed hydraulic
Handbrake	Mechanical
Front brakes (all models except Minx V)...	Two leading shoe
(Minx V)..	Disc
Rear brakes (all models)	Leading and trailing shoe
Linings-Front-Minx I to III, Husky I to III ..	Ferodo DM. 53
-Minx IIIA to IIIC..	Ferodo DM. 53. A
Minx V (pad lining)	Don 55
Rear-Minx I to III, Husky I to III ...	Ferodo DM. 53
-Minx IIIA to V	Ferodo DM53. A
Brake drums - Material	Cast iron
- Diameter	8 in. (20.3 cm) 9 in. (22.8 cm) on Minx IIIC
Brake disc (Minx V - Material	Cast iron
- Diameter...	10.3 in. (26.1 cm)
Brake adjustment location (drum type) ...	Hole in wheel and brake drum
Access to master cylinder...	Under bonnet

TORQUE WRENCH SETTINGS

Drum Brakes

Backplate to carrier	17 lb/ft.
Wheel cylinder to backplate	12 lb/ft.

Disc Brakes

Brake disc to hub	38 lb/ft.
Calliper to adaptor...	52 lb/ft.
Steering arm to carrier and adaptor ...	38 lb/ft.)
	60 lb/ft.)
Adaptor to carrier...	38 lb/ft.
Union nuts (male)	7 lb/ft.
(female)	9 lb/ft.
Wheel cylinder to backplate	12 lb/ft.
Bleed screws	6 lb/ft.

GENERAL DESCRIPTION

The four wheel drum brakes fitted are of the internal expanding type, the shoes of which are expanded against the drum by hydraulic pressure when the brake pedal is applied. Attached to each rear brake operating cylinder is a mechanical expander operated through a cable from the handbrake lever positioned on the floor of the car on the driver's side. Drum brakes need to be adjusted at regular intervals to compensate for the wear which takes place in the shoe friction linings. It will be found that as these linings wear away so the brake pedal needs greater movement towards the floor in order to obtain good stopping power. The hydraulic brake system functions on the application of the brake pedal which sets up a pressure inside the master cylinder, the hydraulic fluid being displaced and forced into each brake operating cylinder by means of a four-way union and a series of rigid pipes and flexible hoses. The hydraulic fluid thus forced into each brake piston moves the shoes outwards toward the drum surface and applies the retarding action to each drum. When the brake pedal is released, return springs fitted to each pair of shoes pull the shoes away from the drum surface, and at the same time the pressure in the hydraulic system is released and the fluid from each brake operating cylinder moves back toward the master cylinder.

2. DRUM BRAKES - MAINTENANCE

1. Every 3,000 miles of service, carefully clean the top of the master brake cylinder, remove the cap and check the level of the fluid in the reservoir. This should be about $\frac{1}{4}$ in. below the bottom of the filler neck. Check

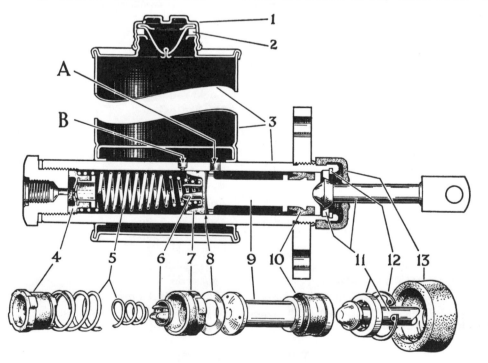

Fig. 9.1. EXPLODED VIEW OF THE BRAKE MASTER CYLINDER.

1 Filler cap. 2 Washer. 3 Master cylinder body. 4 Check valve. 5 Return spring. 6 Spring retainer. 7 Main cup. 8 Washer. 9 Piston. 10 Secondary cup. 11 Pushrod assembly. 12 Circlip. 13 Rubber boot. A Main port. B By-pass port.

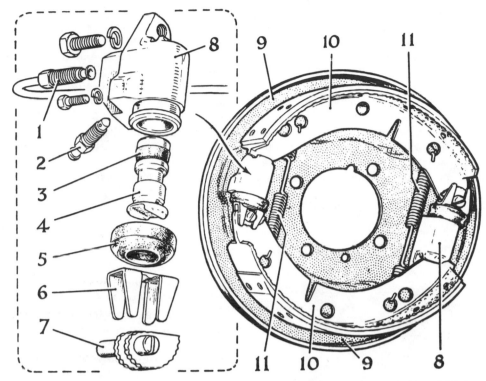

Fig. 9.2. EXPLODED VIEW OF THE FRONT DRUM BRAKE ASSEMBLY - LEFT HAND SIDE SHOWN.

Bridge pipe union nut. 2 Bleed screw. 3 Piston seal. 4 Piston. 5 Rubber boot. 6 Mask. 7 Micram adjuster. 8 Wheel cylinder body. 9 Back plate. 10 Brake shoe assembly. 11 Pull-off spring.

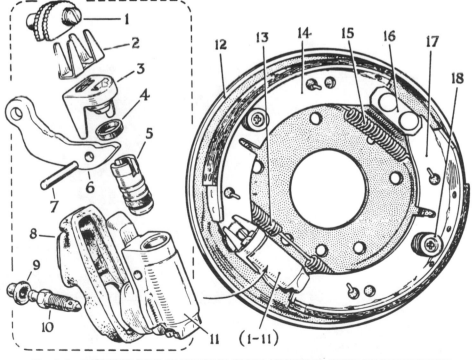

Fig. 9.3. EXPLODED VIEW OF THE REAR BRAKE ASSEMBLY - RIGHT HAND SIDE SHOWN.

1 Micram adjuster. 2 Mask. 3 Outer piston. 4 Seal (outer piston). 5 Inner piston. 6 Handbrake lever. 7 Pivot pin. 8 Rubber boot. 9 Dust cap. 10 Bleed screw. 11 Cylinder body. 12 Backplate. 13 Pull-off spring. 14 Brake shoe assembly. 15 Tension spring. 16 Abutment. 17 Brake shoe assembly. 18 Steady spring assembly.

carefully that the breather holes in the cap are clear, otherwise this will not allow air to escape when the fluid returns from the brake shoe cylinders as mentioned above, and this will result in dragging brakes.

2. If the fluid level is low, top up the reservoir with Lockheed brake fluid. DO NOT USE OIL or any other fluid, because this will rapidly soften the many rubber pistons and seals and result in complete brake failure in a short time.

3. At intervals of 3,000 miles check the brake pedal movement and if necessary adjust the brake shoes to compensate for lining wear.

Fig. 9.4. VIEW OF THE FRONT DRUM BRAKE ASSEMBLY
1 Brake shoe lining. 2 Shoe pull-off spring. 3 hydraulic wheel cylinder. 4 Adjuster unit. 5 Brake backplate. 6 Hub.

3. DRUM BRAKE - ADJUSTMENT

1. Adjustment is carried out by means of adjuster units, access to these being through large holes in the brake drum which enables a screwdriver to be inserted in order to engage a slotted adjuster. This is turned by leverage of the screwdriver against the hole in the drum. (See Fig. 9.5.).

Fig. 9.5. Brake adjustment being carried out through the hole in the drum. The superimposed insets show the two adjusters.

2. Each wheel needs to be jacked up securely in order to allow it to be turned freely. Bring the adjuster hole, which may be in the wheel and evident when the hub cap is removed, or may only be in the drum in line with the slotted head of the adjuster, and then use the screwdriver to turn the adjuster until the shoe contacts the drum. At this point the adjuster needs to be turned back two notches so that the drum can revolve freely. In the case of the front brake drums turn the wheel through 180° to the second adjuster and carry out similar operations.

3. It will be found that there are two adjusters on each front brake, but only one on the rear brake.

4. DRUM BRAKE SHOE - INSPECTION - REMOVAL & REPLACEMENT

1. Every 6,000 miles the brake shoes should be examined, and if the shoe linings are found to be worn to less than one third of their original thickness, then the shoes should be replaced with Factory Exchange units.

2. To remove the brake shoes, first remove the brake drums by unscrewing the countersunk screws set in the drums. Give the drum a light blow on each side with a copper-headed hammer to loosen the drum from the axle hub.

3. Dislodge the pull-off springs from one shoe with the aid of a screwdriver and then remove both shoes carefully, making sure that the pistons are not pulled out of the hydraulic cylinders. Also take care not to damage the adjusters and their masks.

Fig. 9.6. The front drum brake assembly showing the shoe ends correctly fitted into the wheel cylinder and the flexible hose being examined.

4. To refit new shoes, fit the upper return springs into the correct holes in the shoes and make certain that the spring is clear of the shoe webs. If the hydraulic piston plunger has been wired up to prevent it from coming out,

remove the wire carefully and locate the shoe ends against the ends of the cylinder.

5. Assemble the lower springs and then pull the shoes open so that they fit into their respective slots in the cylinder. Once in position pull the shoes against the spring and insert the adjusters and their masks. The assembly can be seen clearly in Fig. 9.5.

5. FLEXIBLE HOSES - INSPECTION - REMOVAL & REPLACEMENT

1. Every 12,000 miles brake hoses need to be inspected for signs of leaking, chafing on adjacent parts or general deterioration. If there is any doubt at all, renew these hoses. At the same time the metal pipes should be carefully checked for signs of chafing or for looseness which will ultimately lead to splitting.

2. It is not always appreciated that the flexible hoses can swell up inside while appearing perfectly alright on the outside. The result of such swelling is to restrict the flow of the fluid in the pipe. For example if the fluid flows through easily under pressure, once the pressure is released, the swollen pipe will restrict the return flow and this will result in the particular brake being very sluggish to come off. Alternatively if the swelling inside one hose is severe it will mean that the brake pedal pressure is only distributed to three brakes, and this will result in uneven braking especially in bad weather conditions or in an emergency.

3. To remove a flexible hose, (Fig. 9.7.) first fit a cap over the master cylinder reservoir on which the vent holes have been stopped up. This will prevent an excessive flow of fluid from the system.

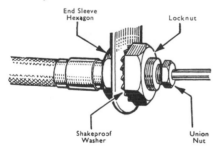

Fig. 9.7. A flexible hose connection.

4. Unscrew the metal pipe union nuts from the connection to the hose, and then hold the hexagon of the hose with a short spanner while with a second spanner, unscrew the attachment nut and washer. The flexible hose is then disconnected from the backplate of the brake drum cylinder. New hose replacement is the reverse of the above procedure.

6. BRAKE SEAL & CYLINDER - INSPECTION & OVERHAUL

If hydraulic fluid is leaking from one of the brake cylinders it will be necessary to dismantle the cylinder and replace the piston rubber and sealing ring. If the brake fluid is found running down the side of the wheel, or it is noticed that a pool of liquid forms alongside one wheel and the level in the master cylinder has dropped, proceed as follows:-

1. Remove the brake drums and brake shoes as detailed in the section headed 'Drum Brake Shoe Inspection, Removal & Replacement.'

2. Ensure that all the other wheels and drums are in place and where two brake operating cylinders are fitted to one backplate, as on the front wheels, securely wire the piston in the cylinder which is not leaking. Remove the piston, piston rubber and seal from the leaking cylinder by applying gentle pressure to the footbrake. Place a quantity of rag under the backplate or a tray to catch the hydraulic fluid as it pours out of the cylinder.

3. Inspect the inside of the cylinder for score marks caused by impurities in the hydraulic fluid. If any are found the cylinder and piston will require renewal.

4. If the cylinder is sound thoroughly clean it out with fresh hydraulic fluid.

5. The old rubbers will probably be swollen and visibly worn. Smear the new rubbers with hydraulic fluid and reassemble in the cylinder the spring, cup filler, cup, piston, sealing ring and dust cover, in that order.

6. Replenish the brake fluid, replace the brake shoes and brake drum, and bleed the hydraulic system as previously detailed.

7. If the cylinder is scored and is to be renewed, remove the flexible hose as detailed in the section 'Flexible Hose Inspection, Removal & Replacement.'

8. In the case of two leading shoe front brakes disconnect the pipe between the two brake cylinders and remove complete with the banjo adaptors. Unscrew from the backplate the two set bolts and spring washers which retain each cylinder in place. The cylinders are now free. Replacement is a direct reversal of this process.

9. In the case of early models with single leading shoe rear brakes remove the bolt which secures the banjo adaptor to the wheel cylinder. Disconnect the handbrake lever rod at the backplate. Move the backplate handbrake lever until its shoulder clears the backplate. Then move the brake operating cylinder forward, turn it about its forward end, and extract the rear end from the slot. To remove

the cylinder, move it backwards so clearing its forward end from the backplate. Reassembly is a direct reversal of this process.

10. In the case of the rear brake assemblies on later models, remove the hydraulic pipe, the flexible cable, bleed screw, and circlip from the cylinder boss which protrudes through the backplate. With the brake drum and brake shoes removed the cylinder can now be released. Reassembly is a direct reversal of this process.

DRUM BRAKE BACKPLATE REMOVAL & REPLACEMENT

1. In the case of the front brakes the backplate can be removed after disconnecting the flexible pipe, by removing the four backplate securing bolts and washers.

2. In the case of the rear brakes the backplate securing bolts can be removed and the backplate lifted away after:-

a) The road wheels, brake drum, handbrake lever rod, and hydraulic pipe have been disconnected.

b) The half shaft and hub assembly have been removed as detailed in Chapter 8.

3. Replacement in both cases is a straightforward reversal of the above.

HANDBRAKE ADJUSTMENT

If the handbrake requires adjustment it is more than likely that the footbrake will require adjustment also. Excess travel in the footbrake is compensated by adjusting the brake shoes, this automatically compensates for excess travel in the handbrake lever also.

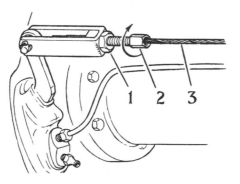

Fig. 9.8. The handbrake cable adjuster. The arrow shows the direction the nut must be rotated to shorten the cable. 1 Locknut. 2 Threaded sleeve. 3 Inner cable.

Never try to adjust the handbrake to compensate for wear on the rear brake linings. It is very seldom that the handbrake will require adjustment, and that only after very high mileages due to slight stretching of the cable.

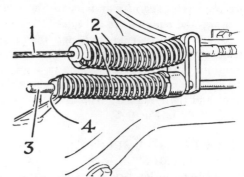

Fig. 9.9. THE RETURN SPRINGS ON THE HANDBRAKE CABLE AND ROD.
1 Inner cable. 2 Return springs. 3 Brake rod. 4 Brake rod bearing.

Usually it is badly worn rear brake linings that lead to excessive handbrake travel. If the rear brake linings are in good condition or have been recently renewed and the handbrake tends to reach the end of its ratchet travel before the brakes come on, adjust the handbrake as follows:-

1. Lock the rear brake shoes by rotating the adjustment screw as far as it will turn clockwise.

2. Apply the handbrake on the third or fourth notch of its ratchet.

3. Remove the slackness in the cable by adjusting the bowden cable sleeve nuts at the front of the compensator bracket. DO NOT OVERTIGHTEN the cables or the rear brakes will bind.

4. Release the handbrake and check that neither of the rear wheels are binding. A certain resistance due to the differential gears is natural.

9. DISC BRAKES - GENERAL DESCRIPTION

Disc brakes are fitted to the front wheels of later models which retain the previous system of single leading shoe drum brakes for the rear wheels, together with the mechanically operated handbrake.

The brakes fitted to the front two wheels are of the rotating disc and static calliper type, with one calliper per disc, each calliper containing two piston operated friction pads, which on application of the footbrake pinch the disc rotating between them.

Application of the footbrake creates hydraulic pressure in the master cylinder and fluid from the cylinder travels via steel and flexible pipes to the cylinders in each half of the callipers, the fluid so pushing the pistons, to which are attached the friction pads, into contact with either side of each disc.

Two rubber seals are fitted to the mouth of the operating cylinders. The outer seal

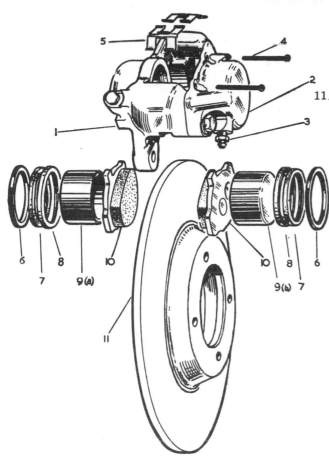

Fig. 9.10. EXPLODED VIEW OF THE DISC BRAKE CALLIPER ASSEMBLY
1 Brake calliper. 2 Brake calliper, rim side. 3 Bleed screw. 4 Split pins. 5 Steady springs. 6 Sealing ring. 7 Dust seal. 8 Dust seal retainer. 9a and b Piston. 10 Brake pad. 11 Brake disc.

prevents moisture and dirt from entering the cylinder, while the inner seal, which is retained in a groove just inside the cylinder, prevents fluid leakage, and provides a running clearance for the pad irrespective of how worn it is, by moving it back a fraction when the brake pedal is released.

As the friction pad wears so the pistons move further out of the cylinders and the level of the fluid in the hydraulic reservoir drops, but disc pad wear is thus taken up automatically and eliminates the need for periodic adjustments by the owner.

10. DISC BRAKES - MAINTENANCE

Every 3,000 miles, check the level of the fluid in the master cylinder reservoir as detailed in the section headed 'Drum Brakes - Maintenance.' In this case, however, use Lockheed disc brake fluid, or if this is not available, a fluid to the specification SAE 70R3 for replenishment purposes.

At the same time examine the wear in the brake disc pads and change them round if one is very much more worn on one side of the rotating disc than on the other.

11. DISC BRAKE FRICTION PAD - INSPECTION, REMOVAL & REPLACEMENT

1. Remove the front wheels and inspect the amount of friction material left on the friction pads. The pads must be renewed when the thickness of the material has worn down to $\frac{1}{16}$ inch.
2. Press down on the pad retaining spring and extract the retaining pad split pins.
3. Take off the spring clip and with a slight rotational movement, remove the friction pads and anti-squeak shims, using a pair of sharp-nosed pliers if necessary.

Fig. 9.11. The 10.3 inch diameter disc brake assembly fitted to the front of later Minx Series V models.

4. Carefully clean the recesses in the calliper in which the friction pad assemblies lie, and the exposed face of each piston from all traces of dirt and rust.
5. Remove the cap from the hydraulic reservoir and place a large rag underneath the unit. Press the pistons in each half of the calliper right in - this will cause the fluid level in the reservoir to rise and possibly to spill over the brim onto the protective rag.
6. After checking that the relieved face of each piston is facing downwards, fit the new friction pads into the callipers and position the anti-squeak shims between the friction pad and the piston.
7. Check that the new friction pad assemblies move freely in the calliper recesses and remove any high spots on the edge of the pressure

plate by careful filing.

8. Check that the retaining spring clips show no sign of damage or loss of tension and then, if sound, replace them, press them down and insert the split pins.

9. Replace the road wheels and remove the jacks. Press the brake pedal several times to adjust the brake. Top up the master cylinder as required.

12. DISC & BRAKE CALLIPER - REMOVAL & DISMANTLING

1. Jack up the car, remove the roadwheel, and disconnect the flexible hydraulic pipe as previously detailed on page 115.

Fig. 9.12. The Lockheed QM disc brake unit showing the brake pads and securing pins in position.

2. Unscrew the nuts which hold the flexible hose retaining plate to the calliper and remove the plate.

3. Remove the disc brake friction pads and anti-squeal shims as previously detailed.

4. Unscrew the two calliper mounting bolts and lockwashers and remove the calliper assembly from the disc.

5. Meticulously clean the calliper, reconnect the flexible hydraulic hose, and place the calliper on a block or similar support, or ask a friend to hold it to avoid it hanging on the hydraulic hose which could damage the latter.

6. Clamp the piston in either the mounting half or the rim half of the calliper with wire or a suitable clamp, depending on which side of the calliper the piston is to be removed from first.

7. Gently apply the footbrake so forcing the unclamped piston out of the calliper until it is in a position where it can be removed by hand.

8. Gently prise the dust seal retainer from the cylinder by carefully inserting a penknife blade between the dust seal retainer and the dust seal, and then extract the seal.

9. Remove the inner hydraulic fluid seal from its groove in the calliper cylinder with a blunt nosed tool. NOTE great care should be taken not to damage or scratch the cylinder bore or fluid seal groove.

10. After the piston and rubber seals in one side of the calliper have been checked and replaced as necessary, and the piston reassembled to the calliper as detailed in the following section, the piston in the other half of the calliper can be removed by clamping the rebuilt piston assembly in place and then repeating the process used to remove the first piston.

11. If it is wished to remove the brake disc first prise off the hub bearing cover, then extract the split pin, unscrew the hub nut, and pull off the hub casing and disc.

12. To separate the hub from the disc, unscrew the four set bolts and lockwashers and lift the disc away from the hub.

13. DISC & BRAKE CALLIPER - REASSEMBLY

1. Replace the disc on the hub casing and tighten down the four set bolts and lockwashers.

2. Refit the hub casing and disc to the swivel axle assembly, at the same time replacing the distance piece, outer hub bearing, retaining washer, castellated nut, split pin, and the bearing hub cap.

3. Check the run out at the outer periphery of the disc. If it exceeds .006 in. (.152 mm.) remove the disc and reposition it on the hub casing.

4. Coat a new rubber fluid seal with Lockheed hydraulic disc brake fluid and fit the seal to the groove in the cylinder.

5. Slacken the bleed screw in the calliper one turn.

6. Lubricate the piston with hydraulic fluid and press the piston into the cylinder carefully with the undercut portion facing downwards and out. Press the piston in squarely until approximately $1/4$ inch protrudes from the cylinder.

7. Smear a new dust seal with hydraulic fluid and fit it to its retainer.

8. Place the dust seal assembly with the seal

resting on the raised portion of the piston and press the piston and seal home with a suitable clamp. Tighten the bleed screw. Repeat this procedure with the remaining cylinder in the other half of the calliper.

9. Refit the calliper to the disc and stub axle.

10. Fit the anti-squeal plates and disc brake friction pads as previously detailed and bleed the hydraulic system. Assembly is now complete.

14. SELF-ADJUSTING REAR BRAKES - GENERAL DESCRIPTION

Later models are fitted with rear drum brakes in which the wheel cylinder consists of four major parts. Fig. 9.13. A screwed tappet and adjusting wheel is freely mounted in the outer piston. The head of the screwed tappet is slotted to accommodate the web of the leading brake shoe and the adjuster wheel has a series of castellations on the outer periphery.

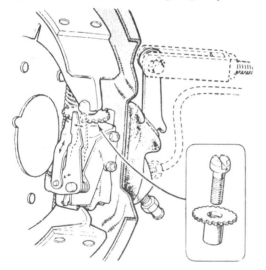

Fig. 9.13. A left-hand self-adjusting wheel cylinder with arrows indicating the direction of travel of the pawl linkage as the brake is applied and released. Inset shows the screwed tappet and adjuster wheel.

A metal pressing is attached to the piston and this has a finger which is parallel with the axis of the operating cylinder towards its closed end.

An adjusting pawl the tip of which rests on the adjuster wheel, pivots on a plate attached to the wheel cylinder body. The adjuster pawl adjacent to the pivot, is connected to the finger of the piston pressing, thus linear movement of the piston and pressing becomes accurate movement at the tip of the adjuster pawl.

The wheel cylinder body has a face on which the adjuster pawl pivot plate is mounted.

When the brakes are applied, the piston moves out of the cylinder body under the pressure of the hydraulic fluid and this causes the

adjuster pawl to pivot on its plate resulting in the tip of the pawl sliding over the periphery of the adjuster wheel. A reactionary movement of the wheel cylinder body travelling in the brake plate slot moves the pawl pivot plate in the opposite direction to the piston and thus increases the movement of the adjuster pawl tip. When the movement is greater than one castellation of the adjuster wheel, the pawl tip will drop behind the castellation, and as the brakes are released the adjuster pawl will return to its rest position taking the adjuster with it and so extending the screwed tappet from the piston and so take up the excessive shoe clearance.

When the movement of the adjuster pawl tip is less than one castellation on the adjuster wheel, this wheel and tappet will remain at rest when the brakes are released.

Power to rotate the adjuster wheel and to return the adjuster pawl to rest is provided by a torsion spring mounted on the adjuster pawl pivot pin.

Fig. 9.14. The Lockheed self adjusting rear brake assembly showing the automatic adjuster (arrowed).

15. ADJUSTMENT

1. It will be appreciated that periodic adjustment of this design of rear drum brake is not required, adjustment only being necessary when the brakes have been disturbed and new shoes are fitted.

2. To bring the adjustment to the correct position, pump the footbrake pedal a number of times, noting that while the shoe/drum clearance is being reduced, each pump action

will be of lesser depth than the previous.

3. Stop the pumping when the pedal reaches a constant depth.

16. REMOVAL & REPLACEMENT OF BRAKE SHOES

1. To remove and refit the brake shoes of the self adjusting brakes, secure the front wheels, release the handbrake, jack up the rear of the car and remove the rear wheel.

2. Remove the brake drum and distance piece where one is fitted, by unscrewing the counter-sunk screw. Hold the head of the shoe steady post and rotate the dished washer to free the steady post.

3. Apply a rubber band or length of wire round the brake cylinder to retain the tappet and adjuster wheel in the head of the cylinder, and mark the four holes in the brake shoe webs which are used to secure the pull off springs.

4. Remove the heel ends of both brake shoes from the location opposite the wheel cylinders, followed by the toe end of the trailing shoe from the wheel cylinder body. This will release the tension in the pull off springs and the leading shoe can be removed from the slot in the tappet. Refitting is the reverse of the removal sequence.

17. WHEEL CYLINDER REMOVAL

1. With the brake shoes removed, detach the handbrake cable or rod from the wheel cylinder lever. Release the hydraulic pipe union nuts and withdraw the pipes from the wheel cylinder.

2. Detach the rubber dust cover and slide the wheel cylinder in the backplate slot toward the piston end and work the opposite end out of the slot. Refitting is the reverse of the removal sequence.

18. HANDBRAKE ADJUSTMENT FOR SELF-ADJUSTING REAR BRAKES

1. The handbrake is set during initial assembly and will not require adjustment until replacement parts are fitted, or the length of the cable has been altered in error. Normally there are 6 clicks of the handbrake lever to bring the handbrake hard on.

2. To make correct adjustment, secure the front wheels, release the handbrake and jack up the rear of the car. Remove the slackness from the handbrake cable by slackening a lock-nut and rotating the threaded sleeve, and then retighten the locknut.

3. Make sure that the brakes do not bind following this adjustment. Check that the brakes are hard on when the handbrake is pulled on.

BRAKING SYSTEM

Cause	Trouble	Remedy
SYMPTOM:	BRAKES TEND TO BIND, DRAG, OR LOCK-ON	
Incorrect adjustment	Brake shoes adjusted too tightly Handbrake cable over-tightened Master cylinder push rod out of adjust-ment giving too little brake pedal free movement	Slacken off brake shoe adjusters two clicks. Slacken off handbrake cable adjustment. Reset to manufacturer's specifications.
Wear or dirt in hydraulic system or incorrect fluid	Reservoir vent hole in cap blocked with dirt Master cylinder by-pass port restricted – brakes seize in 'on' position Wheel cylinder seizes in 'on' position	Clean and blow through hole. Dismantle, clean, and overhaul master cylinder. Bleed brakes. Dismantle, clean, and overhaul wheel cylinder, Bleed brakes.
Mechanical wear	Brake shoe pull off springs broken, stretched or loose	Examine springs and replace if worn or loose.
Incorrect brake assembly	Brake shoe pull off springs fitted wrong way round, omitted, or wrong type used	Examine, and rectify as appropriate.
Neglect	Handbrake system rusted or seized in the 'on' position	Apply 'Plus Gas' to free, clean and lubricate.

CHAPTER TEN
ELECTRICAL SYSTEM

CONTENTS

SPECIFICATIONS

Battery make	Lucas
Type & capacity...	BT. 7A. 38 amp/hr.
Voltage	12
System..	Positive earth
Make & type of coil	Lucas L. A. or H. A. 12
Location of coil...	Right-hand side of engine
Make of generator (dynamo)	Lucas

Type:- Minx I to III, Husky I...	C. 39 PV-2
Minx IIIA, Husky II onwards ...	C. 40-1
Performance - C.39 PV-2-cutting in speed	1050 - 1250 r.p.m. 13 gen. volts
-field resistance	6.1 ohms.
-max. output ...	19 amp. at 1900 - 2150 r.p.m.
-C.40-1-cutting in speed..	1250 - 1450 r.p.m. 13 gen. volts
-field resistance	6.0 ohms.
-max. output ...	22 amp. at 2050 to 2250 r.p.m.
Drive	'V' belt from crankcase
Control of output	C. V-C
Brush spring tension	22/25 oz.
Control box make & type..	Lucas R.B.106/1 or R.B.106/2
Starter motor...	Lucas M.35G/1. Four brush
Control type	Solenoid
Drive type	Lucas 'SB'
Brush spring tension	15/25 oz.
Windscreen wiper - Minx I to III	Lucas DR 2 self parking
- Minx IIIA onwards ..	Lucas DR 3 self parking
all Husky models ...	
Blades	Steel back rainbow
Horns - make & type	Lucas W.T. 618 wind tone
	or HF.1849 high frequency
	or 9H
Fuses	1 or 2 x 35 amp. Lucas 4FJ
	Some series II models have only 1 x 35 amp. fuse
Heater blower fuse (if fitted)	1 x 10 amp.
Lamp bulbs:-	
Headlamps	
Minx I, II, Husky I	Lucas 354 12v 42/36 w.
Minx III onwards, Husky II	Lucas 414 12v 50/40 w.
Later Minx IIIC, Husky II onwards ..	Sealed beam unit
Side and flasher	Lucas 380 12v. 21/6w.
Stop and tail	Lucas 380 12v. 21/6w.
Rear flasher	Lucas 382 12v. 21 w.
Warning lamps - Ignition	Philips 12829 12v. 2 w.
- Oil pressure	Philips 12829 12v. 2 w.
- Flashing indicators ...	Philips 12829 12v. 2 w.
-Beam indicator (where fitted) ...	Philips 12829 12v. 2 w.
Rear number plate...	Lucas 989 12v. 6 w.
Interior	Lucas 254 12v. 6 w. (festoon)
Panel illumination	Lucas 987 12v. 2.2 w.
Side (Minx V, Husky III)..	Lucas 222 12v. 4 w.
Front flasher (Minx V, Husky III).. ...	Lucas 382 12v. 21 w.

1. GENERAL DESCRIPTION

The electrical system is of the 12-volt type and the major components comprise: a 12-volt battery of which the positive terminal is earthed: a voltage regulator and cut-out; a Lucas dynamo which is fitted to the front right-hand side of the engine and is driven by the fan belt from the crankshaft pulley wheel; and a starter motor which is fitted to the end plate and gearbox bellhousing on the right-hand side of the engine.

The six plate 12-volt battery supplies a steady supply of current for the ignition, lighting, and other electrical circuits, and provides a reserve of electricity when the current consumed by the electrical equipment exceeds that being produced by the dynamo.

The dynamo is of the two brush type and works in conjunction with the voltage regulator and cut-out. Two types of dynamo were fitted, the type fitted to your car depending on when it was manufactured. Early models made use of the Lucas C39 PV2 unit, while later models made use of the virtually identical C40-1 unit which has a slightly higher output. The dynamo is cooled by a multi-bladed fan mounted behind the dynamo pulley, and blows air through cooling holes in the dynamo end brackets. The output from the dynamo is controlled by the voltage regulator which ensures a high output if the battery is in a low state of charge or the demands from the electrical equipment high, and a low output if the battery is fully charged and there is little demand from the electrical equipment.

2. BATTERY - REMOVAL & REPLACEMENT

1. Disconnect the positive and then the negative leads from the battery terminals by slackening the retaining nuts and bolts, or by unscrewing the retaining screws if these are fitted.

2. Remove the battery clamp and carefully lift the battery out of its compartment. Hold the battery vertical to ensure that none of the electrolyte is spilled.

3. Replacement is a direct reversal of this procedure. NOTE replace the negative lead before the earth (positive) lead and smear the terminals with petroleum jelly (vaseline) to prevent corrosion. NEVER use an ordinary grease as applied to other parts of the car.

3. BATTERY MAINTENANCE & INSPECTION

1. Normal weekly battery maintenance consists of checking the electrolyte level of each cell to ensure that the separators are covered by $\frac{1}{4}$ in. of electrolyte. If the level has fallen top up the battery using distilled water only. Do not overfill. If the battery is overfilled or any electrolyte spilled immediately wipe away the excess as electrolyte attacks and corrodes any metal it comes into contact with very rapidly.

2. As well as keeping the terminals clean and covered with petroleum jelly, the top of the battery, and especially the top of the cells, should be kept clean and dry. This helps prevent corrosion and ensures that the battery does not become partially discharged by leakage through dampness and dirt.

3. Once every three months remove the battery and inspect the battery securing bolts, the battery clamp plate, tray and battery leads for corrosion (white fluffy deposits on the metal which are brittle to touch). If any corrosion is found, clean off the deposits with ammonia and paint over the clean metal with an anti-rust/anti-acid paint.

4. At the same time inspect the battery case for cracks. If a crack is found, clean and plug it with one of the proprietary compounds marketed by firms such as 'Holts' for this purpose. If leakage through the crack has been excessive then it will be necessary to refill the appropriate cell with fresh electrolyte as detailed later. Cracks are frequently caused to the top of the battery cases by pouring distilled water in the middle of winter AFTER instead of BEFORE a run. This gives the water no chance to mix with the electrolyte and so the former freezes and splits the battery case.

5. If topping up the battery becomes excessive and the case has been inspected for cracks that could cause leakage, but none are found, the battery is being overcharged and the voltage regulator will have to be checked and reset.

6. With the battery on the bench at the three monthly interval check, measure its specific gravity with a hydrometer to determine its state of charge and condition of the electrolyte. There should be very little variation between the different cells and if a variation in excess of 0.025 is present it will be due to either:-
a) Loss of electrolyte from the battery at some time caused by spillage or a leak resulting in a drop in the specific gravity of the electrolyte, when the deficiency was replaced with distilled water instead of fresh electrolyte.
b) An internal short circuit caused by buckling of the plates or a similar malady pointing to the likelihood of total battery failure in the near future.

7. The specific gravity of the electrolyte for fully charged conditions at the electrolyte temperature indicated, is listed in Table A. The specific gravity of a fully discharged battery at different temperatures of the electrolyte is given at Table B.

TABLE A

Specific Gravity - Battery fully charged

1.268 at 100°F or 38°C electrolyte temperature
1.272 at 90°F or 32°C " "
1.276 at 80°F or 27°C " "
1.280 at 70°F or 21°C " "
1.284 at 60°F or 16°C " "
1.288 at 50°F or 10°C " "
1.292 at 40°F or 4°C " "
1.296 at 30°F or -1.5°C " "

TABLE B

Specific Gravity - Battery fully charged

1.098 at 100°F or 38°C electrolyte temperature
1.102 at 90°F or 32°C " "
1.106 at 80°F or 27°C " "
1.110 at 70°F or 21°C " "

1.114 at 60°F or 16°C electrolyte temperature
1.118 at 50°F or 10°C   "   "
1.122 at 40°F or 4°C   "   "
1.126 at 30°F or -1.5°C   "   "

4. ELECTROLYTE REPLENISHMENT

1. If the battery is in a fully charged state and one of the cells maintains a specific gravity reading which is 0.025 or more lower than the others, and a check of each cell has been made with a voltage meter to check for short circuits (a four to seven second test should give a steady reading of between 1.2 to 1.8 volts), then it is likely that electrolyte has been lost from the cell with the low reading at some time.

2. Top the cell up with a solution of 1 part sulphuric acid to 2.5 parts of water. If the cell is already fully topped up draw some electrolyte out of it with a pipette. The total capacity of each cell is ¾ pint. When mixing the sulphuric acid and water NEVER ADD WATER TO SULPHURIC ACID - always pour the acid slowly onto the water in a glass container. IF WATER IS ADDED TO SULPHURIC ACID IT WILL EXPLODE. Continue to top up the cell with the freshly made electrolyte and then recharge the battery and check the hydrometer readings.

5. BATTERY CHARGING

In winter time when heavy demand is placed upon the battery, such as when starting from cold, and much electrical equipment is continually in use, it is a good idea to occasionally have the battery fully charged from an external source at the rate of 3.5 to 4 amps. Continue to charge the battery at this rate until no further rise in specific gravity is noted over a four hour period. Alternatively a trickle charger charging at the rate of 1.5 amps can be safely used overnight. Specially rapid 'boost' charges which are claimed to restore the power of the battery in 1 to 2 hours are most dangerous as they can cause serious damage to the battery plates through overheating. While charging the battery note that the temperature of the electrolyte should never exceed 100°F.

6. DYNAMO - ROUTINE MAINTENANCE

1. Routine maintenance consists of checking the tension of the fan belt, and lubricating the dynamo rear bearing once every 6,000 miles.

2. The fan belt should be tight enough to ensure no slip between the belt and the dynamo pulley. If a shrieking noise comes from the engine when the unit is accelerated rapidly then it is likely that it is the fan belt slipping. On

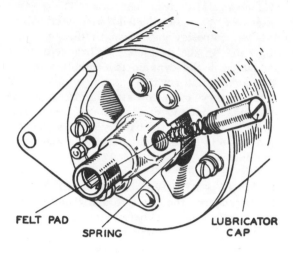

Fig. 10.1. Exploded view of the rear dynamo bearing early wick type lubricator.

FELT PAD   **SPRING**   **LUBRICATOR CAP**

the other hand, the belt must not be too taut or the bearings will wear rapidly and cause dynamo failure or bearing seizure. Ideally ½ in. of total free movement should be available at the fan belt midway between the fan and the dynamo pulley. To adjust the fan belt tension slightly slacken the three dynamo retaining bolts, and swing the dynamo on the upper two bolts outwards to increase the tension, and inwards to lower it. It is best to leave the bolts fairly tight so that considerable effort has to be used to move the dynamo; otherwise it is difficult to get the correct setting. If the dynamo is being moved outwards to increase the tension and the bolts have only been slackened a little, a long spanner acting as a lever placed behind the dynamo with the lower end resting against the block works very well in moving the dynamo outwards. Retighten the dynamo bolts and check that the dynamo pulley is correctly aligned with the fan belt.

3. Lubrication of early model Lucas C39 PV2 dynamos consists of unscrewing the lubricator cap from the end bracket, removing the spring and felt pad from the cap, half filling the cap with high melting point grease, replacing the spring and felt pad in the cap, and screwing home the cap to the dynamo. Lubrication on the C40-1 dynamo consists of inserting three drops of S.A.E. 30 engine oil in the small oil hole in the centre of the commutator end bracket. This lubricates the rear bearing. The front bearing is pre-packed with grease and requires no attention.

7. DYNAMO - TESTING IN POSITION

1. If, with the engine running no charge comes from the dynamo, or the charge is very low, first check that the fan belt is in place and is

not slipping. Then check that the leads from the control box to the dynamo are firmly attached and that one has not come loose from its terminal. The lead from the 'D' terminal on the dynamo should be connected to the 'D' terminal on the control box, and similarly the 'F' terminals on the dynamo and control box should also be connected together.

2. Disconnect the leads from terminals 'D' and 'F' on the dynamo and then join the terminals together with a short length of wire. Attach to the centre of this length of wire the negative clip of a 0-20 volts voltmeter and run the other clip to earth. Start the engine and allow it to idle at approximately 750 r.p.m. At this speed the dynamo should give a reading of about 15 volts on the voltmeter. There is no point in raising the engine speed above a fast idle as the reading will then be inaccurate.

3. If no reading is recorded then check the brushes and brush connections. If a very low reading of approximately 1 volt is observed then the field winding may be suspect. On early dynamos it was possible to remove the dynamo cover band and check the dynamo and brushes in position. With the Lucas C40-1 windowless yoke dynamo, currently fitted to all models, the dynamo has to be removed and dismantled before the brushes and commutator can be attended to.

4. If the voltmeter shows a good reading then with the temporary link still in position connect both leads from the control box to 'D' and 'F' on the dynamo ('D' to 'D' and 'F' to 'F'). Release the lead from the 'D' terminal at the control box end and clip one lead from the voltmeter to the end of the cable, and the other lead to a good earth. With the engine running at the same speed as previously, an identical voltage to that recorded at the dynamo should be noted on the voltmeter. If no voltage is

recorded then there is a break in the wire. If the voltage is the same as recorded at the dynamo then check the 'F' lead in similar fashion. If both readings are the same as at the dynamo then it will be necessary to test the control box.

8. DYNAMO - REMOVAL & REPLACEMENT

1. Slacken the two dynamo retaining bolts, and the nut on the sliding link, and move the dynamo in towards the engine so that the fan belt can be removed.

2. Disconnect the two leads from the dynamo terminals. NOTE if the ignition coil is mounted on top of the dynamo, remove the high tension wire from the centre of the coil by unscrewing the knurled nut, and unscrew the nuts holding the two low tension wires in place.

3. Remove the nut from the sliding link bolt. and remove the two upper bolts. The dynamo is then free to be lifted away from the engine.

4. Replacement is a reversal of the above procedure. Do not finally tighten the retaining bolts and the nut on the sliding link until the fan belt has been tensioned correctly. (See paragraph 2 of 'Dynamo Routine Maintenance').

5. If it is wished to fit a replacement dynamo check the identification marks which will be found on the yoke, and quote these to your local Rootes or Lucas agent prior to handing the dynamo in to ensure a replacement is available.

9. DYNAMO - DISMANTLING & REASSEMBLY

1. Remove the dynamo pulley after unscrewing the nut and lockwasher which retains it to the armature shaft. (It is not necessary to do this if only the brushes and commutator are to be examined).

2. From the commutator end bracket remove the nuts, spring and flat washers from the field terminal post.

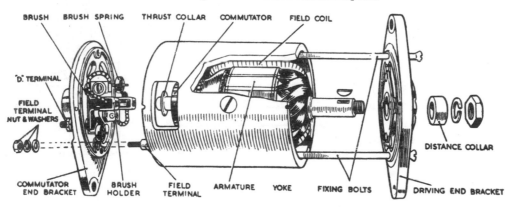

Fig. 10.2. Exploded view of the Lucas C39 PV-2 type dynamo fitted to early models.

3. Unscrew the two through bolts and remove them together with their spring washers.

4. Take off the commutator end bracket, and remove the driving end bracket complete with the armature.

5. Lift the brush springs and draw the brushes out of the brush holders. Unscrew the screws and lockwashers holding the brush leads to the commutator end bracket.

6. The bearings need not be removed, or the armature shaft separated from the drive end bracket unless the bearings or the armature are to be renewed. If it is wished to remove the armature shaft from the drive end bracket and bearing (and this is necessary for bearing renewal) then the bearing retaining plate must be supported securely, and with the woodruff key removed the shaft pressed out of the end bracket.

7. When a new armature is fitted or the old one replaced, it is most important that the inner journal of the ball bearing is supported by a steel tube of suitable diameter so that no undue strain is placed on the bearing as the armature shaft is pressed home.

8. Reassembly is a straightforward reversal of the above process. A point worth noting is that when fitting the commutator end plate with brushes attached, it is far easier to slip the brushes over the commutator if the brushes are raised in their holders and held in this position by the pressure of the springs resting against their flanks rather than on their heads.

10. DYNAMO - INSPECTION & REPAIR

1. First check the brushes for wear. Any brush on early C39 type dynamos less than 11/32 in. long and 9/32 in. long on the C40 unit, must be replaced. Check that the brushes move freely and easily in their holders by removing the retaining springs and then pulling gently on the wire brush leads. If either of the brushes tend to stick in their holders clean the brushes with a petrol moistened rag and if still stiff, lightly polish the sides of the brush with a very fine file until the brush moves quite freely and easily in its holder.

2. If the brushes are but little worn and are to be used again then ensure that they are placed in the same holders from which they were removed. Check the tension of the brush springs with a spring balance. The tension of the springs when new was 20 to 25 oz. on the C39 dynamo and the springs should be renewed if the tension falls below 15 oz. On the C40 unit the tension, new, was 30 oz. falling to 13 oz. when the brush was sufficiently worn to warrant replacement.

3. Secondly, check the condition of the commutator. If the surface is dirty or blackened, clean it with a petrol dampened rag. If the commutator is in good condition the surface will be smooth and quite free from pits or burnt areas, and the insulated segments clearly defined.

4. If, after the commutator has been cleaned pits and burnt spots are still present, then

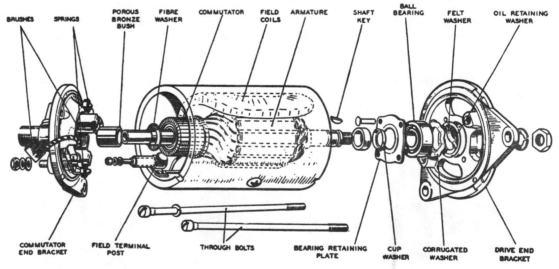

Fig. 10.3. Exploded view of the Lucas C40-1 type dynamo fitted to later models.

wrap a strip of glass paper round the commutator and rotate the armature.

5. In extreme cases of wear the commutator can be mounted in a lathe and with the lathe turning at high speed, a very fine cut may be taken off the commutator. Then polish the commutator with glass paper. If the commutator has worn so that the insulators between the segments are level with the top of the segments, then undercut the insulators to a depth of 1/32 in. (.8 mm.). The best tool to use for this purpose is half a hacksaw blade ground to the thickness of the insulator, and with the handle end of the blade covered in insulating tape to make it comfortable to hold.

6. Thirdly, check the armature for open or short circuited windings. It is a good indication of an open circuited armature when the commutator segments are burnt. If the armature has short circuited the commutator segments will be very badly burnt, and the overheated armature windings badly discoloured. If open or short circuits are suspected then test by substituting the suspect armature for a new one.

7. Fourthly, check the resistance of the field coils. To do this, connect an ohmmeter between the field terminal and the yoke and note the reading on the ohmmeter which should be about 6 ohms. If the ohmmeter reading is infinity this indicates an open circuit in the field winding. If the ohmmeter reading is below 5 ohms this indicates that one of the field coils is faulty and must be replaced.

8. Field coil replacement involves the use of a wheel operated screwdriver, a soldering iron, caulking and riveting and this operation is considered to be beyond the scope of most owners. Therefore, if the field coils are at fault either purchase a rebuilt dynamo, or take the casing to a reputable electrical engineering works for new field coils to be fitted.

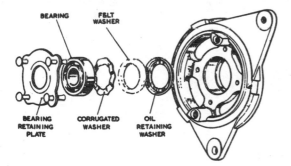

Fig. 10.4. Exploded view of the dynamo front end bracket and bearing assembly.

11. DYNAMO BEARINGS - INSPECTION, REMOVAL & REPLACEMENT

With the dynamo partially stripped down, check the condition of the bearings. They must be renewed when wear has reached such a state that they allow visible side movement of the armature shaft. A bush bearing is fitted to the commutator end bracket and a ball bearing to the drive end bracket. To renew the bush bearing proceed as follows:-

1. With a suitable extractor pull out the old bush from the commutator end bracket. Alternatively screw a 3/8 in. tap into the C39 bush and a 5/8 in. tap into the C40 bush and pull out the bush together with the tap.

2. NOTE when fitting the new bush bearing that it is of the porous bronze type, and it is essential that it is allowed to stand in S.A.E.30 engine oil for at least 24 hours before fitment.

3. Carefully fit the new bush into the end plate, pressing it in until the end of the bearing is flush with the inner side of the end plate. If available press the bush in with a smooth shouldered mandrel the same diameter as the armature shaft. To renew the ball bearing fitted to the drive end bracket remove the armature from the end bracket as detailed in the section headed 'Dynamo Dismantling & Reassembly', and then proceed as follows:-

1. Drill out the rivets which hold the bearing retainer plate to the end bracket and lift off the plate.

2. Press out the bearing from the end bracket and remove the corrugated washers, felt washer, and oil retaining washer from the bearing housing.

3. Thoroughly clean the bearing housing, and the new bearing and pack with high melting-point grease.

4. Place the oil retaining washer, felt washer and corrugated washer in that order in the end bracket bearing housing, and then press in the new bearing.

5. Replace the plate and fit new rivets opening out the rivet ends to hold the plate securely in position. (NOTE that on the C40 dynamo the rivets are fitted from the outer face of the end bracket).

12. STARTER MOTOR - GENERAL DESCRIPTION

The starter motor is mounted on the right-hand lower side of the engine end plate, and is held in position by two bolts which also clamp the bellhousing flange. The motor is of the four field coil, four pole piece type, and utilises four spring-loaded commutator brushes. Two of these brushes are earthed, and the other two are insulated and attached to the field coil ends.

13. STARTER MOTOR - TESTING ON ENGINE

1. If the starter motor fails to operate then check the condition of the battery by turning on the headlamps. If they glow brightly for several seconds and then gradually dim, the battery is in an uncharged condition.

2. If the headlamps glow brightly and it is obvious that the battery is in good condition then check the tightness of the battery wiring connections (and in particular the earth lead from the battery terminal to its connection on the bodyframe). Check the tightness of the connections at the relay switch and at the starter motor. Check the wiring with a voltmeter for breaks or shorts.

3. If the wiring is in order then check that the starter motor switch is operating. To do this press the rubber covered button in the centre of the relay switch under the bonnet. If it is working the starter motor will be heard to 'click' as it tries to rotate. Alternatively check it with a voltmeter.

4. If the battery is fully charged, the wiring in order, and the switch working and the starter motor fails to operate then it will have to be removed from the car for examination. Before this is done, however, ensure that the starter pinion has not jammed in mesh with the flywheel. Check by turning the square end of armature shaft with a spanner. This will free the pinion if it is stuck in engagement with the flywheel teeth.

14. STARTER MOTOR - REMOVAL & REPLACEMENT

1. Disconnect the battery earth lead from the positive terminal.

2. Disconnect the starter motor cable from the terminal on the starter motor end plate.

3. Remove the distributor as detailed in Chapter 4.

4. Unscrew the two starter motor bolts after removing the starter motor dirt deflector where this is fitted.

5. Lift the starter motor out of engagement with the teeth on the flywheel ring.

6. Replacement is a straightforward reversal of the removal procedure.

15. STARTER MOTOR - DISMANTLING & REASSEMBLY

1. With the starter motor on the bench, loosen the screw on the cover band and slip the cover band off. With a piece of wire bent into the shape of a hook, lift back each of the brush springs in turn and check the movement of the brushes in their holders by pulling on the flexible connectors. If the brushes are so worn that their faces do not rest against the commutator, or if the ends of the brush leads are exposed on their working face, they must be renewed.

2. If any of the brushes tend to stick in their holders then wash them with a petrol moistened cloth and, if necessary, lightly polish the sides of the brush with a very fine file, until the brushes move quite freely in their holders.

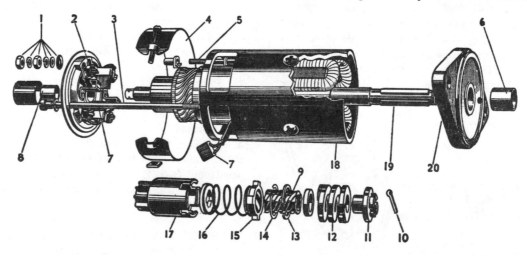

Fig. 10.5. EXPLODED VIEW OF THE STARTER MOTOR AND STARTER MOTOR DRIVE.
1 Terminal nuts and washers. 2 Brush spring. 3 Through-bolt. 4 Band cover. 5 Terminal post. 6 Bearing bush. 7 Brushes 8 Bearing bush. 9 Sleeve. 10 Split pin. 11 Shaft nut. 12 Main spring. 13 Retaining ring. 14 Washer. 15 Control nut. 16 Restraining spring. 17 Pinion and barrel. 18 Yoke. 19 Armature shaft. 20 Driving end bracket.

3. If the surface of the commutator is dirty or blackened, clean it with a petrol dampened rag. Secure the starter motor in a vice and check it by connecting a heavy gauge cable between the starter motor terminal and a 12-volt battery.

4. Connect the cable from the other battery terminal to earth on the starter motor body. If the motor turns at high speed it is in good order.

5. If the starter motor still fails to function or if it is wished to renew the brushes, then it is necessary to further dismantle the motor.

a) Lift the brush springs with the wire hook and lift all four brushes out of their holders one at a time.

b) Remove the terminal nuts and washers from the terminal post on the commutator end bracket.

c) Unscrew the two through bolts which hold the end plates together and pull off the commutator end bracket. Also remove the driving end bracket which will come away complete with the armature.

6. At this stage if the brushes are to be renewed their flexible connectors must be unsoldered and the connectors of new brushes soldered in their place. Check that the new brushes move freely in their holders as detailed above. If cleaning the commutator with petrol fails to remove all the burnt areas and spots then wrap a piece of glass paper round the commutator and rotate the armature. If the commutator is very badly worn remove the drive gear as detailed in the following section. Then mount the armature in a lathe and with the lathe turning at high speed, take a very fine cut out of the commutator and finish the surface by polishing with glass paper. DO NOT UNDERCUT THE MICA INSULATORS BETWEEN THE COMMUTATOR SEGMENTS.

7. With the starter motor dismantled, test the four field coils for an open circuit. Connect a 12-volt battery with a 12-volt bulb in one of the leads between the field terminal post and the tapping point of the field coils to which the brushes are connected. An open circuit is proved by the bulb not lighting.

8. If the bulb lights, it does not necessarily mean that the field coils are in order, as there is a possibility that one of the coils will be earthing to the starter yoke or pole shoes. To check this, remove the lead from the brush connector and place it against a clean portion of the starter yoke. If the bulb lights the field coils are earthing. Replacement of the field coil calls for the use of a wheel operated screwdriver, a soldering iron, caulking and

riveting operations and is beyond the scope of the majority of owners. The starter yoke should be taken to a reputable electrical engineering works for new field coils to be fitted. Alternatively, purchase an exchange Lucas starter motor.

9. If the armature is damaged this will be evident after visual inspection. Look for signs of burning, discolouration, and for conductors that have lifted away from the commutator. Reassembly is a straightforward reversal of the dismantling procedure.

16. STARTER MOTOR DRIVE - GENERAL DESCRIPTION

The starter motor drive is of the outboard type. When the starter motor is operated the pinion moves into contact with the flywheel gear ring by moving in towards the starter motor.

If the engine kicks back, or the pinion fails to engage with the flywheel gear ring when the starter motor is actuated no undue strain is placed on the armature shaft, as the pinion sleeve disengages from the pinion and turns independently.

17. STARTER MOTOR DRIVE — REMOVAL & REPLACEMENT

1. Extract the split pin from the shaft nut on the end of the starter drive.

2. Holding the squared end of the armature shaft at the commutator end bracket with a suitable spanner, unscrew the shaft nut which has a right-hand thread, and pull off the mainspring.

3. Slide the remaining parts with a rotary action off the armature shaft.

4. Reassembly is a straightforward reversal of the above procedure. Ensure that the split pin is refitted. NOTE It is most important that the drive gear is completely free from oil, grease and dirt. With the drive gear removed, clean all the parts thoroughly in paraffin. UNDER NO CIRCUMSTANCES OIL THE DRIVE COMPONENTS. Lubrication of the drive components could easily cause the pinion to stick.

18. STARTER MOTOR BUSHES - INSPECTION, REMOVAL & REPLACEMENT

1. With the starter motor stripped down check the condition of the bushes. They should be renewed when they are sufficiently worn to allow visible side movement of the armature shaft.

2. The old bushes are simply driven out with a suitable drift and the new bushes inserted by the same method. As the bearings are of the

phosphor bronze type it is essential that they are allowed to stand in S.A.E.30 engine oil for at least 24 hours before fitment.

19. CONTROL BOX - GENERAL DESCRIPTION

The control box comprises the voltage regulator and the cut-out. The voltage regulator controls the output from the dynamo depending on the state of the battery and the demands of the electrical equipment, and ensures that the battery is not overcharged. The cut-out is really an automatic switch and connects the dynamo to the battery when the dynamo is turning fast enough to produce a charge. Similarly it disconnects the battery from the dynamo when the engine is idling or stationary so that the battery does not discharge through the dynamo. Ordinary screw-type terminals are used on early Lucas control boxes but later modified RB 106/2 types make use of Lucar connectors.

20. CUT - OUT & REGULATOR CONTACTS - MAINTENANCE

Every 12,000 miles check the cut-out and regulator contacts. If they are dirty or rough or burnt place a piece of fine glass paper (DO NOT USE EMERY PAPER OR CARBORUNDUM PAPER) between the cut-out contacts, close them manually and draw the glass paper through several times.

2. Clean the regulator contacts in exactly the same way, but use emery or carborundum paper and not glass paper. Carefully clean both sets of contacts from all traces of dust with a rag moistened in methylated spirits.

21. VOLTAGE REGULATOR ADJUSTMENT

1. If the battery is in sound condition, but is not holding its charge, or is being continually overcharged, and the dynamo is in sound condition, then the voltage regulator in the control box must be adjusted.

2. Check the regulator setting by removing and joining together the cables from the control box terminals A1 and A. Then connect the negative lead of a 20-volt voltmeter to the 'D' terminal on the dynamo and the positive lead to a good earth. Start the engine and increase its speed until the voltmeter needle flicks and then steadies. This should occur at about 2,000 r.p.m. If the voltage at which the needle steadies is outside the limits listed below, then remove the control box cover and turn the adjusting screw in the illustration, clockwise, a quarter of a turn at a time to raise the setting, and a similar amount, anti-clockwise, to lower it.

Air Temperature	Type RB106/1 Open circuit Voltage	Type RB106/2 Open circuit Voltage
10°C or 50°F	16.1 to 16.7	16.1 to 16.7
20°C or 68°F	15.8 to 16.4	16.0 to 16.6
30°C or 86°F	15.6 to 16.2	15.9 to 16.5
40°C or 104°F	15.3 to 15.9	15.8 to 16.4

3. It is vital that the adjustments be completed within 30 seconds of starting the engine as otherwise the heat from the shunt coil will affect the readings.

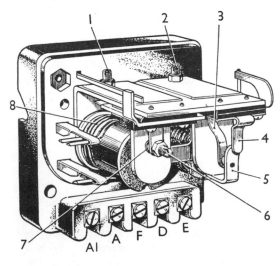

Fig. 10.6. VIEW OF THE CONTROL BOX FITTED TO EARLY MODELS.

1 Regulator adjusting screw. 2 Cut-out adjusting screw. 3 Fixed contact blade. 4 Stop arm. 5 Armature tongue and moving contact. 6 Regulator moving contact. 7 Fixed contact. 8 Regulator series windings.

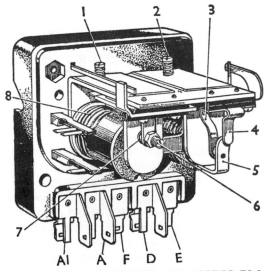

Fig. 10.7. VIEW OF THE CONTROL BOX FITTED TO LATER MODELS WITH LUCAR CONNECTORS.

1 Regulator adjusting screw. 2 Cut-out adjusting screw. 3 Fixed contact blade. 4 Stop arm. 5 Armature tongue and moving contact. 6 Regulator fixed contact screw. 7 Regulator moving contact. 8 Regulator series windings.

22. CUT-OUT ADJUSTMENT

1. Check the voltage required to operate the cut-out by connecting a voltmeter between the control box terminals 'D' and 'E'. Remove the control box cover, start the engine and gradually increase its speed until the cut-outs close. This should occur when the reading is between 12.7 to 13.3 volts. If the reading is outside these limits turn the cut-out adjusting screw in the illustration a fraction at a time clockwise to raise the voltage, and anti-clockwise to lower it. To adjust the drop off voltage bend the fixed contact blade carefully. The adjustment to the cut-out should be completed within 30 seconds of starting the engine as otherwise heat build-up from the shunt coil will affect the readings.

2. If the cut-out fails to work, clean the contacts, and if there is still no response renew the cut-out and regulator unit.

23. FUSES - GENERAL

Two fuses are fitted to a separate fuse holder positioned adjacent to the control box. The fuse marked A1 - A2 protects the electrical items such as the horn and lights, which function irrespective of whether the ignition is on or not.

The fuse marked A3 - A4 protects the ignition system and items which only operate when the ignition system is switched on, i.e. the stop lights, fuel gauge, flasher unit, and windscreen wiper motor.

If either of these fuses blow due to a short circuit or similar trouble, trace and rectify the cause before renewing the fuse.

In later models a 10 amp fuse is fitted in the pilot and tail light circuit and is fitted in a tube located in the wiring loom beneath the regulator. To expose the fuse, twist and press in one end then pull the assembly apart and remove the fuse.

24. FLASHER CIRCUIT - FAULT TRACING & RECTIFICATION

The flasher unit is located inside the car and is plugged into a socket on the underside of the fascia. The unit is actuated by the direction indicator switch.

If the flasher unit fails to operate, or works very slowly or very rapidly, check out the flasher indicator circuit as detailed below before assuming there is a fault in the unit itself.

1. Examine the direction indicator bulbs front and rear for broken filaments.

2. If the external flashers are working but the internal flasher warning light has ceased to function check the filament of the warning bulb and replace as necessary.

3. With the aid of the wiring diagram check all the flasher circuit connections if a flasher bulb is sound but does not work.

4. In the event of total direction indicator failure check the A3 - A4 fuse.

5. With the ignition turned on check that current is reaching the flasher unit by connecting a voltmeter between the 'plus' or 'B' terminal and earth. If this test is positive connect the 'plus' or 'B' terminal and the 'L' terminal and operate the flasher switch. If the flasher bulb lights up the flasher unit itself is defective and must be replaced as it is not possible to dismantle and repair it.

25. WINDSCREEN WIPER MECHANISM - MAINTENANCE

1. Renew the windscreen wiper blades at intervals of 12,000 miles, or more frequently if necessary.

2. The cable which drives the wiper blades from the gearbox attached to the windscreen wiper motor is pre-packed with grease and requires no maintenance. The washer round the wheelbox spindle can be lubricated with several drops of glycerine every 6,000 miles.

26. WINDSCREEN WIPER MECHANISM - FAULT DIAGNOSIS & RECTIFICATION

1. Should the windscreen wipers fail to park or park badly then check the limit switch on the gearbox cover. Loosen the four screws which retain the gearbox cover and place the projection close to the rim of the limit switch in line with the groove in the gearbox cover. Rotate the limit switch anti-clockwise 25° and tighten

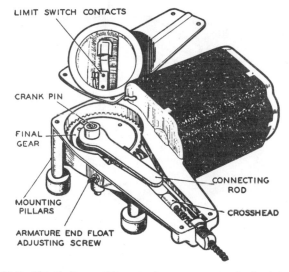

Fig. 10.8. The windscreen wiper gearbox cover removed, showing the limit switch contacts.

the four screws retaining the gearbox cover. If it is wished to park the windscreen wipers on the other side of the windscreen rotate the limit switch 180° clockwise.

2. Should the windscreen wipers fail, or work very slowly, then check the current the motor is taking by connecting up a 1-20 volt voltmeter in the circuit and turning on the wiper switch. Consumption should be between 2.3 to 3.1 amps.

3. If no current is passing through check the A3 - A4 fuse. If the fuse has blown replace it after having checked the wiring of the motor and other electrical circuits serviced by this fuse for short circuits. If the fuse is in good condition check the wiper switch and the current operated thermostat by substitution.

4. If the wiper motor takes a very high current check the wiper blades for freedom of movement. If this is satisfactory check the gearbox cover and gear assembly for damage and measure the armature end float which should be between .008 to .012 in. (.20 to .30 mm.). The end float is set by the adjusting screw. Check that excessive friction in the cable connecting tubes caused by too small a curvature is not the cause of the high current consumption.

5. If the motor takes a very low current ensure that the battery is fully charged. Check the brush gear after removing the commutator end bracket and ensure that the brushes are bearing on the commutator. If not, check the brushes for freedom of movement and if necessary renew the tension spring. Check the

armature by substitution if this unit is suspected.

27. WINDSCREEN WIPER MOTOR & GEARBOX - REMOVAL & REPLACEMENT

1. To remove the windscreen wiper motor, disconnect the battery and lift off the wiper arms. The wiper motor is mounted on a bracket secured to the front of the bulkhead, being secured in place with three nuts and spring washers.

2. Release the large nut securing the rigid outer cable to the motor and then unscrew the three nuts securing the motor to its bracket. The cable is disconnected at the snap connectors. Refit in the reverse order.

3. The sequence of operation for the removal of the wiper wheel boxes varies slightly between models, but the following is the general sequence.

4. Detach the wiper blades, unscrew the large plated nuts retaining the wiper blade spindles and take away the weather grommets.

5. Remove the screws securing the air intake grille to the scuttle on the leading edge of the grille, and lift away the grille. In some models it will be necessary to remove the wiper motor from its mounting in order to release the large nut securing the rigid outer tubing from the motor. Then push the wiper spindles into the fresh air box together. Where the wiper wheel boxes are secured to the spindles it is necessary to remove the wheel retaining brackets

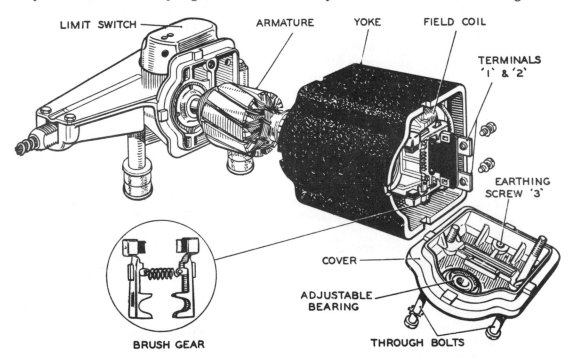

LIMIT SWITCH ARMATURE YOKE FIELD COIL

TERMINALS '1' & '2'

EARTHING SCREW '3'

COVER

ADJUSTABLE BEARING

THROUGH BOLTS

BRUSH GEAR

Fig. 10.9. A view of the windscreen wiper motor partly dismantled.

which are secured by two screws.

6. Cable and rack tube. If the wiper does not function smoothly, check the cable rack and tube for damage by removing the wiper arms and blades, disconnecting the rack from the motor and securing a light spring balance to the motor end of the rack. A steady pull should give a reading of not more than 6 lbs on the balance. If there are any kinks in the tube these must be removed, and at the same time check that this tube is not bent to a radius of less than 9 inches at any change in direction.

28. FUEL & TEMPERATURE GAUGES

1. On models fitted with fuel and temperature gauges the bimetal resistance equipment consists in each case of an indicator head or gauge and a transmitter unit connected to a common voltage regulator. This regulator is sited behind the instrument panel.

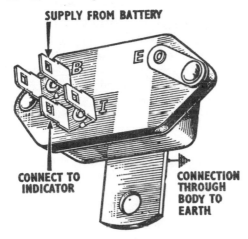

Fig. 10.10.   INSTRUMENT VOLTAGE REGULATOR

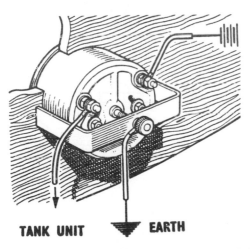

Fig. 10.11.   FUEL GAUGE ELECTRICAL CONNECTIONS

2. The mean voltage between terminals E and I on the regulator should be 10 volts. If this voltage is not obtained the regulator must be renewed. (See Fig. 10.10.)

3. If no reading is obtained check that the gauge earth is sound. (See Fig. 10.11.)

4. Also check that the lead to the tank transmitter unit has not chafed so that it is creating a short circuit. (See Fig. 10.12.)

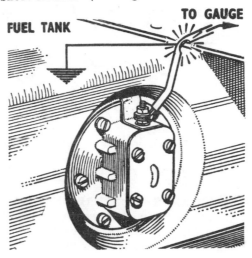

Fig. 10.12.   FUEL TANK SENDER UNIT SHOWING CHAFED WIRE

5. To test a gauge. Disconnect the T terminal switch on ignition and check that the gauge reads Full, or Empty when the terminal T is earthed. (See Fig. 10.13.)

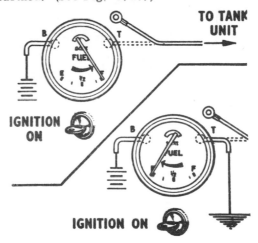

Fig. 10.13.   CHECKING GAUGE READING

6. To test tne tank unit, connect up as shown and note that the gauge should show relative to the float arm movement. (See Fig. 10.14.

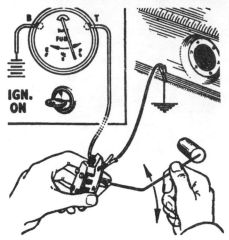

Fig. 10.14. FUEL GAUGE & SENDER UNIT.

29. HEADLAMPS - GENERAL DESCRIPTION

On earlier models the headlamps are of the flush fitting type. 'Pre-focus' bulbs are used and provided the bulb is properly located no adjustment of focusing is required, as provision is made for headlamp beam adjustment. Dipping of the headlamps is achieved by the use of double filament bulbs

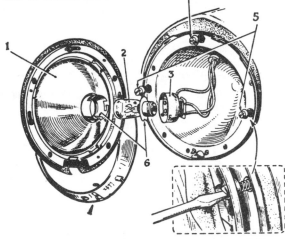

Fig. 10.15. EXPLODED VIEW OF THE HEADLAMP ASSEMBLY ON EARLY MODELS.
1 Reflector. 2 Bulb. 3 Bulb adaptor. 4 Vertical adjustment screw. 5 Lateral adjustment screw. 6 Bulb location.

Later models (see specifications) employ the 'sealed beam light unit'. The light unit is of an all glass construction with an aluminised glass reflector which is fused to the front lense. The two filaments one for 'main' beam and the other for 'dipped' beam are installed in a gas filled chamber which comprises the light unit. In the event of headlamp failure on a 'sealed beam' unit, and should the fault not be traced to loose or broken connections, the

fault will lie in the unit itself and the whole unit will have to be replaced. DO NOT on any account attempt to dismantle the 'sealed beam' unit.

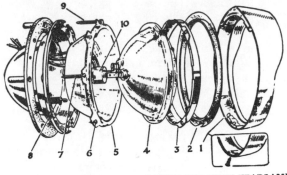

Fig. 10.16. EXPLODED VIEW OF THE SEALED BEAM HEADLAMP ASSEMBLY ON LATER MODELS.
1 Front rim. 2 Sealing ring. 3 Retaining rim. 4 Sealed beam light unit. 5 Seating rim. 6 Retaining rim screw. 7 Lateral adjusting screw. 8 Tensioning screw. 9 Vertical adjusting screw. 10 Slotted connector plug.

30. REMOVAL & REPLACEMENT OF BULBS - EARLY UNITS

1. Take out the screw at the bottom of the rim with a screwdriver. The lamp front can now be removed by hand.
2. Grasp the glass and reflector assembly. (See Fig. 10.15.) with both hands, depress rearwards and turn slightly anti-clockwise thus releasing the three key-hole apertures in its rear edge from the three spring loaded screws. Do not turn or remove these screws (See Fig. 10.15.) as they also control the beam settings.
3. The bulb can now be removed and replaced, care being taken to ensure that the new bulb is of the correct type (see specifications).

31. HEADLAMP BEAM ADJUSTMENT

1. Ideally the headlamp beams should be set on an optical-type beam setter. Where this is not available however, a fair degree of accuracy can be obtained by using a suitable wall or 'aiming board'. (See Fig. 10.17.)

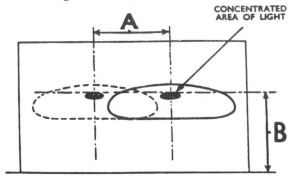

Fig. 10.17. HEADLAMP ALIGNMENT CHART
A - Distance between headlamp centres.
B - Height of headlamp above ground.

2. Stand the car on level ground exactly 25 feet from the wall or aiming board to be used.

3. Measure the height of the filaments of the headlamps from the ground and also the distance between the headlamps.

4. These measurements are then transfered to the aiming board (A and B in Fig.10.17.)

5. Ensure that the front of the car is parallel to the aiming board.

6. Remove the front rim from both headlamps, which will expose the adjusting screws (three on earlier models, 2 on 'sealed beam' units, (See Figs.10.15. and 10.16.)

7. Ensure that the headlamps are on main beam, mask off one lamp and by carefully manipulating the adjusting screws set the beam as in Fig.10.17. Repeat for the other headlamp and then recheck both beams together.

32. SIDELAMPS

1. Three different types of sidelamp assembly were used on the range of cars covered by this manual.

2. On Minx Series I, II & III and Husky I & II the rim and glass are retained by shaped lips formed in the rubber body. See Fig.10.18. for details.

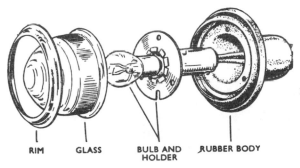

RIM   GLASS   BULB AND HOLDER   RUBBER BODY

Fig. 10.18. View of the sidelamps fitted to Minx Series I, II and III and Husky Series I and II.

3. To replace the bulb first remove the rim by easing back the rubber lip by means of a screwdriver, and then remove the glass by the same method.

4. The bulb can then be replaced. It will be noted that the bulb has staggered pins thus ensuring that the bright filament is connected to the flasher circuit.

5. Reassembly is the reversal of the above procedure.

6. On Minx Series IIIA, IIIB and IIIC models the assembly seen in Fig.10.19.is used. Access to the bulb is very easily obtained by removing the two screws, rim and glass.

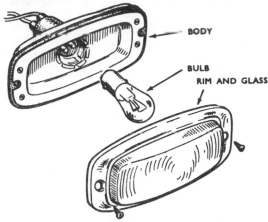

BODY

BULB

RIM AND GLASS

Fig. 10.19. View of the sidelamps fitted to Minx Series IIIA, IIIB and IIIC.

7. Minx Series V and Husky Series III use the assembly detailed in Fig.10.20. To renew a defective bulb, remove the two screws and detach the white and amber lenses.

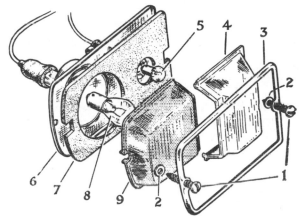

Fig. 10.20. Exploded view of the sidelamp and front flasher unit fitted to the Minx Series V and Husky Series III.

8. Renew the bulb and refit the lenses, making sure that the rubber seat (7) is correctly located.

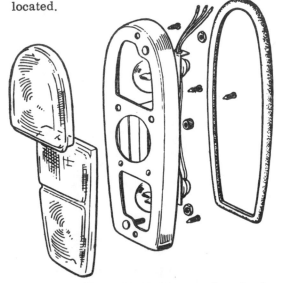

Fig. 10.21. Stop tail and flasher lamp details as fitted to early Series I models.

Fig. 10.23. Stop tail and flasher lamp details as fitted to Series IIIA, IIIB, IIIC and V models.

33. STOP, TAIL & FLASHER LAMPS

On all models the bulbs are accessible for renewal from inside the boot. Later Series I II and III Minx models have a detachable bulb-holder assembly retained to the body by a single screw. See Fig.10.22) From Series IIIA onwards individual bulbholders are used which are a push fit in the lamp body as shown in Fig.10,23.

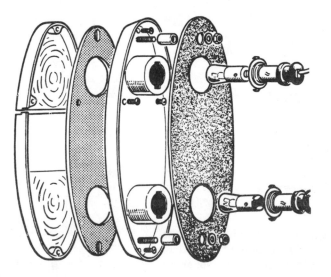

Fig. 10.22. Stop tail and flasher lamp details as fitted to later Series I, Series II and II models.

FAULT FINDING CHART

Cause	Trouble	Remedy
SYMPTOM:	STARTER MOTOR FAILS TO TURN ENGINE	
No electricity at starter motor	Battery discharged	Charge battery.
	Battery defective internally	Fit new battery.
	Battery terminal leads loose or earth lead not securely attached to body	Check and tighten leads.
	Loose or broken connections in starter motor circuit	Check all connections and tighten any that are loose.
	Starter motor switch or solenoid faulty	Test and replace faulty components with new.
Electricity at starter motor: faulty motor	Starter motor pinion jammed in mesh with flywheel gear ring	Disengage pinion by turning squared end of armature shaft.
	Starter brushes badly worn, sticking, or brush wires loose	Examine brushes, replace as necessary, tighten down brush wires.
	Commutator dirty, worn, or burnt	Clean commutator, recut if badly burnt.
	Starter motor armature faulty	Overhaul starter motor, fit new armature.
	Field coils earthed	Overhaul starter motor.
SYMPTOM:	STARTER MOTOR TURNS ENGINE VERY SLOWLY	
Electrical defects	Battery in discharged condition	Charge battery.
	Starter brushes badly worn, sticking, or brush wires loose	Examine brushes, replace as necessary, tighten down brush wires.
	Loose wires in starter motor circuit	Check wiring and tighten as necessary.
SYMPTOM:	STARTER MOTOR OPERATES WITHOUT TURNING ENGINE	
Dirt or oil on drive gear	Starter motor pinion sticking on the screwed sleeve	Remove starter motor, clean starter motor drive.
Mechanical damage	Pinion or flywheel gear teeth broken or worn	Fit new gear ring to flywheel, and new pinion to starter motor drive.
SYMPTOMS:	STARTER MOTOR NOISY OR EXCESSIVELY ROUGH ENGAGEMENT	
Lack of attention or mechanical damage	Pinion or flywheel gear teeth broken or worn	Fit new gear teeth to flywheel, or new pinion to starter motor drive.
	Starter drive main spring broken	Dismantle and fit new main spring
	Starter motor retaining bolts loose	Tighten starter motor securing bolts. Fit new spring washer if necessary.
SYMPTOM:	BATTERY WILL NOT HOLD CHARGE FOR MORE THAN A FEW DAYS	
Wear or damage	Battery defective internally	Remove and fit new battery.
	Electrolyte level too low or electrolyte too weak due to leakage	Top up electrolyte level to just above plates
	Plate separators no longer fully effective	Remove and fit new battery.
	Battery plates severely sulphated	Remove and fit new battery.
Insufficient current flow to keep battery charged	Fan/dynamo belt slipping	Check belt for wear, replace if necessary, and tighten.
	Battery terminal connections loose or corroded	Check terminals for tightness, and remove all corrosion.
	Dynamo not charging properly	Remove and overhaul dynamo.
	Short in lighting circuit causing continual battery drain	Trace and rectify.
	Regulator unit not working correctly	Check setting, clean, and replace if defective.
SYMPTOM:	IGNITION LIGHT FAILS TO GO OUT, BATTERY RUNS FLAT IN A FEW DAYS	
Dynamo not charging	Fan belt loose and slipping, or broken	Check, replace, and tighten as necessary.
	Brushes worn, sticking, broken, or dirty	Examine, clean, or replace brushes as necessary.
	Brush springs weak or broken	Examine and test. Replace as necessary.
	Commutator dirty, greasy, worn, or burnt	Clean commutator and undercut segment separators.

	Armature badly worn or armature shaft bent	Fit new or reconditioned armature.
	Commutator bars shorting	Undercut segment separations.
	Dynamo bearings badly worn	Overhaul dynamo, fit new bearings.
	Dynamo field coils burnt, open, or shorted.	Remove and fit rebuilt dynamo.
	Commutator no longer circular	Recut commutator and undercut segment separators.
	Pole pieces very loose	Strip and overhaul dynamo. Tighten pole pieces.
Regulator or cut-out fails to work correctly	Regulator incorrectly set	Adjust regulator correctly.
	Cut-out incorrectly set	Adjust cut-out correctly.
	Open circuit in wiring of cut-out and regulator unit	Remove, examine, and renew as necessary.

Failure of individual electrical equipment to function correctly is dealt with alphabetically, item by item, under the headings listed below:

FUEL GAUGE

Fuel gauge gives no reading	Fuel tank empty!	Fill fuel tank.
	Electric cable between tank sender unit and gauge earthed or loose	Check cable for earthing and joints for tightness.
	Fuel gauge case not earthed	Ensure case is well earthed.
	Fuel gauge supply cable interrupted	Check and replace cable if necessary.
	Fuel gauge unit broken	Replace fuel gauge.
Fuel gauge registers full all the time	Electric cable between tank unit and gauge broken or disconnected	Check over cable and repair as necessary.

HORN

Horn operates all the time	Horn push either earthed or stuck down	Disconnect battery earth. Check and rectify source of trouble.
	Horn cable to horn push earthed	Disconnect battery earth. Check and rectify source of trouble.
Horn fails to operate	Blown fuse	Check and renew if broken. Ascertain cause.
	Cable or cable connection loose, broken or disconnected	Check all connections for tightness and cables for breaks.
	Horn has an internal fault	Remove and overhaul horn.
Horn emits intermittent or unsatisfactory noise	Cable connections loose	Check and tighten all connections.
	Horn incorrectly adjusted	Adjust horn until best note obtained.

LIGHTS

Lights do not come on	If engine not running, battery discharged	Push-start car, charge battery.
	Light bulb filament burnt out or bulbs broken	Test bulbs in live bulb holder.
	Wire connections loose, disconnected or broken	Check all connections for tightness and wire cable for breaks.
	Light switch shorting or otherwise faulty	By-pass light switch to ascertain if fault is in switch and fit new switch as appropriate.
Lights come on but fade out	If engine not running battery discharged	Push-start car, and charge battery.
Lights give very poor illumination	Lamp glasses dirty	Clean glasses.
	Reflector tarnished or dirty	Fit new reflectors.
	Lamps badly out of adjustment	Adjust lamps correctly.
	Incorrect bulb with too low wattage fitted	Remove bulb and replace with correct grade
	Existing bulbs old and badly discoloured	Renew bulb units.
	Electrical wiring too thin not allowing full current to pass	Rewire lighting system.

ELECTRICAL SYSTEM

Cause	Trouble	Remedy
Lights work erratically – flashing on and off, especially over bumps	Battery terminals or earth connection loose Lights not earthing properly Contacts in light switch faulty	Tighten battery terminals and earth connection. Examine and rectify. By-pass light switch to ascertain if fault is in switch and fit new switch as appropriate.
WIPERS		
Wiper motor fails to work	Blown fuse Wire connections loose, disconnected, or broken Brushes badly worn Armature worn or faulty Field coils faulty	Check and replace fuse if necessary. Check wiper wiring. Tighten loose connections. Remove and fit new brushes. If electricity at wiper motor remove and overhaul and fit replacement armature. Purchase reconditioned wiper motor.
Wiper motor works very slowly and takes excessive current	Commutator dirty, greasy, or burnt Drive to wheelboxes too bent or un-lubricated Wheelbox spindle binding or damaged Armature bearings dry or unaligned Armature badly worn or faulty	Clean commutator thoroughly. Examine drive and straighten out severe curvature. Lubricate. Remove, overhaul, or fit replacement. Replace with new bearings correctly aligned. Remove, overhaul, or fit replacement armature.
Wiper motor works slowly and takes little current	Brushes badly worn Commutator dirty, greasy, or burnt Armature badly worn or faulty	Remove and fit new brushes. Clean commutator thoroughly. Remove and overhaul armature or fit replacement.
Wiper motor works but wiper blades remain static	Driving cable rack disengaged or faulty Wheelbox gear and spindle damaged or worn Wiper motor gearbox parts badly worn	Examine and if faulty, replace. Examine and if faulty, replace. Overhaul or fit new gearbox.

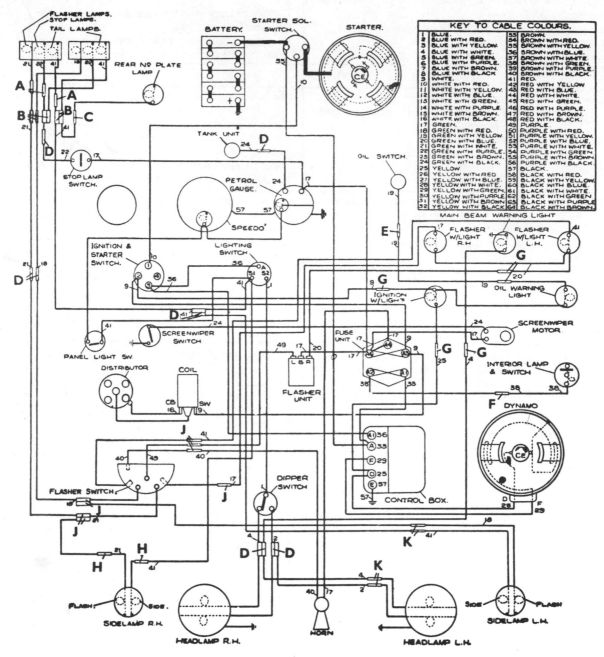

KEY TO CABLE COLOURS.

1 BLUE.	33 BROWN.
2 BLUE WITH RED.	34 BROWN WITH RED.
3 BLUE WITH YELLOW.	35 BROWN WITH YELLOW.
4 BLUE WITH WHITE.	36 BROWN WITH BLUE.
5 BLUE WITH GREEN.	37 BROWN WITH WHITE.
6 BLUE WITH PURPLE.	38 BROWN WITH GREEN.
7 BLUE WITH BROWN.	39 BROWN WITH PURPLE.
8 BLUE WITH BLACK.	40 BROWN WITH BLACK.
9 WHITE.	41 RED.
10 WHITE WITH RED.	42 RED WITH YELLOW
11 WHITE WITH YELLOW.	43 RED WITH BLUE.
12 WHITE WITH BLUE.	44 RED WITH WHITE.
13 WHITE WITH GREEN.	45 RED WITH GREEN.
14 WHITE WITH PURPLE.	46 RED WITH PURPLE.
15 WHITE WITH BROWN.	47 RED WITH BROWN.
16 WHITE WITH BLACK.	48 RED WITH BLACK.
17 GREEN.	49 PURPLE.
18 GREEN WITH RED.	50 PURPLE WITH RED.
19 GREEN WITH YELLOW.	51 PURPLE WITH YELLOW.
20 GREEN WITH BLUE.	52 PURPLE WITH BLUE.
21 GREEN WITH WHITE.	53 PURPLE WITH WHITE.
22 GREEN WITH PURPLE.	54 PURPLE WITH GREEN.
23 GREEN WITH BROWN.	55 PURPLE WITH BROWN.
24 GREEN WITH BLACK.	56 PURPLE WITH BLACK.
25 YELLOW.	57 BLACK.
26 YELLOW WITH RED.	58 BLACK WITH RED.
27 YELLOW WITH BLUE.	59 BLACK WITH YELLOW.
28 YELLOW WITH WHITE.	60 BLACK WITH BLUE.
29 YELLOW WITH GREEN.	61 BLACK WITH WHITE.
30 YELLOW WITH PURPLE.	62 BLACK WITH GREEN.
31 YELLOW WITH BROWN.	63 BLACK WITH PURPLE.
32 YELLOW WITH BLACK.	64 BLACK WITH BROWN.

LOCATIONS OF SNAP CONNECTORS

A Top left-hand corner of luggage locker.   B Top right-hand corner of luggage locker.   C In luggage locker under parcel tray.
D Under fascia on left-hand side of car.   E Adjacent to oil switch.   F Behind left-hand side quarter light trim panel.   G Under fascia
behind the lamp.   H Right-hand side wing valance.   J Under fascia in line with steering column.   K Left-hand side wing valance.

MINX (I) De-Luxe

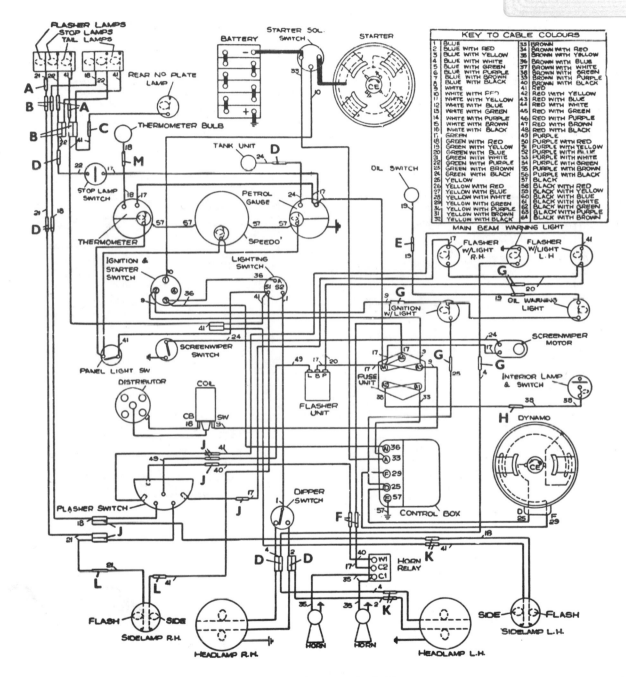

KEY TO CABLE COLOURS

1	BLUE	33	BROWN
2	BLUE WITH RED	34	BROWN WITH RED
3	BLUE WITH YELLOW	35	BROWN WITH YELLOW
4	BLUE WITH WHITE	36	BROWN WITH BLUE
5	BLUE WITH GREEN	37	BROWN WITH WHITE
6	BLUE WITH PURPLE	38	BROWN WITH GREEN
7	BLUE WITH BROWN	39	BROWN WITH PURPLE
8	BLUE WITH BLACK	40	BROWN WITH BLACK
9	WHITE	41	RED
10	WHITE WITH RED	42	RED WITH YELLOW
11	WHITE WITH YELLOW	43	RED WITH BLUE
12	WHITE WITH BLUE	44	RED WITH WHITE
13	WHITE WITH GREEN	45	RED WITH GREEN
14	WHITE WITH PURPLE	46	RED WITH PURPLE
15	WHITE WITH BROWN	47	RED WITH BROWN
16	WHITE WITH BLACK	48	RED WITH BLACK
17	GREEN	49	PURPLE
18	GREEN WITH RED	50	PURPLE WITH RED
19	GREEN WITH YELLOW	51	PURPLE WITH YELLOW
20	GREEN WITH BLUE	52	PURPLE WITH BLUE
21	GREEN WITH WHITE	53	PURPLE WITH WHITE
22	GREEN WITH PURPLE	54	PURPLE WITH GREEN
23	GREEN WITH BROWN	55	PURPLE WITH BROWN
24	GREEN WITH BLACK	56	PURPLE WITH BLACK
25	YELLOW	57	BLACK
26	YELLOW WITH RED	58	BLACK WITH RED
27	YELLOW WITH BLUE	59	BLACK WITH YELLOW
28	YELLOW WITH WHITE	60	BLACK WITH BLUE
29	YELLOW WITH GREEN	61	BLACK WITH WHITE
30	YELLOW WITH PURPLE	62	BLACK WITH GREEN
31	YELLOW WITH BROWN	63	BLACK WITH PURPLE
32	YELLOW WITH BLACK	64	BLACK WITH BROWN

LOCATIONS OF SNAP CONNECTORS

A Top right-hand corner of luggage locker. **B** Top left-hand corner of luggage locker. **C** In luggage locker under parcel tray.
D Under fascia on left-hand side of car. **E** Adjacent to oil switch. **F** Adjacent to horn relay. **G** Under fascia behind the lamp.
H Behind left-hand side quarter light trim panel. **J** Behind fascia in line with steering column. **K** Left-hand side wing valance.
L Right-hand sidewing valance. **M** Adjacent to transmitter on water pump.

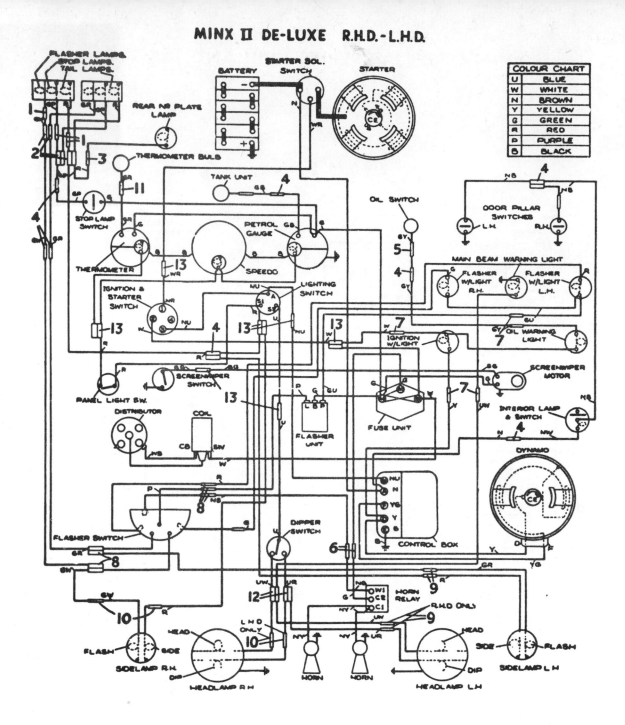

LOCATIONS OF SNAP CONNECTORS

1 Top right-hand corner of luggage boot. **2** Top left-hand corner of luggage boot. **3** In luggage boot under parcel shelf. **4** Under **fascia** at left-hand side of car. **5** Adjacent to oil switch. **6** Adjacent to horn relay. **7** Under fascia behind warning light panel. **8 Behind** fascia in line with steering column. **9** Left-hand side wing valance (front). **10** Right-hand side wing valance (front). **11 Adjacent** to transmitter on water pump. **12** At left-hand wing valance L.H.D. At right-hand wing valance R.H.D. **13** Behind fascia adjacent to instruments.

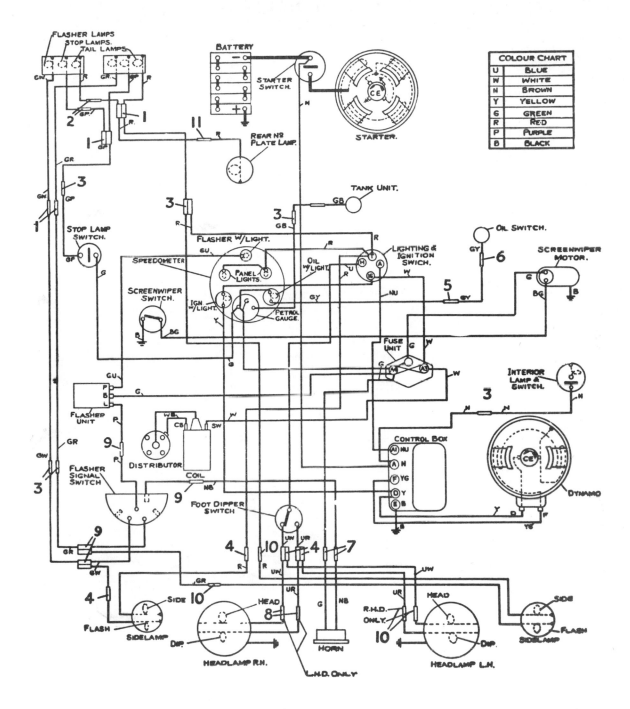

LOCATIONS OF SNAP CONNECTORS

1 Top right-hand corner of boot/behind lamp.   2 Top left-hand corner of boot/behind lamp.   3 Under fascia at left-hand side of car.
4 At left-hand wing valance on L.H.D.   At right-hand wing valance on R.H.D.   5 Behind instrument panel.   6 Adjacent to oil switch.
7 Adjacent to horn.   8 Right-hand side wing valance (front).   9 Under fascia in line with steering column.   10 Left-hand side wing valance (front).   11 Inside luggage boot under parcel shelf.

MINX III DE-LUXE R.H.D. and L.H.D.

COLOUR CHART

U	BLUE
W	WHITE
N	BROWN
Y	YELLOW
G	GREEN
R	RED
P	PURPLE
B	BLACK

LOCATIONS OF SNAP CONNECTORS

1 Top left-hand corner of luggage boot. 2 Under fascia of left-hand side of car. 3 Adjacent to control unit. 4 Adjacent to left-hand rear lamp. 5 Adjacent to right-hand rear lamp. 6 Left-hand wing valance. 7 Right-hand wing valance. 8 Under fascia near steering column. 9 Under fascia on right-hand side. 10 Adjacent to tank unit.

MINX IIIA and IIIB (early) DE-LUXE R.H.D. and L.H.D.

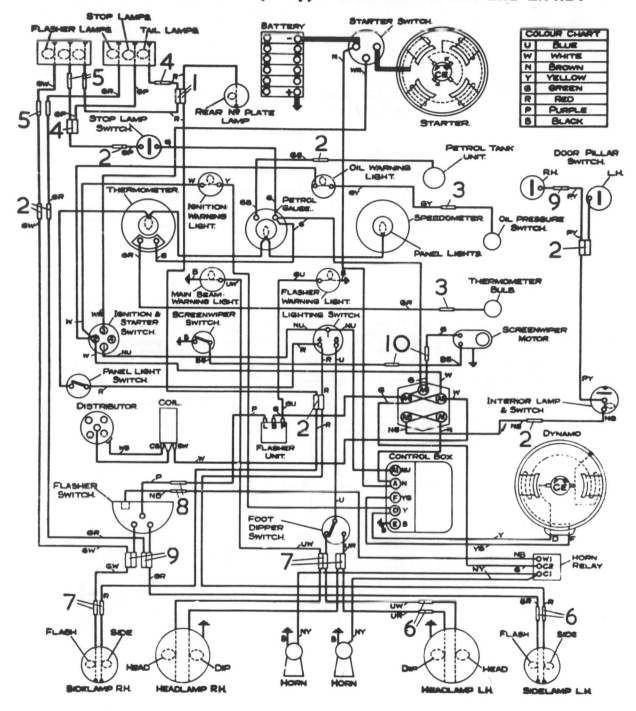

LOCATIONS OF SNAP CONNECTORS

1 Top left-hand corner of luggage boot. 2 Under fascia at left-hand side of car. 3 Adjacent to control unit. 4 Adjacent to left-hand rear lamp. 6 Left-hand wing valance. 7 Right-hand wing valance. 8 Under fascia near steering column. 9 Under fascia on right-hand side. 10 Adjacent to wiper motor.

MINX IIIB SPECIAL and DE-LUXE (late)
MINX IIIC

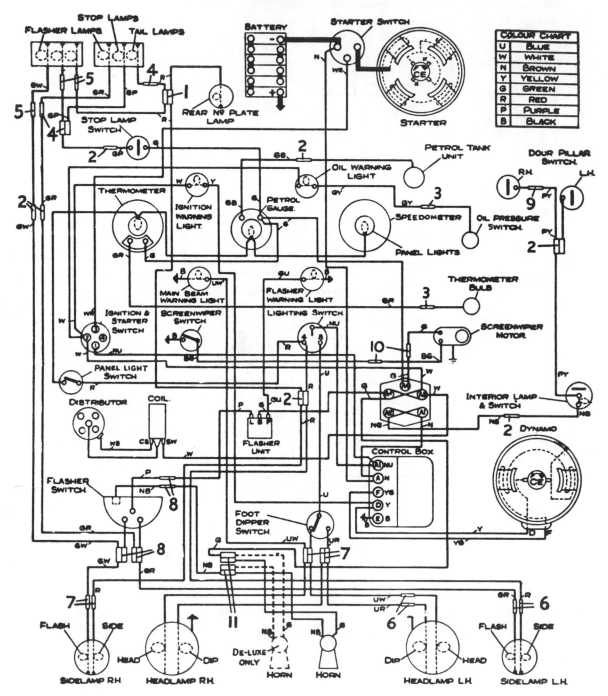

COLOUR CHART	
U	BLUE
W	WHITE
N	BROWN
Y	YELLOW
G	GREEN
R	RED
P	PURPLE
B	BLACK

LOCATIONS OF SNAP CONNECTORS

1 Top left-hand corner of luggage boot. 2 Under fascia at left-hand side of car. 3 Adjacent to control unit. 4 Adjacent to left-hand rear lamp. 5 Adjacent to right-hand rear lamp. 6 Left-hand wing valance. 7 Right-hand wing valance. 8 Under fascia near steering column. 9 Under fascia on right-hand side. 10 Adjacent to wiper motor. 11 Adjacent to left-hand horn.

MINX SERIES V (EARLY MODELS)

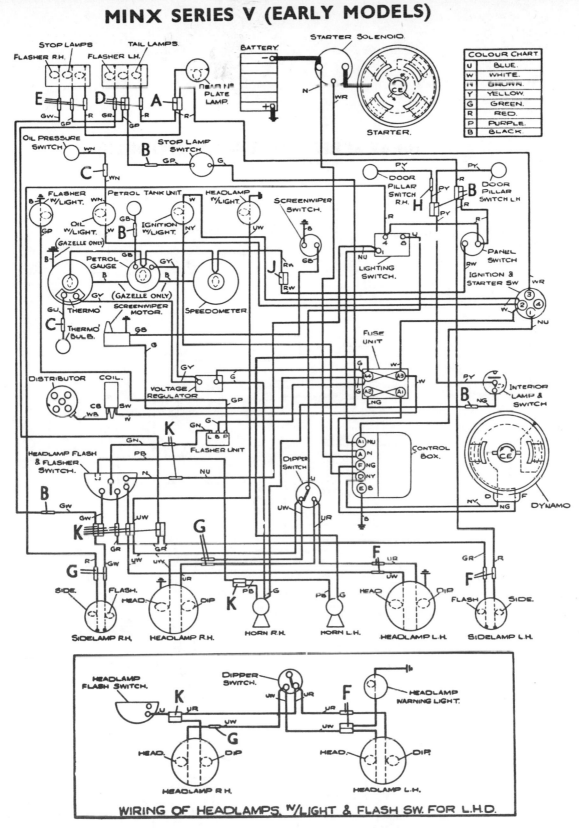

HUSKY SERIES III (EARLY MODELS)

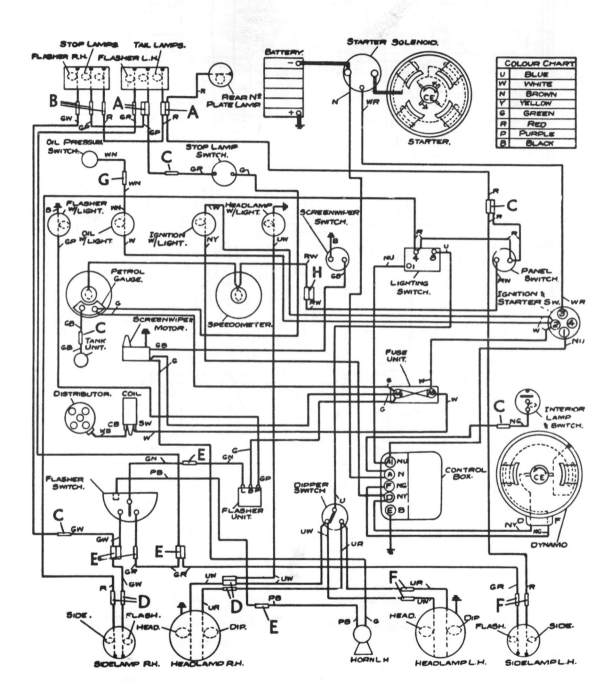

LOCATIONS OF SNAP CONNECTORS

A At rear of left-hand tail lamp cluster. **B** At rear of right-hand tail lamp cluster. **C** Beneath fascia of left-hand side. **D** On front wing valance at right-hand side. **E** Beneath fascia adjacent to steering column. **F** On front wing valance at left-hand side. **G** Under bonnet adjacent to control box. **H** Adjacent to instrument at rear.

CHAPTER ELEVEN

SUSPENSION – DAMPERS – STEERING

CONTENTS

SPECIFICATIONS

Front Suspension

Type	Independant. Coil spring with unequal length wishbones
Spring - Outer diameter	
- Minx I to IIIc, Husky I & II ...	4.46 in. (11.3 cm.)
- Minx V	4.56 in. (11.6 cm.)
- Husky III	4.53 in. (11.5 cm.)
- Static laden length	
- Minx I to IIIc, Husky I & II ...	7.75 in. $\pm$ 0.1 in. (19.7 $\pm$ .2 cm.)
- Minx V, Husky III	7.9 in. $\pm$ 0.1 in. (20 $\pm$ .2 cm.)
- Free length	
Minx I to IIIc	11.52 in. (29.2 cm.)
Minx V	12.75 in. (32.3 cm.)
Husky I and II	11.03 in. (28 cm.)
Husky III	12.04 in. (30.5 cm.)

Castor Angle

- Minx I early Minx II	2^O 15' $\pm$ 15'
- Later Minx II onwards	30' $\pm$ 15'
- Minx estate cars	1^O 40' $\pm$ 15'
- Husky	2^O $\pm$ 15'

Wheel camber angle..	30' $\pm$ 15'
King pin inclination	5° 15' $\pm$ ¼^O
Wheel lock angle	25° on each outer lock
Toe-in	⅛ in. (3 mm.)
Hub bearings - Inner	Timken 1988/1922
- Outer	Timken L.M. 11949/L.M. 11910
- End float..	.002 to .007 in. (.05 to .18 mm.)

Length of top link ... ...   7.625 in. (193.7 mm.)
Length of bottom link ... ...   12.85 in. (326.4 mm.)
Shock absorbers ... ...   Telescopic direct acting
Linkage ... ...   Rubber bushed

Rear Suspension

Type.. ... ...   Semi-elliptic
Springs – Length between centres
     – Minx I to V ... ...   46.95 in. (119.2 cm.)
     – Husky I and II... ... ...   43.95 in. (111.6 cm.)
     – Husky III... ... ...   43.45 in. (110.3 cm.)
     – Width
     – Minx I to V, Husky I and II ...   1.5 in. (3.8 cm.)
     – Husky III... ... ...   2 in. (5 cm.)
     – Depth
     – Minx I to IIIc – Cars ... ...   1.72 in. (4.3 cm.)
                  – Estate cars ...   2.43 in. (6.2 cm.)
     – Minx V ... ...   1.66 in. (4.2 cm.)
     – Husky I and II... ... ...   1.62 in. (4.1 cm.)
     – Husky III... ... ...   1.28 in. (3.2 cm.)
     – Bushes ... ...   Steel and rubber
     – Eyes.. ... ...   Rolled

Number of leaves:
     – Minx I to IIIc – Cars ... ...   6 at $^{15}/_{64}$ in.   1 at $^{5}/_{16}$ in.
                  – Estate cars ...   7 at $^{1}/_{4}$ in.   2 at $^{11}/_{32}$ in.
     – Minx V ... ...   5 at $^{7}/_{32}$ in.   1 at $^{1}/_{4}$ in.   1 at $^{5}/_{16}$ in.
     – Husky I and II... ... ...   6 at $^{7}/_{32}$ in.   1 at $^{5}/_{16}$ in.
     – Husky III... ... ...   4 at $^{3}/_{16}$ in.   1 at $^{9}/_{32}$ in. 1 at $^{1}/_{4}$ in.

Number of clips   3
Shock absorbers – All Minx models ...   Telescopic direct acting
              – Husky.. ... ...   Armstrong hydraulic

Steering

Make.. ... ...   Burman 'P' or 'F'
Type.. ... ...   Worm and nut or recirculating ball
Steering wheel – Type ... ...   2 spoke
             – Diameter ... ...   16.5 in. (41.91 cm.)
Turns lock to lock ... ...   'P' Type   'F' Type
                                    2.5   3.15
Steering box ratio (straight ahead).. ...   15.7   14.5
                                         (16.4 from chassis No. B.0310448)
Rocker arm end float adjustment ... ...   Adjusting screw   Shim

Wheels & Tyres

Type .. ..   Pressed steel 4 studs fixing
Sizes –
        All models except Minx V ... ...   4J x 15
                   Minx V ... ...   4½J x 13
Tyres – Type ... ...   Standard 4 ply (tubeless)
Sizes –
        –Husky ... ...   5.00 x 15
        –Minx cars and Husky from
            Chassis No. F.68197 ... ...   5.90 x 15
        –Minx estate cars... ... ...   5.90 x 15
        –Minx V only... ... ...   6.00 x 13

SUSPENSION – DAMPERS – STEERING

TORQUE WRENCH SETTINGS

Front Suspension

Fulcrum pin to crossmember mounting (upper)	48 lb/ft.
Fulcrum pin to crossmember mounting (lower)	32 lb/ft.
Eyebolt – trunnion to link	40 lb/ft.)
	85 lb/ft.)
Ball pin – stub carrier to link..	52 lb/ft.
Ball pin – housing to link..	32 lb/ft.
Shock absorber to spring pan	6 lb/ft.
Crossmember to frame	62 lb/ft
Road wheel nuts	48 lb/ft.

Rear Suspension

Rear spring 'U' bolts – Minx...	16 lb/ft.
– Husky..	35 lb/ft.

Steering

Box to frame	30 lb/ft.
Relay lever to frame	30 lb/ft.
Steering crosstube ball pin – centre	30 lb/ft.
– outer..	28 lb/ft.

1. GENERAL DESCRIPTION

The front suspension is of the coil spring and unequal length wishbone type, and employs long inner fulcrum pins threaded at each end to carry the bushes of the upper and lower links. Provision for camber adjustment is made, this being accomplished by the insertion of shims between the upper fulcrum pin and its bracket location on the crossmember as seen in Fig.11.1. The stub axle is located by

Fig. 11.1. Layout of the front suspension.

means of a ball socket assembly secured directly into the outer end of the upper link and by means of a short swivel pin into the trunnion. A short threaded outer fulcrum pin completes the connection between the trunnion and the lower link. Thrust is taken to the lower face of the stub axle swivel by means of a nut and a thrust washer.

The steering gear on earlier models, the Burman 'P' type operates on the nut and worm principle, while the Burman 'F' type of steering gear is of the recirculating ball type and is

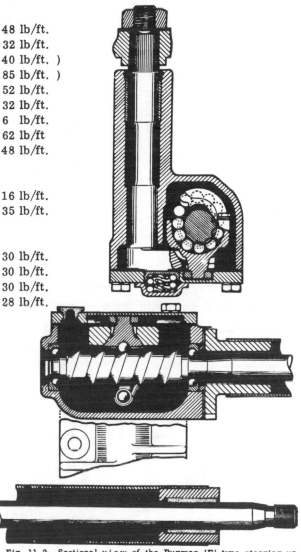

Fig. 11.2. Sectional view of the Burman 'F' type steering un

secured to the underframe side member with bolts. Screw threads of the unified series are used on this unit. The rear suspension spring eyes and shackle brackets are fitted with bushes of the steel/bonded rubber type, and the suspension is controlled by telescopic direct acting shock absorbers on all Minx models and by Armstrong hydraulic shock absorbers on Husky models.

2. SUSPENSIONS & STEERING – MAINTENANCE

1. On earlier models the front suspension track rod joints and suspension pivots should be greased at every 3,000 miles with a grease gun filled with Castrolease L.M. Shell Retinax A or Esso Multipurpose H grease. Grease points will be found on each steering rod joint. front and rear of each wishbone pivot and at the top and underneath each steering king pin.

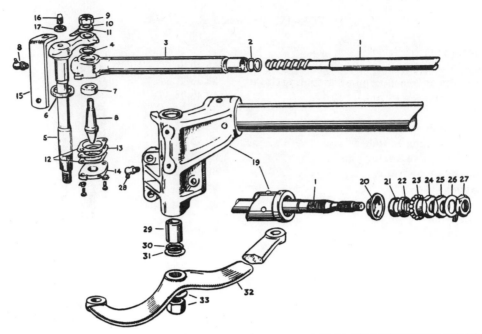

Fig. 11.3. EXPLODED VIEW OF THE BURMAN 'P' TYPE STEERING GEAR AS FITTED TO MINX AND HUSKY I AND EARLY MINX II MODELS.

1 Inner column. 2 Seal. 3 Sleeve assembly. 4 Seal. 5 Rocker shaft. 6 Felt seal. 7 Bush—ball peg. 8 Ball peg. 9 Nut.
10 Washer. 11 'Oil only' tab. 12 Joint. 13 Shim. 14 Base plate. 15 Adjustment bracket. 16 Adjusting screw. 17 Locknut.
18 Greaser. 19 Main casing. 20 Seal. 21 Collar. 22 Lower track. 23 Balls. 24 Adjusting nut. 25 Locknut. 26 Trafficator
cancelling ring. 27 Locknut. 28 Greaser. 29 Bush. 30 Seal. 31 Backing washer. 32 Swing lever. 33 Nut and washer.

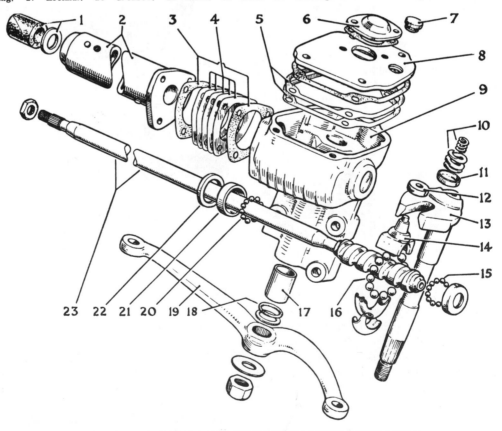

Fig. 11.4. EXPLODED VIEW OF THE BURMAN 'F' TYPE STEERING UNIT.

1 Felt bush and washer. 2 Outer column. 3 Paper gaskets (joint washers) 4 Shims. 5 Shims. 6 Spring cap. 7 Filler plug.
8 Top cover. 9 Steering box. 10 Double coil spring. 11 Damper button. 12 Guide roller. 13 Rocker shaft. 14 Nut. 15 Steel
balls (lower track). 16 Steel balls (nut). 17 Rocker shaft bush. 18 Oil seal. 19 Drop arm (swing lever). 20 Steel balls (upper
track). 21 Upper track. 22 Distance piece. 23 Inner column and worm.

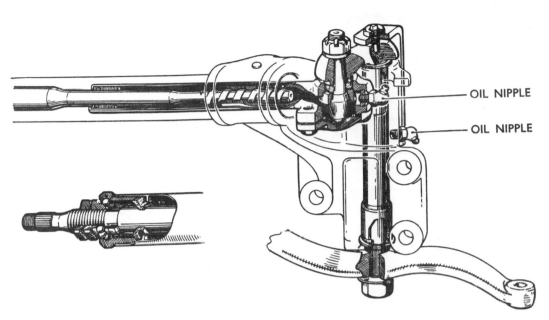

OIL NIPPLE

OIL NIPPLE

Fig. 11.5. Sectional view of the Burman 'P' type steering unit.

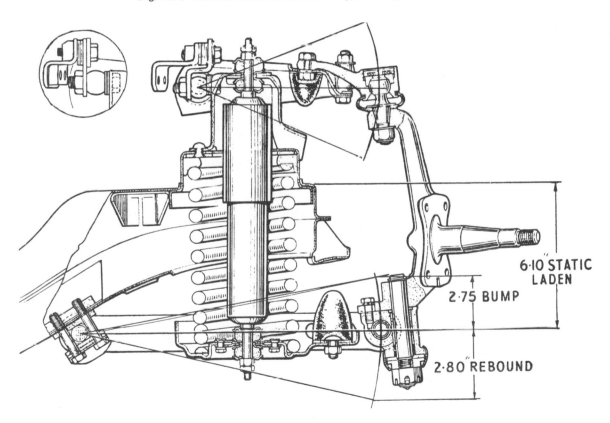

6.10" STATIC LADEN

2.75 BUMP

2.80" REBOUND

Fig. 11.6. Sectional view of the front suspension as fitted to Minx Series I to IIIC and Husky Series I and II.

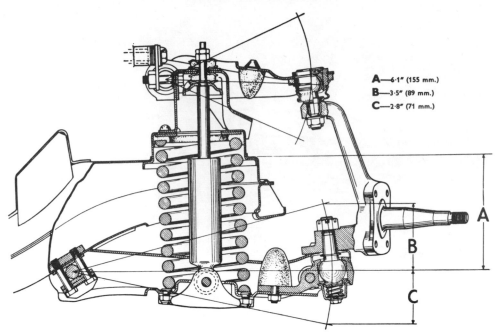

A—6·1" (155 mm.)
B—3·5" (89 mm.)
C—2·8" (71 mm.)

Fig. 11.7. Sectional view of the front suspension as fitted to Minx Series V and Husky Series III.

During greasing it will be found of practical advantage to jack up each front wheel in order to take the weight from the bottom thrust and allow the grease to spread over the thrust area. No grease nipples are fitted to the rear suspension pivots and shackle bolts.

2. Every 6,000 miles it is a safeguard to check that the rear suspension 'U' bolts are really tight. Each spring should be wiped with an oily rag and checked for any broken blades, and if, during dry weather there is a persistant squeak from the rear spring shackles, apply a spray of hydraulic brake fluid over each rubber bonded bush. This will eliminate the squeak without causing deterioration of the rubber, as is the case if these bushes are treated with normal lubricating oil.

3. On later models the metal bushes have been superseded by self-lubricating synthetic bushes, and the track rod joints are of the sealed type. No grease nipples are fitted to any of these joints. On these models the only parts requiring regular lubrication are the front wheel hubs, and the steering idler lever.

3. FRONT & REAR DAMPERS - MAINTENANCE
1. The damper units used on the Minx models are sealed units and no routine servicing is

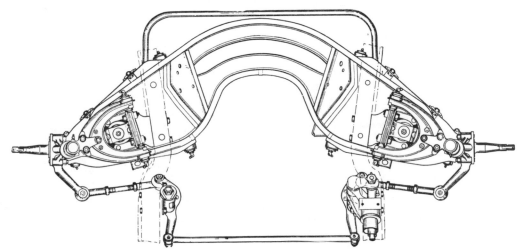

Fig. 11.8. Plan view of the steering linkage.

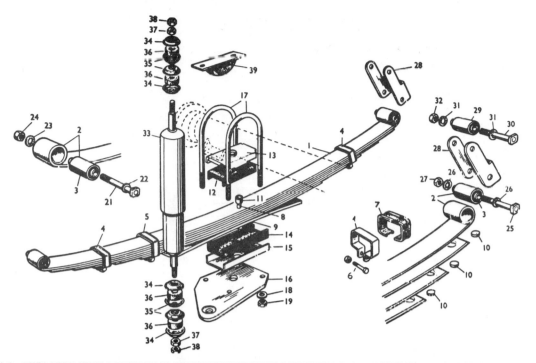

Fig. 11.9. EXPLODED VIEW OF THE REAR SUSPENSION WITHOUT ECCENTRIC BUSH, AS FITTED TO MINX CARS UP TO SERIES IIIC
1 Rear spring assembly. 2 Main leaf. 3 Spring eye bush. 4 Spring clip. 5 Spring clip. 6 Bolt and nut—clip to spring. 7 Rubber lining. 8 Dowel bolt. 9 Dowel bolt securing nut. 10 Thrust buttons. 11 Dowel bolt sleeve. 12 Top spring clamp rubber. 13 Rubber retainer. 14 Bottom spring clamp rubber. 15 Rubber retainer. 16 Spring clamp plate. 17 'U' bolts. 18 Washer. 19 Nyloc nut. 21 Pivot pin—front spring eye to frame. 22 Washer. 23 Washer. 24 Nut. 25 Shackle pin—rear spring eye to frame. 26 Washer. 27 Nut. 28 Shackle. 29 Shackle bush. 30 Shackle pin—shackle to frame. 31 Washer. 32 Nut. 33 Shock absorber. 34 Retaining washer. 35 Separating washer. 36 Rubber washer. 37 Nut—shock absorber to frame and axle. 38 Locknut. 39 Rubber bump stop.

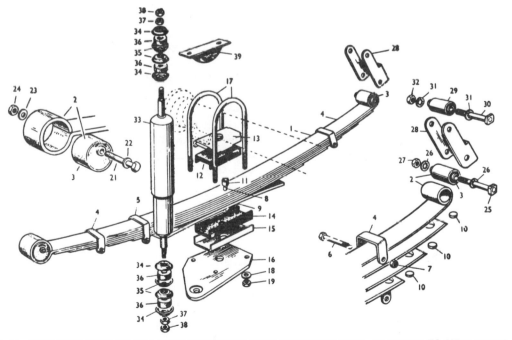

Fig. 11.10. EXPLODED VIEW OF THE REAR SUSPENSION WITH ECCENTRIC BUSH, AS FITTED TO MINX SERIES IIIC AND V.
1 Rear spring assembly. 2 Main leaf. 3 Eccentric spring eye bush. 4 Spring clip. 5 Spring clip. 6 Bolt and nut - clip to spring. 7 Rubber lining. 8 Dowel bolt. 9 Dowel bolt securing nut. 10 Thrust buttons. 11 Dowel bolt sleeve. 12 Top spring clamp rubber. 13 Rubber retainer. 14 Bottom spring clamp rubber. 15 Rubber retainer. 16 Spring clamp plate. 17 'U' bolts. 18 Washer. 19 Nyloc nut. 21 Pivot pin - front spring eye to frame. 22 Washer. 23 Washer. 24 Nut. 25 Shackle pin—rear spring eye to frame. 26 Washer. 27 Nut. 28 Shackle. 29 Shackle bush. 30 Shackle pin—shackle to frame. 31 Washer. 32 Nut. 33 Shock absorber. 34 Retaining washer. 35 Separating washer. 36 Rubber washer. 37 Nut—shock absorber to frame and axle. 38 Locknut. 39 Rubber bump stop.

possible or required. When it is evident that wear has taken place inside a unit, by the fact that the car pitches on its springs and such pitching movement is continuous and excessive, then the unit must be removed and replaced.

2. On Husky models it is possible to top up the hydraulic fluid levels on the rear dampers, but to do this job satisfactorily they should be removed from the car. The damper should then be placed in a vice, and the damper arm moved up and down during filling to remove all the air bubbles.

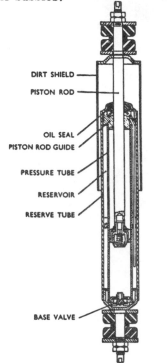

DIRT SHIELD
PISTON ROD
OIL SEAL
PISTON ROD GUIDE
PRESSURE TUBE
RESERVOIR
RESERVE TUBE
BASE VALVE

Fig. 11.11. Sectional view of the telescopic shock absorber.

4. **INSPECTING THE SUSPENSION & STEERING**

1. To check the tie-rod ball joints for wear, put the car over a pit, and have someone else rock the steering wheel from side to side. As this movement takes place examination of each tie-rod ball joint will show if the movement is excessive. Similarly by taking a firm grip on the front wheel and attempting to move it about the king pin will soon show up slackness in the tie-rod joints.

2. If each wheel is jacked up it will be possible to check for looseness in the king pin by grasping the road wheel at the top and bottom while someone observes the movement of the stub axle in relation to the upper and lower links.

3. Because of the pressure exerted by the coil springs, it is not so easy to check that the link pivot bushes are worn, but where this is the case it is usually evident, because of the peculiar tyre wear pattern which develops.

4. The dampers can be checked for correct

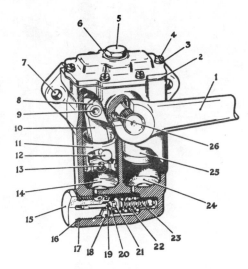

Fig. 11.12. EXPLODED VIEW OF THE ARMSTRONG HYDRAULIC SHOCK ABSORBER AS FITTED TO ALL HUSKY MODELS.
1 Arm. 2 Gasket. 3 Shakeproof washer. 4 Lid screw. 5 Filler plug. 6 Filler plug washer. 7 Mounting holes. 8 Crank plate. 9 Crank pin. 10 Connecting rod. 11 Compression piston. 12 Piston pin. 13 Recuperation valve. 14 Compression or bump cylinder. 15 Valve screw. 16 Valve screw compression washer. 17 Rubber "O" ring. 18 Valve screw inner seal. 19 Rebound valve. 20 Leak groove. 21 Compression valve. 22 Compression spring. 23 Rebound spring. 24 Rebound cylinder. 25 Rebound piston. 26 Gland packing.

operation by bouncing the front end of the car and noting how many bounces continue after your pressure is released. If more than about $1\frac{1}{2}$ bounces take place, then the dampers are not carrying out their function, and if the car continues to move up and down for a number of times, then the dampers are useless.

5. Excessive play in the steering gear will lead to front wheel wobble, and the amount of play is checked by noting any lost movement between the end of the steering column and the steering drop arm. By turning the steering wheel back and forth, the amount of movement inside the box can be seen by relating this steering wheel turning to the movement of the steering drop arm, which is the arm used to change the revolving movement of the steering wheel into a to-and-fro movement necessary at the steering tie-rods.

5. **STABILISER BAR - REMOVAL & REPLACEMENT**

1. To remove the front stabiliser bar, raise up the front of the car to a reasonable working height, remove the bolts, nuts and washers securing four retaining clips to the lower wishbone links, noting that the two $\frac{3}{16}$ in. thick washers are on the outer clips. The retaining clips can be eased from their locating slots with a screwdriver.

2. When replacing the bar, offer it up into position and check the alignment of the rubber

bushes with the slots in the lower links. When correctly aligned the bar must just protrude beyond the two outer bushes. Insert the tongues of the retaining clips into the slots in the lower links and then use a G clamp to compress the rubber bushes so that the securing bolts can be inserted in the holes in both clips and links.

6. **STUB AXLE – REMOVAL & REPLACEMENT**
1. Any removal work on the front suspension units where the coil spring is to be removed, calls for the use of a spring compressor tool capable of being inserted in the place of the front damper unit, and used to compress and release from compression, the large coil spring.

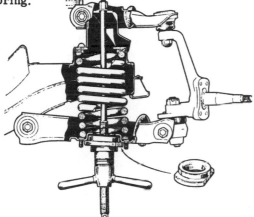

Fig. 11.13. Front suspension unit in the static

laden position with spring compressing tool in position.

2. When it is necessary to remove a stub axle, the operations amount to an almost complete dismantling of the unit, and the sequence of operation given below can be stopped at any point where the repair work requires.
3. First jack up the front of the car, and load the front seats with some form of weights, such as a sack of potatoes or heavy weights in order to avoid straining the damper and its mounts, and then undo the two nuts at the upper spindle fixing and lift off the rubber and cup washers.
4. Slacken the two nuts at the lower spindle fixing but do not remove these.
5. Now unscrew the nuts around the damper lower plate, lift the plate clear of the series of studs and turn it through about 90⁰ to allow it to pass through the lower link spring pan, bringing the damper with it.
6. Now remove the road wheel and the brake drum, and unscrew the hydraulic brake hose from its connection at the chassis bracket. Cover the end of the hose with a wad of clean rag secured in place with a rubber band, or bung up the end of the hose with a cork. This will retain the hydraulic fluid and also prevent any dirt from entering this pipe.
7. Next remove the large castellated nut securing the front hub to the stub axle, and remove the hub and bearings.
8. Remove the four nuts and bolts holding the oil catcher, backplate and steering arm to the stub axle flange, and at this point fit the spring compressor tool mentioned earlier by passing it up through the coil spring in the position of the normal damper. With this compressor take the load imposed by the coil spring, to enable the stub axle assembly to be released from the upper and lower links.
9. Remove the split pin, locknut and adjusting nut and thrust washer from the base of the lower swivel pin and then remove the upper swivel assembly from the stub axle. This may require the use of a drawer tool.
10. The stub axle with its pin can now be lifted from the bush in the lower link, leaving the upper swivel in the link. Refitting is the reverse procedure, and during the reassembly fit the thrust washer and screw on the adjusting nut to give an end float of between 0.15 and 0.18 in., this being checked with a feeler gauge. Having obtained this end float, fit the locking nut and screw it up by hand until it is in contact with the adjusting nut, and then turn until the split pin hole is exposed. Fit this pin in position and then using two spanners, hold the locknut and slacken back the adjuster nut until the two nuts are firmly locked together.

7. **REAR SPRINGS – REMOVAL & REPLACEMENT**
1. Jack up the rear of the car and support it by means of chassis stands or suitable blocks of wood placed under the underframing just forward of the spring front anchorages. Remove the road wheel and then clean the projecting threads of the 'U' bolts, dampers and mounting bolts with a wire brush and apply a soaking of penetrating oil.
2. Remove the nuts securing the shock absorber and lift this away. On the early models the upper securing bolts are accessible from inside the luggage boot.
3. Remove the securing nuts, and, in the case of earlier models the washers, in the case of later models self-locking Nyloc nuts, from the 'U' bolts and then place a jack under the axle and jack up until the axle parts from the spring. Lift off the 'U' bolts and clamp plate.
4. Remove the nut from the lower shackle pin, remove the shakeproof washer and tap out the pin, and lower the spring to the ground. The front pin can be removed in exactly the

same manner, and the spring lifted away. Refitting is the direct reversal of the removal sequence.

8. **FRONT WHEEL HUBS - REFITTING**

1. Removal of the front hubs has already been mentioned, and when these are to be replaced, the following points are important. All parts must be clean, and if new bearings are to be fitted, press into the hub the outer shells of each of the two taper roller bearings, with the larger internal diameter outwards from the respective ends of the hub. The rollers and inner races of both bearings should be packed with grease and the inner bearing roller race placed in position in the hub together with the distance piece and seal.

2. Grease should then be packed evenly in the hub shell, and the hub fitted back onto the stub axle, the front roller bearing being placed in position.

3. The hub cap should not be filled with grease, and in some models these caps will be found to have a small $\frac{1}{16}$ in. diameter hole drilled in the centre to permit any excess grease to seep out and so relieve the pressure which would otherwise be built up in the hub.

4. To adjust these roller bearings the hub nut should be tightened using a torque wrench to obtain a reading of 15-20 lb/ft. Now release the nut 1 to $1\frac{1}{2}$ flats to ensure a small amount of end float and also to line up one of the split pin holes in the stub axle with slots in the nut. The castle nut must be locked in position with a new split pin, otherwise the nut could work off and the wheel fly from the car during running.

9. **STEERING WHEEL - REMOVAL**

1. Before removing the steering wheel, disconnect the battery. Slacken the three screws around the steering wheel hub and draw out the horn push button, or horn ring, and pull apart a snap connector located inside the steering wheel boss. Remove the centre nut, and pull the steering wheel from the splines on the top of the column. If the wheel has not been removed for some time it may be necessary to obtain a steering wheel drawer in order to loosen the wheel, but it may also be possible to squirt penetrating oil down the splines in order to release any corrosion which may be holding the two parts.

2. Where a ring type of horn switch is employed, this consists of a circular central plate to which the outer ring is secured, and this assembly is secured with the upper and lower contact plates, to the underside of the centre cover by three screws. The two contact plates are held apart by three light coil springs.

10. **STEERING GEAR - REMOVAL & REPLACEMENT**

1. Disconnect the car battery, jack up the front wheel on the steering gear side, and unscrew the outer track rod from the drop arm. Normally this joint is very tight, and requires the use of a drawer tool in order to free the drop arm.

2. Slacken the three screws around the steering wheel hub and remove the horn ring, and then remove the self tapping screw on the side of the steering wheel column cowl, which secures the warning light panel to the cowl, and ease the panel from its key location in the cowl by pulling towards you.

3. Disconnect the wire connectors behind the warning light, and then remove the two screws which will be found on the side of the cowl. This will allow one side of the cowl to be taken away, and the second side can then be eased from the trafficator switch. The trafficator switch can then be removed and disconnected, followed by the steering wheel.

4. Now unscrew the parcel tray at its inner corner to allow it to drop clear of the steering column. This will give access to the rubber grommet around the column where this passes through the bulkhead.

5. The gearshift linkage on cars with steering wheel gear change mechanism is now disconnected at the lower end of the column by removing a square headed bolt in the lower lever and driving out the pin from the operating boss for the cable linkage. The lever and shaft can now be moved upwards into the car.

6. Remove two bolts securing the lower support bracket to the steering box and ease this bracket towards the engine in order to clear the column.

7. Now unscrew the bolts securing the column hanger clip at the dash panel, leaving the hanger in position. Move the front seat back as far as it will go, unscrew the bolts securing box to the underframe side member, and pull the unit forward to expose the centre track rod ball joint which should be extracted.

8. Now raise the lower end of the steering column and ease it forward out of the scuttle hole, lifting it forward over the front wing. Refitting of the steering column and steering gear is the reverse of the removal procedure.

11. **ROCKER SHAFT ADJUSTMENT**

1. Rocker shaft end float adjustment may be carried out with the steering gear fitted in

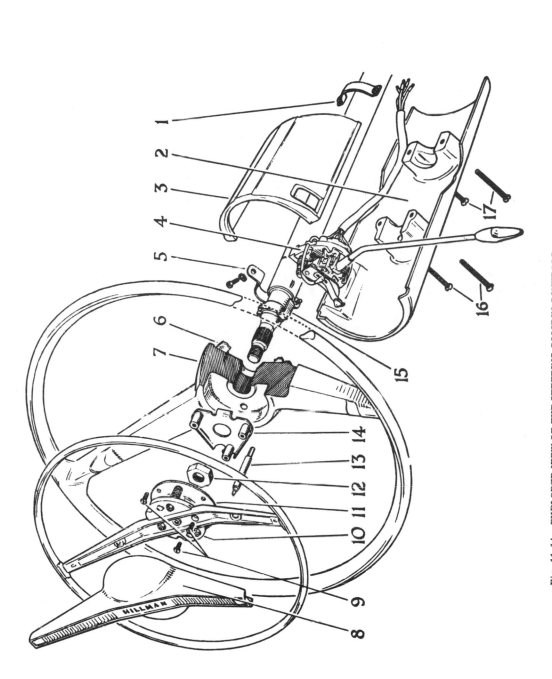

Fig. 11.14. EXPLODED VIEW OF THE STEERING COLUMN CONTROLS.

1 Clip. 2 Column cowling (lower). 3 Column cowling (upper). 4 Indicator switch. 5 Clip. 6 Slip ring. 7 Steering wheel. 8 Cover and motif assembly. 9 Screws. 10 Upper contact plate. 11 Lower contact plate. 12 Nut—steering wheel. 13 Plunger. 14 Horn carrier. 15 Striker ring. 16 Screws. 17 Screws.

position in the car.

2. Under the cover plate will be found a quantity of shims. To carry out the adjustment, with the spring cap removed from the cover, which is fitted back onto the box without any shims, measure the gap between the rocker shaft and the top cover with a feeler gauge, with the steering gear in the straight ahead position.

3. There should be 0.004 to 0.008 in rocker shaft end float, but the shaft must be free to rotate.

4. Now remove the top cover and adjust the thickness of the shims to achieve the required clearance. Shims are obtainable in three thicknesses, 0.002 in., 0.005 in. and 0.010 in.

5. With the cover refitted, replace the damper button, or thrust cup with springs and flange plate, which control the rocker shaft dampening, securing this with the two screws.

12. FRONT WHEEL ALIGNMENT

1. The front wheels are correctly aligned when they toe-in at the front $\frac{1}{8}$ in. Adjustment is made by slackening the locknuts on each outer track rod ball joint.

2. Adjust the track by rotating each track rod equally, which in fact calls for expensive track rod alignment bar, or optical equipment, and is therefore best carried out by your local Rootes Group dealer.

3. Misalignment of the front wheels can cause a most distinctive wear pattern on the tyre largely because the wheel is not running straight and the tread is being ground off in such a manner as to leave a feathered lip on the edge of each tread pattern rib.

4. If the misalignment is serious, due perhaps to a bent track rod, then the steering will be heavy and stiff, and the car will not run along a level surface in a straight line.

CHAPTER TWELVE

BODYWORK AND UNDERFRAME

CONTENTS

1. MAINTENANCE — BODYWORK & UNDERFRAME

The condition of your car's bodywork is of considerable importance as it is on this that the second hand value of the car will mainly depend. It is very much more difficult to repair neglected bodywork than to renew mechanical assemblies. The hidden portions of the body, such as the wheel arches and the underframe and the engine compartment are equally important, though obviously not requiring such frequent attention as the immediately visible paintwork.

Once a year or every 12,000 miles, it is a sound scheme to visit your local main agent and have the underside of the body steam cleaned. This will take about 1½ hours and costs about £4. All traces of dirt and oil will be removed and the underside can then be inspected carefully for rust, damaged hydraulic pipes, frayed electrical wiring and similar maladies. The car should be greased on completion of this job.

At the same time the engine compartment should be cleaned in the same manner. If steam cleaning facilities are not available then brush 'Gunk' or a similar cleanser over the whole engine and engine compartment with a

stiff paint brush, working it well in where there is an accumulation of oil and dirt. Do not paint the ignition system and protect it with oily rags when the Gunk is washed off. As the Gunk is washed away it will take with it all traces of oil and dirt, leaving the engine looking clean and bright.

The wheel arches should be given particular attention as undersealing can easily come away here and stones and dirt thrown up from the road wheels can soon cause the paint to chip and flake, and so allow rust to set in. If rust is found, clean down to the bare metal with wet and dry paper, paint on an anti-corrosive coating such as Kurust, or if preferred, red lead, and renew the paintwork and undercoating.

The bodywork should be washed once a week or when dirty. Thoroughly wet the car to soften the dirt and then wash the car down with a soft sponge and plenty of clean water. If the surplus dirt is not washed off very gently in time it will wear the paint down as surely as wet and dry paper. It is best to use a hose if this is available. Give the car a final wash down and then dry with a soft chamois leather to prevent the formation of spots.

Spots of tar and grease thrown up from the

road can be removed with a rag dampened with petrol.

Once every six months, or every three months if wished, give the bodywork and chromium trim a thoroughly good wax polish. If a chromium cleaner is used to remove rust on any of the car's plated parts remember that the cleaner also removes part of the chromium, so use sparingly.

2. MAINTENANCE - UPHOLSTERY & CARPETS

Remove the carpets and thoroughly vacuum clean the interior of the car every three months or more frequently if necessary. Beat out the carpets and vacuum clean them if they are very dirty. If the headlining or upholstery is soiled apply an upholstery cleaner with a damp sponge and wipe off with a clean dry cloth.

3. MINOR BODY REPAIRS

At some time during your ownership of your car it is likely that it will be bumped or scraped in a mild way, causing some slight damage to the body. Major damage must be repaired by your local Rootes Group agent, but there is no reason why you cannot successfully beat out, repair and respray minor damage yourself. The essential items which the owner should gather together to ensure a really professional job are:-
a) A plastic filler such as Holts 'Cataloy'.
b) Paint whose colour matches exactly that of the bodywork, either in a can for application by a spray gun, or in an aerosol can.
c) Fine cutting paste.
d) Medium and fine grade wet and dry paper.

Never use a metal hammer to knock out small dents as the blows tend to scratch and distort the metal. Knock out the dent with a mallet or rawhide hammer and press on the underside of the dented surface a metal dolly or smooth wooden block roughly contoured to the normal shape of the damaged area.

After the worst of the damaged area has been knocked out, rub down the dent and surrounding area with medium wet and dry paper and thoroughly clean away all traces of dirt.

The plastic filler comprises a paste and a hardener which must be thoroughly mixed together. Mix only a small portion at a time as the paste sets hard within five to fifteen minutes depending on the amount of hardener used.

Smooth on the filler with a knife or stiff plastic to the shape of the damaged portion and allow to thoroughly dry - a process which takes about six hours. After the filler has dried it is likely that it will have contracted slightly so spread on a second layer of filler if necessary.

Smooth down the filler with fine wet and dry paper wrapped round a suitable block of wood and continue until the whole area is perfectly smooth and it is impossible to feel where the filler joins the rest of the paintwork. Spray on from an aerosol can, or with a spray gun, an anti-rust undercoat, smooth down with wet and dry paper, and then spray on two coats of the final finishing using a circular motion. When thoroughly dry polish the whole area with a fine cutting paste to smooth the resprayed area into the remainder of the wing and to remove the small particles of spray paint which will have settled round the area. This will leave the wing looking perfect with not a trace of the previous unsightly dent.

4. MAJOR BODY REPAIRS

Because the body is built on the monocoque principle and is integral with the underframe, major damage must be repaired by competent body repairers having the necessary welding, cutting and straightening equipment.

Whenever the shell has received a severe impact it is vital that it be correctly aligned by being fitted to an alignment/repair jig, which is a part of the equipment in the bodyshop of main Rootes Service departments.

5. MAINTENANCE - DOOR LOCKS & HINGES

Every six months, the door, bonnet and boot hinges should be given several drops of oil, and the striker plates smeared with grease.

If the locks become stiff to operate and so function badly the mechanism can be checked and oiled by first easing away the door trim after the handles have been removed.

The trim is secured in position with some type of spring clip, and it is essential to work progressively round the door to free these clips, otherwise there is the chance that the spring will tear away from the trim panel rather than slide out of the hole.

With an oil can give all the working pivots of the lock and the remote control rod a few drops of oil while working the lock.

6. DOOR LOCKS - REMOVAL

Several types of door lock have been used on the different models throughout the range of cars and the following methods outline the operations required to remove a door lock.

With the door handles and trim removed, unscrew the three screws holding the remote control to the door and swing the unit on its connecting link downwards so that the link can be unhooked from the lock. Remove the screws on the shut face of the door and then press

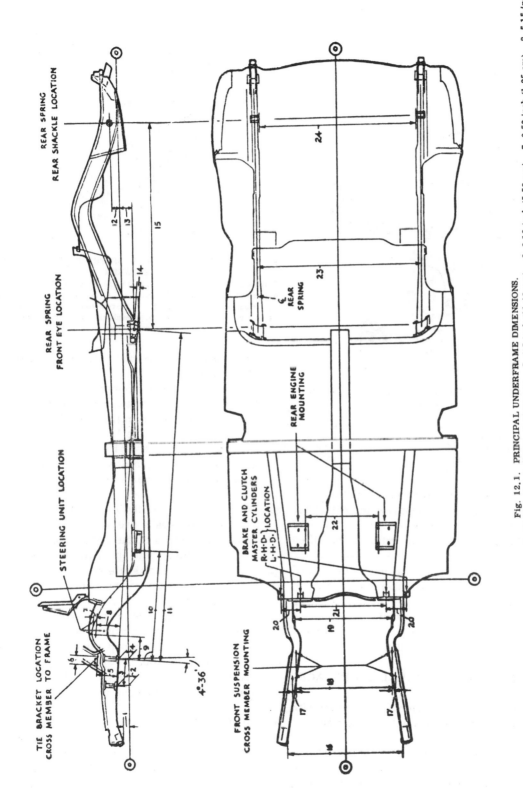

TIE BRACKET LOCATION
CROSS MEMBER TO FRAME

STEERING UNIT LOCATION

REAR SPRING
FRONT EYE LOCATION

REAR SPRING
REAR SHACKLE LOCATION

FRONT SUSPENSION
CROSS MEMBER MOUNTING

BRAKE AND CLUTCH
MASTER CYLINDERS
R·H·D·
L·H·D· LOCATION

REAR ENGINE
MOUNTING

Ç REAR
SPRING

4°-36'

Fig. 12.1.   PRINCIPAL UNDERFRAME DIMENSIONS.

1 1.66 inch (4.21 cm).   2 3.12 inch (7.92 cm).   3 6.0 inch (15.24 cm).   4 2.64 inch (6.70 cm).   5 4.5 inch (11.43 cm).   6 2.18 inch (5.53 cm).   7 0.53 inch (1.35 cm).   8 5.15 inch (13.08 cm).   9 5.56 inch (14.12 cm).   10 24.36 inch (61.87 cm).   11 74.16 inch (188.36 cm).   12 1.38 inch (3.50 cm).   13 2.96 inch (8.51 cm).   14 0.34 inch (0.86 cm).   15 46.44 inch (117.96 cm).   16 27.12 inch (69.36 cm).   17 0.88 inch (2.23 cm).   18 22.56 inch (57.30 cm).   19 22.34 inch (56.74 cm).   20 5.0 inch (12.7 cm).   21 19.64 inch (49.9 cm).   22 16. inch (41.9 cm).   23 37.5 inch (95.25 cm).   24 35.84 inch (91.03 cm).

down the lock safety catch. Where applicable, unscrew the knob of this catch and swing the control wire against the knob so that this is now free to be withdrawn through the lock opening.

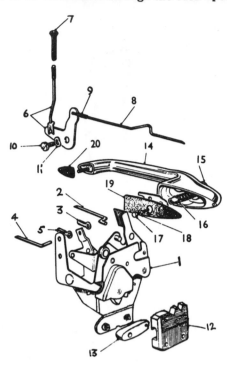

Fig. 12.2. EXPLODED VIEW OF THE REAR DOOR LOCK MECH-ANISM.
1 Lock assembly. 2 Sill control rod (with 8). 3 Clip attachment. 4 Remote control rod. 5 Clip attachment. 6 Sill control. 7 Knob. 8 Sill control rod (with 2)   9 Clip. 10 Screw. 11 Washer. 12 Striker. 13 Dovetail. 14 Exterior handle. 15 Push button. 16 Spring. 17 Screw (plunger). 18 Nut (lock). 19 Washer. 20 Washer.

If the lock is fitted with a push button operating mechanism first unscrew the nut at the front and then the screw behind and this will allow the handle and push button to be lifted away.

If the trouble is that the push button will not operate the lock, on the reverse side of the button will be found an adjustable plunger which is secured with a locknut. Release this locknut and turn the plunger in or out as required and retighten the locknut.

BUMPER BARS - REMOVAL & REPLACE-MENT

The bumpers can be removed complete with their mounting brackets or without the mounting brackets.

However, it is essential to mention that if you take the bumper from the car and intend to run on the road with the brackets projecting from the car, there is a possibility of being summoned for having a vehicle on the road which could be dangerous. This legal point

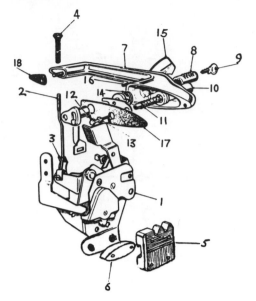

Fig. 12.3. EXPLODED VIEW OF THE FRONT DOOR LOCK MECHANISM
1 Lock assembly. 2 Sill control link. 3 Clip. 4 Knob. 5 Striker. 6 Dovetail. 7 Exterior handle. 8 Locking cylinder. 9 Key. 10 Push button. 11 Spring. 12 Screw (plunger). 13 Nut (lock). 14 Centralising spring. 15 Weathershield. 16 Spring. 17 Washer. 18 Washer.

has already been argued out, to the detriment of the motorist.

To remove the bumper and its mounting brackets, remove the two nuts, spring washers and plain washers from the back of each mounting bar, and lift the bumper away. Where overriders are fitted these are secured by nuts, spring and plain washers which screw onto studs in the overriders.

8. ## DOOR SEALS - REMOVAL & REPLACEMENT

The door seals are retained in channels around the edges of the doors and to remove them ease up a joint and pull the whole seal out. Replacing such seals needs a screwdriver to assist the entry of the seal flange into its channel in the door. If the furflex piping around the door opening is to be renewed, the sill tread plates will have to be removed, and as these are retained by pop-rivets, these rivets should be drilled out to release the plates. The plates can be re-secured with self tapping screws once the new piping has been fitted.

9. ## WINDOW REGULATOR - REMOVAL

To remove a window winder, remove the trim, and bring the window winding handle to a position where the window is about half down. Support the window with a piece of wood and then remove the screws which secure the regulator unit to the inner door panel. This will allow the operating arm of the regulator to

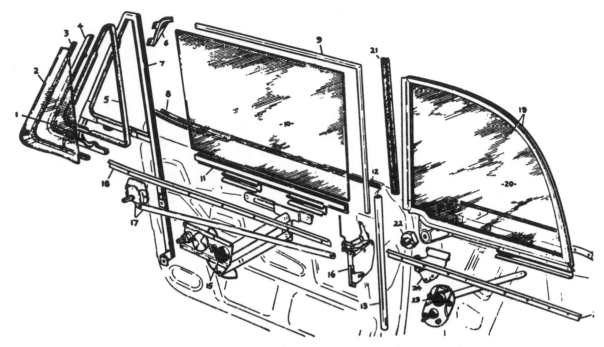

Fig. 12.4. EXPLODED VIEW OF THE COUPE DOOR GLASSES AND MECHANISM.

1 Drain channel. 2 Glass. 3 Glazing rubber. 4 Inner frame. 5 Weatherstrip. 6 Rain deflector. 7 Outer frame. 8 Weatherstrip. 9 Winding window frame. 10 Winding window. 11 Glass channel and camplate. 12 Seal. 13 Glass run channel. 15 Window regulator. 16 Door lock. 17 Remote control. 18 Retainer (trim pad). 19 Quarter light frame. 20 Glass. 21 Weatherstrip. 22 Special nut. 23 Regulator. 24 Mounting bracket. 25 Retainer (trim pad). 26 Guide buffer.

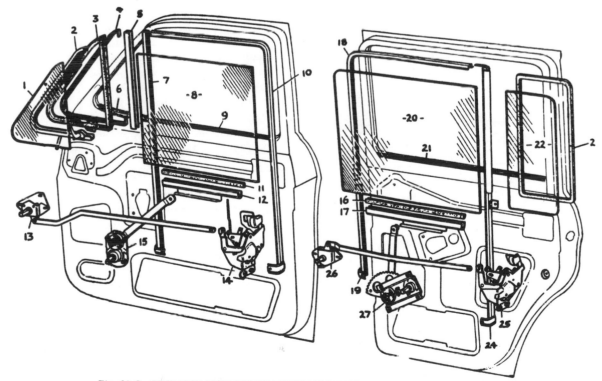

Fig. 12.5. EXPLODED VIEW OF THE ESTATE CAR DOOR GLASSES AND MECHANISM.

1 Glass. 2 Inner frame. 3 Weatherstrip. 4 Outer frame. 5 Centre channel. 6 Weatherstrip. 7 Glass run channel. 8 Winding window. 9 Seal. 10 Glass run channel. 11 Glazing rubber. 12 Glass channel and camplate. 13 Remote control. 14 Door lock. 15 Window regulator. 16 Glazing rubber. 17 Glass channel and camplate. 18 Glass run channel. 19 Glass run channel. 20 Winding window. 21 Seal. 22 Fixed glass. 23 Weatherstrip. 24 Glass run channel. 25 Door lock. 26 Remote control. 27 Window regulator.

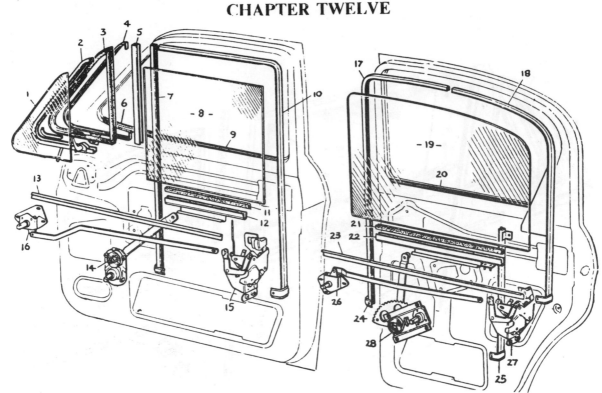

Fig. 12.6. EXPLODED VIEW OF THE SALOON DOOR GLASSES AND MECHANISM.

1 Glass. 2 Inner frame. 3 Weatherstrip. 4 Outer frame. 5 Centre channel. 6 Weatherstrip. 7 Glass run channel. 8 Winding window. 9 Seal. 10 Glass run channel. 11 Glazing rubber. 12 Glass channel and camplate. 13 Retainer (trim pad). 14 Window regulator. 15 Door lock. 16 Remote control. 17 Glass run channel. 18 Glass run channel. 19 Winding window. 20 Seal. 21 Glazing rubber. 22 Glass channel and camplate. 23 Retainer (trim pad). 24 Glass run channel. 25 Glass run slide channel. 26 Remote control. 27 Door lock. 28 Window regulator.

slide from its location in the bottom channel of the window glass.

Reverse these operations for replacement, giving the operating arm ball a smear of grease to provide easy running in the channel.

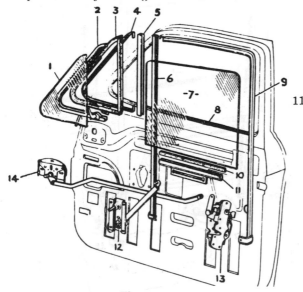

Fig 12.7. EXPLODED VIEW OF THE HUSKY DOOR GLASSES AND MECHANISM

1 Glass. 2 Inner frame. 3 Weatherstrip. 4 Outer frame. 5 Centre channel. 6 Glass channel. 7 Winding window. 8 Finisher. 9 Glass channel. 10 Glazing rubber. 11 Glass channel and camplate. 12 Window regulator. 13 Door lock. 14 Remote control.

10. REAR DOOR FIXED WINDOW - REMOVAL (WHERE FITTED)

To remove the glass, first remove the winding window and then remove the upper glass channel from its retaining clips in the window frame.

If the window is intact, grasp it firmly at the top rear edge and pull down towards the window opening.

Refitting is the reverse of this sequence.

11. HEATING & VENTILATING SYSTEM

The Smith's heating system, where fitted supplies fresh air to the interior of the car by drawing it over a small radiator which is connected to and heated by, the water cooling system of the engine.

The air is distributed and regulated by controls on the dashboard, and if all is working well, the unit will provide a flow of unheated air during the warm weather, and a constant supply of hot air during the cold weather, as seen in Fig. 12.6.

If, however, hot air is brought into the car when the control is set to 'Cold', then the water control valve is either not operating by the lever or has ceased to function.

To replace this valve, remove the control from the side of the heater unit after draining the water, and refit a new one. The control unit is a small cast unit into which the inflow water hose is connected.

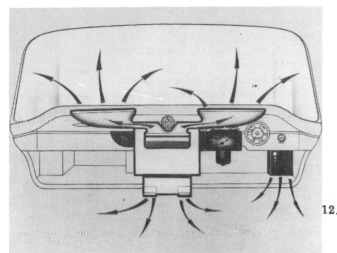

Fig. 12.8. Diagram of the airflow through the heating and ventilating system.

If, after the cooling system of the engine has been drained, the heater refuses to provide hot air, this will mean the air has entered the system and is preventing water from circulating. To check, when the cooling water has heated up switch on the heater motor and then check the temperature of the heater return hose, which should be warming up fairly fast. If this hose shows no signs of getting hot then the method to be used to remove any air lock, is first to remove the return hose at its connection with the bottom water hose. Next obtain a length of hose which will enable the hose to return water to the system through the radiator filler cap. Plug the hole at the bottom of the radiator main hose with a cork, start up the engine, making sure of course that the cooling system is full, and watch for the water to be pumped around until it flows out of the temporary hose and down into the filler cap. At first this will bring with it large air bubbles, but after a few minutes these will subside.

At this stage switch off the engine and, keeping as much water as possible in the hose while reconnecting it to the main hose after removing the cork. Make sure that the hose clips are secured. Now start up the engine again, top up the cooling system and check for any water leaks, and then check the heater hose to make sure that it is warming up.

12. CONVERTIBLE COUPE - MAINTENANCE

On models having a folding head, the only maintenance normally needed is to give a spot of oil regularly on the locks, hinges and pivots, and to wash down the top at the same time as the rest of the bodywork is cleaned.

During the summer months a regular washing once a month, with warm water and a small amount of neutral soap, and then drying with a cloth will keep the material in sound condition.

In general there is nothing to be gained from using such things as wax polishes or furniture cream on the material. Do not under any circumstances use clear cleaners, petrol, naphtha or bleaching agents. If tar spots or similar local stains are evident, a limited amount of methylated spirits will usually remove most of the stain, used on a clean rag.

INDEX

INDEX